Selling
Social Change
(Without
Selling Out)

Selling
Social Change

(Without Selling Out)

Earned Income Strategies for Nonprofits

ANDY ROBINSON

with contributions from

JENNIFER LEHMAN and **TERRY MILLER**

JOSSEY-BASS
A Wiley Company
www.josseybass.com

Published by

JOSSEY-BASS
A Wiley Company
989 Market Street
San Francisco, CA 94103-1741

www.josseybass.com

Jossey-Bass books and products are available through most bookstores. To contact Jossey-Bass directly, call (888) 378-2537, fax to (800) 605-2665, or visit our website at www.josseybass.com.

Substantial discounts on bulk quantities of Jossey-Bass books are available to corporations, professional associations, and other organizations. For details and discount information, contact the special sales department at Jossey-Bass.

Credits appear on page 230.

Library of Congress Cataloging-in-Publication Data

Robinson, Andy.
    Selling social change (without selling out): earned income strategies for nonprofits / Andy Robinson, with contributions from Jennifer Lehman and Terry Miller.
       p. cm.— (The Chardon Press series)
Includes bibliographical references and index.
    ISBN 0-7879-6216-3
    1. Nonprofit organizations—Finance. 2. Charities—Finance. 3. Voluntarism—Finance. 4. Social service—Finance. 5. Fund raising. 6. Nonprofit organizations—United States—Finance—Case studies. 7. Charities—United States—Finance—Case studies. I. Title: Earned income strategies for nonprofits. II. Lehman, Jennifer, date– III. Miller, Terry, date– IV. Title. V. Series.
    HG4027.65.R63 2002
    361.7'63'0681—dc21
                                   2002001858

first edition
PB Printing   10 9 8 7 6 5 4 3 2 1

THE CHARDON PRESS SERIES

Fundamental social change happens when people come together to organize, advocate, and create solutions to injustice. Chardon Press recognizes that communities working for social justice need tools to create and sustain healthy organizations. In an effort to support these organizations, Chardon Press produces materials on fundraising, community organizing, and organizational development. These resources are specifically designed to meet the needs of grassroots nonprofits—organizations that face the unique challenge of promoting change with limited staff, funding, and other resources. We at Chardon Press have adapted traditional techniques to the circumstances of grassroots nonprofits. Chardon Press and Jossey-Bass hope these works help people committed to social justice to build mission-driven organizations that are strong, financially secure, and effective.

Kim Klein, Series Editor

THE FINANCIAL STATEMENT MUST FINALLY GIVE WAY TO THE NARRATIVE, WITH ALL ITS

EXCEPTIONS, SPECIAL CASES, IMPONDERABLES. IT MUST FINALLY GIVE WAY TO THE STORY....

Stanley Crawford
A Garlic Testament: Seasons on a Small New Mexico Farm

For my father, salesman and storyteller

Contents

Preface

. . . .

I have a confession to make: I don't trust capitalism. Indeed, I've spent most of my professional life dealing with the messes created or abetted by our market economy—poverty, inequity, militarism, and environmental troubles, to name a few. So what I'm about to write surprises even me.

Commerce—at least the small-scale, neighborhood-grown variety—can be an instrument for social change. As you will read in this book, many progressive organizations across North America are developing and selling goods and services that support and extend their missions. Ironically, many of these groups are anti-capitalist—actively challenging the economic assumptions that that drive our society   yet they have also found ways to earn significant income from sales. In doing so, they are discovering new strategies for educating their communities, activating their constituents, and expanding their budgets.

The purpose of this book is to help you increase your effectiveness and financial self-sufficiency by applying earned income strategies to your own work. We discuss the growing importance of "social entrepreneurship" in the nonprofit sector and identify specific steps to help you generate more money from your programs, including how to

- Create an "entrepreneurial culture" within your organization

- Brainstorm and evaluate potential earned income projects

- Develop and use a business plan

- Raise enough money to get started

- Successfully market your goods and services

A series of worksheets will guide you through the process, step by step. You'll also learn about corporate partnerships and the tax implications of earned income, and find suggestions for managing your venture once it's up and running (and making money). Finally, we review several nonprofit enterprises that failed and discuss what you can learn from their mistakes.

This project began with a search for good stories. I interviewed people at nearly two dozen nonprofit organizations, visiting half of them in the course of my travels. I talked with staff, board members, and customers. I read their literature, scanned their Web sites, reviewed news articles about their work, and in many instances purchased their goods and services. I quote many of those I spoke with in this book and cite sources for written material I used. Throughout the book, I refer to the work of these profiled organizations.

These nonprofits are the heart of this project. They demonstrate the variety of ways that progressive groups can participate in commerce and still be true to their values. Their stories offer a wealth of tangible, practical ideas you can put to work with your own nonprofit. As you read about these groups, you might ask yourself two questions: How is this relevant to my organization? What can we learn from these folks?

To apply the lessons offered by these organizations, you may need to shift your thinking. Many activists, community organizers, and nonprofit managers think of their program work as separate from their fundraising, and they find the idea of combining mission and money to be strange, if not downright offensive. Like them, you may be suspicious of terms like *market segmentation* and *entrepreneurship*. When you look past the words, however, you'll discover this book is really about *power*. By honoring your principles and tapping into your passion, you can develop economic power for your organization and your community.

Read this book, apply what you learn, and use that power to create a healthy, equitable, sustainable world.

Tucson, Arizona   Andy Robinson
February 2002

Acknowledgments

▪ ▪ ▪ ▪ ▪ ▪ ▪ ▪ ▪ ▪ ▪ ▪ ▪ ▪ ▪ ▪ ▪

This book took shape over the course of many years and many conversations. The following folks were generous with their time and their ideas, and I am grateful to them: John Anner, Peter Barnes, Jan Cohen, Lee Davis, Mark Dowie (a self-described "free market anti-capitalist"), Jed Emerson, Nicole Etchart, Si Kahn, David Morris, and Richard Steckel.

The wonderful librarians at the Tucson-Pima Public Library dug up citations and obscure facts. Lisa Kirvin, Jason McBriarty, and Pat Munoz helped to locate crucial materials, some of which found their way into the book. Jennifer Lehman and Terry Miller went a step further, committing their wisdom to paper. On behalf of the readers, I thank them for their willingness to share. Fun working with you both!

Research time was underwritten, in part, by the Foundation for Deep Ecology and the Dove Fellowship Program, which is administered by the Indiana University Center on Philanthropy. The Blue Mountain Center (special thanks to Harriet Barlow) and the Mesa Refuge offered quiet places to work. This book would not exist without their nurturing energy, lovely landscapes, and good food…but mostly the blessed quiet.

Four anonymous readers reviewed an earlier draft, and I've incorporated many of their suggestions. As one reader noted, "Capitalism is here to stay, and we need to figure out how to work with it, rather than continuing to allow ourselves to be marginalized while capitalists with no ethics take over the world." Thanks to you all for your thoughtful and practical insights.

Given the endless detours that accompanied this project, it's hard to overstate my gratitude to Stephanie Roth and Kim Klein of Chardon Press, who remained cheerful and supportive throughout. It's always a privilege to work with editor Nancy Adess (the best in the business) and production editor Carolyn Uno. Thanks also to Johanna Vondeling and her many colleagues at Jossey-Bass for their professionalism and enthusiasm for this project.

A bow to my beloved, Jan Waterman, and my father, Rocky Robinson. If a "sales gene" exists, my father passed it along to me. Some years ago, I innocently asked him, "Hey, Dad, what did you sell?" He reeled off a long list recounting his life as a salesman. He was paid to market merchandise, but he also volunteered to sell benefit tickets and solicit other charitable gifts. "I was once at a convention," he said, "and this guy finished his speech by saying, 'Nothing happens in this world until somebody makes a sale.' The place went nuts." As well as anything can, my father's story captures the impulse behind this book.

Finally, I'd like to acknowledge the many terrific organizations that allowed me to share their stories in this book. Your work inspires me.

A.R.

The Author

Andy Robinson describes himself as "an anticapitalist with great business instincts."
He has been raising money for social change since 1980. As a trainer and consultant,
he has assisted nonprofits in forty states and Canada, leading workshops on
fundraising, grantwriting, board development, strategic planning, marketing, and
earned income strategies.

He specializes in the needs of organizations promoting human rights, social
justice, and environmental conservation. In addition to hundreds of local and
regional groups, his clients include the American Friends Service Committee,
National Network of Grantmakers, Patagonia Inc., National Wildlife Federation,
Sierra Club, National Trust for Historic Preservation, Neighborhood Reinvestment,
and the Evangelical Lutheran Church in America. He also serves as training and
outreach director for the New England Grassroots Environment Fund in Montpelier,
Vermont. You can reach him at andyfund@earthlink.net.

Robinson is a former columnist for the *NonProfit Times* and a regular con-
tributor to the *Grassroots Fundraising Journal*. *City Limits* called his first book,
Grassroots Grants: An Activist's Guide to Proposal Writing, "a manual for people who
want to change the world." *Grassroots Grants* is available from Jossey-Bass.

The Contributors

Jennifer Lehman, based in Denver, is a senior consultant with AddVenture Network and an adviser to nonprofit organizations across the country. She also works with corporations and philanthropic foundations on strategic planning and innovative marketing. She is coauthor (with Richard Steckel) of *In Search of America's Best Nonprofits* (Jossey-Bass, 1997).

Terry Miller received his B.A. from Antioch College and his M.B.A. from the University of Portland. For twenty-five years, he has worked as a financial manager, consultant, and trainer with a wide variety of nonprofit organizations. Miller directed the financial management training program for the Youth Project, a national foundation supporting grassroots organizers. Later, he was chief financial officer of a $5 million business league in downtown Portland, then a senior paralegal at Silk, Adler & Colvin, a prominent San Francisco corporate and tax law firm serving nonprofits. He is the author of *Managing for Change: A Common Sense Guide to Evaluating Financial Management Health for Grassroots Organizations* (1990).

Chapter 1

Selling your cause
without selling out

▪　　▪　　▪

Capitalism: 1. The economic system in which all or most of the means of production and distribution, as land, factories, railroads, etc., are privately owned and operated for profit, originally under fully competitive conditions. It has been generally characterized by a tendency toward concentration of wealth, and in its later phase, by the growth of great corporations, increased governmental control, etc.

2. The principles, methods, interests, power, influence, etc. of capitalists, especially of those with large holdings.

—WEBSTER'S NEW WORLD DICTIONARY

When I was seven years old, I loaded my unwanted toys into my red Radio Flyer wagon and went door to door trying to sell them to the other kids in the neighborhood. My inventory consisted of one yellow dump truck filled with a few choice rocks; a plastic golf club; a whiffle ball with teeth marks courtesy of our dog; a racecar with a little decapitated man behind the wheel; a parrot that said, "Polly want a cracker," when you pulled the string, except the string was gone and the bird was mute; a boxing glove, right hand; a Bozo the Clown drinking cup; and a rubber tarantula. I can't tell you how much I earned—probably a dollar or two—or how I spent it, but the experience of pulling that wagon up and down the street is burned into my brain.

Was I a capitalist? Hardly. Was I a salesman? Absolutely. I sold lemonade in the summer, raked leaves in the fall, shoveled snow in the winter, and shined my father's shoes for a quarter whenever he asked. (As I grew older and became a better negotiator, the price went up to fifty cents and later a dollar.) Again, I don't remember how I spent the money, because the money wasn't the point. Doing the work and getting paid for my effort made me feel grown up. In a small but important way, it gave me power.

In this chapter you'll learn that commerce and capitalism are not necessarily the same thing, and that the power of selling can be used effectively for worthy causes, like yours.

Biologists have yet to discover a "sales gene," but perhaps some day they will. My grandfather was a salesman. Over the course of a long career, my father marketed women's apparel, sporting goods, and tools and instruments for the jewelry trade. For the past twenty-plus years, I've been raising money for social change. My "products" are social justice, human rights, compassion, dignity, equity, clean air and water, a healthy ecosystem, wild places, artistic expression, and a culture that embraces diversity. These are terrific products and I've been proud to sell them.

We're all in sales

When I lead fundraising workshops, I often talk about the relationship between fundraising and sales. This discussion makes a lot of folks, especially progressive activists, uncomfortable. For many people, the word *sales* brings to mind manipulation, obsequiousness, dishonesty, aggressive behavior, false friendship, and poorly tailored suits. In public polls that measure respect for certain professions, sales consistently ranks near the bottom.

If you distrust salespeople, you're not alone. If the idea of *being* a salesperson makes you nervous, you're reading the right book.

Furthermore, if you don't believe that capitalism works, there's plenty of evidence to support you. For starters, the tax code is designed to promote and reward concentration of wealth and power, especially corporate and military power. As documented by the War Resisters League, nearly half of our federal income tax payments go directly or indirectly to the military, including staggering sums for weapons of mass destruction.[1] The way we allocate our tax money explains, in part, the abysmal state of our schools, the appalling rates of child poverty, the institutionalization of racism, the foul air that covers our cities, the clear-cuts that decimate our forests, the paucity of public support for the arts, the shameful number of people wasting away in our prisons, and many more such disgraces.

The distribution of wealth in this country is extremely lopsided. According to a recent study from United for a Fair Economy, the richest 1 percent of the American population controls 38 percent of the wealth, while the bottom forty percent controls only 0.2 percent (that's two-tenths of one percent). From 1983 to 1998, the top 1 percent of the population enjoyed an increase in net worth of 42 percent, while the bottom 40 percent saw their net worth decrease by 76 percent.[2] (This is the *real* story of the recent economic boom: the poor got poorer.)

The U.S. accounts for less than 5 percent of the planet's population, but Americans consume one-third of the Earth's resources.[3] We lead the world in waste. Our priorities are screwy, and the way our economy is structured is both a cause and a reflection of these problems.

I have two goals for this book. First, to distinguish commerce from capitalism and in doing so redeem commerce as an instrument of social change. I'm proud to be an anticapitalist, but I also have good business instincts that I apply daily to the work of repairing the world. This leads me to goal number two: to help you think and act like a salesperson—perhaps you prefer the word *entrepreneur*—so you can figure out how to earn money from your mission and do your work more effectively. The key is to combine commerce with your mission so that one supports the other.

"Martin Luther King, Jr. called himself a drum major for justice," says Si Kahn of Grassroots Leadership, one of the organizations profiled in this book. "Well, we're salespeople for justice."

Commerce, not capitalism

In *The Ecology of Commerce,* Paul Hawken writes, "One of the reasons we like the term 'market economy' is because we picture the agora, the market square, farmers and craftspeople—the smells, scents and tastes of the piazza and the souks and bazaars of ancient cultural history and tradition, where economic fairness and competition resulted in a vibrant, human atmosphere."[4]

The activities of buying, selling, and trading are as old as our species. Whenever and wherever people gather, commerce has been a part of human behavior. Throughout much of the world, business is still done the old-fashioned way, through barter: trading one product or service for another without the use of coins or currency. Barter is perhaps the opposite of capitalism. In a barter-based system, it's harder to concentrate wealth—to acquire something, you have to give something away.

Once money changes hands, the transaction feels different. I've known dozens of volunteers who were terrified of asking for contributions but had no problem soliciting in-kind goods and services. Many activists believe that fundraising—even the process of physically collecting and handling the funds—somehow corrupts their work. The taboos surrounding money are endless, and endlessly fascinating.

I began a recent fundraising seminar by tearing up a $20 bill. (Yes, it was real currency.) I heard a few gasps, followed by an edgy silence. The pieces floated to the ground. "Where's the tape?" someone muttered. Another person spoke up: "I felt my mother coming back from the grave. She whispered in my ear, 'You make him stop!'" We proceeded to talk our way through the list of taboos: money is dirty, money is scarce, money is private, money is sacred, money is the root of all evil. (The correct quote—it's from the Bible—emphasizes the *love* of money as the root of evil.) And, perhaps most telling, asking for money is seen as a sign of weakness and shame.

"Traditional nonprofits are distrustful of money," says Richard Steckel in *Filthy Rich: How to Turn Your Nonprofit Fantasies Into Cold, Hard Cash.* "They fear money will pollute their mission."[5]

"Grow up," writes Jed Emerson in *New Social Entrepreneurs.* "Money is valueless; it's what people do with money that counts."[6] Adds Steckel, "Entrepreneurial nonprofits control it, not the other way around."[7]

As any good solicitor knows, fundraising is not about money—it's about relationships. Commerce, when conducted honestly and openly, operates on the same principle. If money makes you crazy, think about your customers and not their wallets. According to Hawken, "The promise of business is to increase the general well-being of humankind through service, a creative invention, and ethical philosophy. Making money, on its own terms, is totally meaningless."[8] (Indeed, one of the more disturbing aspects of our age is the number of people who seem to ascribe real meaning to money and its acquisition.)

The organizations profiled in this book are all engaged in different aspects of social change work. Some emphasize service, others advocacy and community organizing, but they're all working to challenge the status quo. Several groups use earned income strategies to protect and restore the environment. For others, it's a means to build community and preserve traditional culture. Still others participate in commerce to create an alternative economic system that benefits the people who've been left behind. Richard Oulahan of Esperanza Unida says that nonprofit enterprise "is our answer to the question, 'How do you level the playing field in a capitalist society?'"[9] In the next chapter, we'll examine in more detail how commerce can benefit your group, and we'll consider the range of options for entering the marketplace.

Yes, your organization can earn money and honor its principles at the same time. If I can't convince you, perhaps these terrific nonprofits can.

Bad Jokes, Great Service

OUR COMMUNITY BIKES

VANCOUVER, BRITISH COLUMBIA

WWW.PEDALPOWER.ORG

ANNUAL BUDGET: $200,000

EARNED INCOME: 100%

EARNED INCOME STRATEGIES

- CONSUMER SERVICES
- CONSUMER GOODS: RETAIL
- TRAINING AND CONSULTING FOR NONPROFITS AND OTHER INSTITUTIONAL CUSTOMERS

Our Community Bikes is a nonprofit bicycle shop dedicated to encouraging people to get out of their cars and onto their bicycles. Founded in 1993 as a project of Better Environmentally Sound Transportation, or BEST, the shop has assembled hundreds of cycles from donated materials: unwanted or outgrown two-wheelers, bikes abandoned at dormitories and apartment buildings, parts scrounged from yard sales and wrecks, factory cast-offs, and unwanted components from other stores. As project manager Richard Andrews told *The Vancouver Courier,* "We never know what we'll get from day to day. It's like having an insane supplier who keeps sending more and more."[1]

Restored, ready-to-ride bicycles fill the rack in front of the store. Dozens more cover the floor of the tiny shop. In the back, two storage rooms overflow with old bikes and parts, while Andrews and his crew—four other paid staff and a team of volunteers—work overtime tearing them apart and putting them back together. "We have a happy arrangement between order and chaos. We never really achieve either one," Andrews told the *Courier.* "However, we've gotten really good at making up weird, monstrous bikes that I've never seen before."[2]

In addition to salvaging old cycles and parts, Our Community Bikes (OCB) pursues its mission—and earns income—through a wide range of strategies:

1. *Low prices.* A restored bicycle—monstrous or otherwise—costs between $25 and $250, which is well below the price of a new one. By keeping prices down, OCB strives to eliminate "price resistance" and make bicycling affordable for everyone. Of course, these low prices are possible thanks to donated parts, modest salaries, and extensive use of volunteers, who collectively contribute 60 hours per week in the shop.

When asked about competition, Andrews says he used to hear complaints that Our Community Bikes was undercutting other stores. Over time, however, the retailers came to recognize two different markets: one for new (expensive) cycles, another for used (cheap) ones. "Now the local bike shops like us. In fact, one of our 'competitors' just gave us 24 forks they can't use. At $10–$20 each, that's a donation of at least $250." Andrews argues that, by encouraging new cyclists, he's expanding the market. Eventually some of OCB's customers move up to new bikes and buy from other stores.

2. *Full-service repairs.* For $40 per hour, a skilled mechanic will fix a customer's bike. A percentage of this fee supports OCB's operations and community education programs.

3. *Fix it yourself.* For those who don't have their own tools or think they know what they're doing, but wouldn't mind having an experienced mechanic looking over their shoulder, customers can drop in, repair their own cycles, and solicit advice from the helpful staff. The fee is $5 to $15 per hour depending on the amount of help needed. Half of OCB's 20 daily customers do their own repairs.

4. *Classes.* On the last Monday of each month, Our Community Bikes opens the store for a "tune-up your cycle" class. Several hundred people have attended this course over the past two years, paying $35 each. The group also organizes classes in the community. Working through a partner organization, PEDAL (Pedal Energy Development Alternatives), OCB staff and colleagues present workshops for local employers seeking to improve employee fitness and reduce traffic and parking problems near the office. In a seminar on urban cycling, participants learn how to deal with everything from rude drivers to Vancouver's moist climate. The emergency repairs program covers flat tires, broken spokes, loose chains, and so on. To date, more than a dozen employers—including BC Hydro, the Vancouver School Board, and Pacific Blue Cross—have contracted for on-site employee training at $150 per seminar.

5. *Promoting pedal power overseas.* Given their overflowing inventory, Our Community Bikes is constantly scrambling to get bicycles out the door. One solution: ship them to developing countries. Staff and volunteers make regular trips to Guatemala, where they deliver truckloads of bicycles and parts to Cakchiquel and Quiche villages in the highlands. In another venture, with funding from the Canadian International Development Agency, the folks at OCB invented a pedal-powered machine to pump water, another to grind corn or make soy milk, and a third that creates cement roof tiles. OCB and PEDAL work in partnership with five Guatemalan organizations to provide the machines to rural community groups. In the newsletter *Spoke 'n' Word,* Andrews wrote,

"This project seemed a natural extension of our work: devising further uses for Vancouver's bicycle waste while helping disadvantaged people elsewhere do tasks normally done by fossil fuel or electric power."[3]

Our Community Bikes and their Guatemalan partners have applied for a patent in Guatemala; OCB will soon do the same in Canada and the United States. Eventually, the group hopes to manufacture these machines in Canada and market them to both international relief agencies and North Americans who want to reduce their reliance on electricity and fossil fuel.

6. *New products.* Based on their overseas experience and in response to local demand, the group is opening a workshop to design, build, and sell pedal-powered devices, local carriers, and custom cycles for the British Columbia market. The search for seed money—venture capital—is under way. If successful, these new products could generate a stream of regular income for years to come.

Our Community Bikes is 100 percent self-funded—the entire budget is earned from sales and services. What's the secret of their success? "Bad jokes and great service," Andrews says. Indeed, puns abound throughout the *Spoke 'n' Word* and other written materials. One article urges readers to "Join the Velorution," a corruption of "revolution." ("Velo" is the Latin root for cycle.) Another headline borrows a well-known gay rights slogan to promote cyclists' rights: "We're here, we're in gear, get used to it!" A newsletter advertisement features a lawyer dressed in a black robe and white lawyer's wig (yes, they still wear those old-fashioned wigs in Canada) while sitting on his bike. "Bicycle injury?" he asks. "I'll be your Spokesman!"

Our Community Bikes proves that you can save the world, earn money, and have fun—all at the same time.

THINGS TO THINK ABOUT

• *Love thine enemy?* Through diplomacy and careful "niche marketing," Our Community Bikes has turned potential competitors—other bike shops—into suppliers and sources of new clients. Don't assume that similar businesses are automatically competitors. If you work with them and try to meet their needs, they may turn out to be valuable partners.

• *If appropriate to your business venture, use goods to promote services and services to promote goods.* People who buy bicycles need bicycle repairs; people who receive bicycle training may want a new bike or accessories to make the ride more enjoyable. If you're selling goods, can you add a relevant service to meet customer needs? If you're selling services, what goods can you develop to support those services?

• *Live your values and your business will prosper.* By creating a casual atmosphere in the store–repair shop and producing entertaining, amusing materials, OCB reinforces the same message again and again: cycling is *fun.* (When was the last time you thought of commuting to work as fun?)

Our Community Bikes is the only group featured in this book that *earns 100 percent of its budget through business activities.* Reflecting your values in your workplace is—surprise!—good for business. You want to live in a just, equitable, enjoyable world? Build your earned income strategies on justice, equity, and fun. As Gandhi, that well-known sales consultant said, "We must be the change we wish to see."[4]

Chapter 2

How earned income can benefit your mission

▪   ▪   ▪

Today, there's a lot of talk about entrepreneurial nonprofits, but the idea of nonprofits starting businesses is nothing new. Guess when the following excerpt was published.

> When mulling over topics for…training sessions recently, we called a friend who is a community organizer in Seattle.
>
> "If we hold a training session in the Pacific Northwest this year, what should be the subject?" we asked. "Media strategy and PR? Community organizing? Or maybe organizational management?"
>
> "Those all sound good," she said, "but do you really want to know what's on people's minds here?"
>
> "What's that?"
>
> "Survival. We are all terrified that the money is going to dry up. And we're all scrambling to figure out new ways to keep our organizations alive."
>
> Organizers discussing fundraising are often just like farmers discussing the price of wheat. They complain a lot. But activists have reason to complain—and to worry—about money….With the virtual end to Federal funding for worthwhile projects…citizen organizations around the country are struggling to make ends meet.
>
> Many groups that failed to plan for self-sufficiency years ago, and have traditionally relied on grants, are churning out proposals to private foundations. But the competition is fierce…and foundations only have enough money to fund a few [organizations].
>
> The funding crisis is sparking some creative solutions.…For several years, there has been an undercurrent of interest in profit-oriented business ventures as a potential source of funds for nonprofit citizen organizations.…The funding crisis has made business ventures an important topic within the citizen movement.[1]

Charles Cagnon wrote this report for the Northern Rockies Action Group in 1982. The Reagan administration had drastically reduced government support for progressive initiatives, bringing on a "funding crisis." However, this excerpt could have been written yesterday. Thousands of organizations are in a perpetual "funding crisis." Many more "have failed to plan for self-sufficiency." How many of your colleagues are "terrified that the money is going to dry up?" And everyone in the nonprofit world—not just community organizers—likes to complain about fundraising.

As you'll discover in this chapter, charitable organizations have been earning income for as long as they've been around. By learning about the risks and rewards of the marketplace, and the continuum of ways that nonprofits can participate in commerce, you can begin to assess the relevance of these strategies to your organization.

First, a little history. In *Successful Fundraising*, Joan Flanagan writes, "Medieval churches made money by selling ales brewed in the church house and renting out vestments to other churches for funerals and festivals. In Cornwall, England, the parish accounts from 1526 show that gypsies stayed at the Stratton church house several times, and the 'keepers of the bear' paid one pence rent for it."[2] As she points out, today's churches—especially those near sports stadiums—continue the tradition by selling parking spaces to fans going to the big game.

Flanagan estimates that "fees charged for services account for 42–45% of total budgets of nonprofits other than religious congregations, although this is higher for some fields like education and health services, and lower for others like advocacy and community organizing."[3] She reported in *The Grantsmanship Center Magazine* in 1999 that fee income "is now the fastest growing source of revenue for nonprofits in the United States, Canada, and the United Kingdom."[4]

In many fields, such as job training and development of affordable housing, nonprofits have been charging for services for decades. The performing arts provide another obvious example. According to an annual survey prepared by the Theatre Communications Group, nonprofit theater companies earn 62 percent of their income from ticket sales, concessions, auditorium rentals, and so on.[5] Another instance is publications. Magazines such as *Mother Jones* (published by the nonprofit Foundation for National Progress) and *Whole Earth* (published by Point Foundation) rely to a substantial degree on subscription fees.

Many organizations also market consumer goods. According to an Urban Institute report cited by author Edward Skloot, roughly 15 percent of the secular nonprofits in the United States sell products, though these sales account for less than 5 percent of their income.[6]

Some nonprofit products are legendary. Reproductions of artwork from the Metropolitan Museum of Art—greeting cards, posters, calendars, address books, postcards, datebooks, refrigerator magnets, and the like—are sold around the world. The World Wildlife Fund licenses its panda logo for children's books, calendars, and other educational products that promote conservation. The characters from Sesame Street, created by the Children's Television Workshop, have been licensed to toy manufacturers for more than thirty years.

The Girl Scouts have created perhaps the best-known example of nonprofit commerce. In 2000, Girl Scout volunteers (both children and adults) sold an estimated 250 million boxes of cookies. In terms of sales volume, Girl Scout cookies, taken as a single product, are reputed to be the number two cookie in America—and they're only available six weeks a year. According to Flanagan, here's how this program meets their mission: "The Scouts use cookie sales as more than a moneymaker; selling cookies is considered a program activity to teach girls goal setting, decision making, and responsibility."[7]

This dynamic marketing program, the envy of cookie corporations everywhere, began as a local bake sale in the 1920s. Within a decade, these bake sales were so common that the national office grew concerned about having a consistent, high-quality product. They contracted with a commercial bakery—and the modern Girl Scout cookie was born.

The moral of the story: your modest earned income venture could grow up to be something bigger than you imagined.

Earned income: It's a movement

In recent years, the sharp line that once divided for-profit enterprises from nonprofit organizations has blurred. Corporations have moved aggressively into several areas, such as early childhood education, job training, and hospital care, that were once the exclusive province of nonprofits and government agencies. Nonprofits have reacted by becoming more entrepreneurial: learning to think and behave like businesses. This response is based, in part, on a desire to protect their traditional turf.

As a result of this convergence, we see a lot of hybrid organizations, sometimes called "social purpose businesses." In the words of Jed Emerson, co-founder of the Roberts Enterprise Development Fund, these groups strive to meet "a double bottom line" of both social mission and profitability. Environmental activist and business entrepreneur Boleslaw Rok of Poland pushes this metaphor even further, promoting a "triple bottom line of people, planet, and profit."[8]

Some of these hybrids are structured as for-profit corporations, such as Patagonia, The Body Shop, Stonyfield Farms, Ben & Jerry's, and Newman's Own, whose motto is "Shameless exploitation in pursuit of the common good." As Laura Scher of Working Assets told one interviewer, "Social change is our reason for being. Profit is simply a means to that end."[9]

Others, including groups featured in this book—Our Community Bikes, Global Exchange, and Esperanza Unida—are structured as nonprofits but designed to generate income by fulfilling their social missions. Indeed, non-governmental organizations in every corner of the world are discovering and experimenting with enterprise strategies.

The "earned income for nonprofits" movement has become its own growth industry. Dozens of organizations and consultants are available to help you figure out how to sell goods and services that support your mission. A conference is organized each year (www.natlgathering.org) to discuss the topic. Academics are studying the phenomenon and churning out articles and dissertations. A growing number of business schools—including heavyweights like Stanford and Harvard universities—now include specialties in nonprofits and earned income.

Every social or professional movement has its own specialized jargon, and this one is no different. Indeed, the practitioners are still searching for a common language that describes their work. Here are some examples:

- Jim Thalhuber and his predecessor Jerr Boschee use the term *social entrepreneurship* at the National Center for Social Entrepreneurs. As Boschee has written on the group's Web site, www.socialentrepreneurs.org, "Social entrepreneurs are nonprofit executives who pay increasing attention to market forces without losing sight of their underlying missions."[10] He now heads another organization, the Institute for Social Entrepreneurs.

- Jed Emerson and co-editor Fay Twersky titled their Roberts Foundation study, *New Social Entrepreneurs.*

- Bill Shore of Share our Strength coined the phrase "community wealth enterprises."

- Nicole Etchart and Lee Davis of the Nonprofit Enterprise and Self-sustainability Team (NESsT), who work internationally, prefer the term "self-financing." One of their workbooks is titled *Profits for Nonprofits.*

- Richard Steckel, author of several books on the subject, calls these groups "entrepreneurial nonprofits" whose projects are managed by "enterprise champions."

- Edward Skloot, now with the Surdna Foundation, edited a collection of essays entitled *The Nonprofit Entrepreneur.*

- The National Center on Nonprofit Enterprise, headed by Dennis Young, uses the phrase "nonprofit enterprise."

- A recent book series by J. Gregory Dees, Jed Emerson, and Peter Economy is titled *Enterprising Nonprofits.*

Most of the organizations profiled in this book don't use these terms, and some would have a hard time defining them. I've borrowed these words from time to time, so I want to give credit where it's due, but let's strive to keep things simple: these groups sell goods and services. More important, the goods and services they sell epitomize their social missions. *What they sell is what they do.*

As the experts emphasize, "being entrepreneurial" is not merely about selling; it's a way of thinking. These organizations tend to consider their work in terms of its value—both social and monetary—and view their members, donors, clients, beneficiaries, partners, funders, and even the community at large as customers or perhaps shareholders. Indeed, several of the groups featured in these pages now sell what they used to give away, which is one way of defining entrepreneurial.

"There are a lot of new names for earning money," wrote Cagnon in 1982. "They all mean the same thing: work late, buy low, and sell a quality product that customers want."[11]

The value of funding diversity

Nonprofit organizations can raise money three ways: by soliciting individual donors, writing grant proposals, or earning income.

INDIVIDUALS

- Membership and donor programs
- Major gifts
- Monthly giving (through electronic funds transfer or credit/debit cards)
- Benefit events
- Workplace giving (payroll plans; United Way, Earthshare, and similar organizations)
- Planned gifts (bequests, life insurance policies, trusts, real property, and the like)

GRANTS

- Foundations
- Corporations
- Government
- Service clubs (Rotary, Kiwanis, Soroptimist, and similar organizations)
- Faith-based (from local congregations to national funding programs)

EARNED INCOME

- Goods
- Services
- Publications
- Investment income
- Cause-related marketing and business partnerships (see Chapter Eight)

While not every organization can generate income from all categories, diversity is the key to survival. Having a broad and diverse funding base—

especially money raised from your community—is the most effective way to ensure the longevity and good health of your organization. Earned income may be an important part of your "diversification strategy."

The pros and cons of earned income

Advantages

The reasons for creating and selling goods and services are as varied as the organizations that do it. In addition to diversifying your revenue, here are some other advantages:

1. *Expanded donor base.* Like fundraising, selling is based on relationships. Customers are good prospects for additional donations because they know your work first-hand, they believe in your mission, and they have already used a credit card or written a check to your group. Global Exchange (profiled in Chapter Three) reports that nearly all major donors—folks who contribute $250 or more per year—are customers who have participated in one of the organization's "reality tours."

The inverse is also true: with modest effort, members can be converted to buyers. Native Seeds/SEARCH, which sells traditional garden seeds, foods, and crafts, and is profiled after this chapter, finds that members spend 60 percent more on purchases than customers who have not joined the group. Familiarity breeds sales.

2. *Less reliance on grants.* Grants are problematic for at least three reasons. First, foundations and corporations combined provide only 17 percent of the private-sector money given to U.S. charities, so groups that rely on funding from these sources are chasing a small piece of a very large pie.[12] Second, fewer than 20 percent of all proposals submitted are actually funded, which makes for lousy odds.[13] Finally, grants are known as soft money because they are seldom renewable.

By developing a range of grassroots fundraising strategies, including earned income, nonprofits have more control over their destiny, instead of relying on luck and the good will of grants officers. (Ironically, a diverse funding base makes it easier to get grants, since most grantmakers prefer to invest in successful groups that already have broad support.)

3. *Tighter focus.* The marketplace has little tolerance for fuzzy thinking or sloppy work. To be successful, you'll need to take a hard look at your mission, your programs, and your markets: who benefits, or might benefit, from your work. The process of business planning forces many groups to examine their weaknesses as well as their assets, and to address those weaknesses.

"If it strengthens the business, it's going to strengthen the program," says Peggy Driscoll of the Women's Bean Project, profiled in Chapter Eight. "Ninety percent of the time, the reverse is also true." Even if you ultimately decide that enterprise is not for you, a serious review of the possibilities will make your organization stronger.

4. Better compensation for staff. In the best cases, successful earned income strategies help to improve salaries and benefits—especially if you create a bonus or incentive plan—by generating new, unrestricted dollars. Better compensation means less turnover and brain drain within your venture, your organization, and the social change movement.

5. Publicity and advocacy opportunities. The creation of goods and services provides handles for promoting your cause as well as your products. With creativity and persistence, you can get a lot of free publicity from the news media (see Chapter Seven).

6. Skill building and leadership development. To do this work successfully, your group will need expertise in market research, graphic design, advertising, promotions, accounting, customer service—it's a long list. Since you need most of those skills anyway to run any sort of nonprofit, the process of developing and selling products can have a positive ripple effect throughout the organization. Along the way, you'll discover and create opportunities to challenge, involve, and train your staff, board, and key volunteers. Your focus on earned income may also attract new, enterprise-minded talent to your board.

Disadvantages

If all this sounds too good to be true, it probably is. Here are six reasons that an earned income strategy might not be appropriate for your organization:

1. Don't you have enough work already? Accountant and trainer Terry Miller, who has advised many nonprofits, is wary of most earned income activities and often counsels nonprofits against them. "Nonprofits are rarely well enough managed to run their regular projects," he says. By adding more work, he contends, they tend to divert management time and energy away from their main programs. Because of the potential for overload and burnout, he concludes, "most groups are not good candidates to add any sort of business venture."

2. Mission creep. Do you know what happens when you start shifting your goals and programs to take advantage of funding opportunities? If you're not careful, the tail (the need for money) starts wagging the dog (your mission). While this problem is most evident in the search for grant money, it can also arise through the sales of goods and services.

3. Internal conflict. Not everyone is comfortable with commerce. Some people (often long-time staff and board members) may view entrepreneurial behavior as a betrayal of the mission. As Jed Emerson writes in *New Social Entrepreneurs,* the process can create "profound organizational, personal and professional changes. In the words of one executive director, 'If you like your board, staff, and clients, don't do this, because they will all change!'"[14]

4. *Up-front costs.* You've heard it before: you have to spend money to make money. If you don't have start-up capital, nothing happens. You might identify a grantmaker or major donor who will subsidize the venture—either as an outright gift or a "program-related investment," through which a limited number of foundations loan money at a low interest rates—but the research and application process will take at least six months. After all the work and waiting, your chances of getting funded are not good. (For more information on financing your venture, see Chapter Six.)

5. *Potential tax liability.* Even tax-exempt charities are liable for federal taxes on net income from sales of items or other business ventures unrelated to their mission. This is known as unrelated business income tax (UBIT). State and local taxes are also added in many areas. For a more detailed discussion of tax issues, turn to Chapter Nine.

6. *Sometimes they lose money.* No one has the precise number—it's a topic of debate among economists—but it's safe to assume that at least three out of four small businesses will fail. Even the best ideas, implemented with skill, savvy, and sufficient cash, are not always profitable.

Every earned income strategy involves risk; how much risk can your organization handle? Stated another way, how much time and money can you afford to lose? Since both are precious, it pays to be cautious.

Balancing Mission and Money:
Resource Center of the Americas

■　　■　　■　　■　　■　　■　　■　　■　　■　　■　　■　　■　　■　　■　　■

The Resource Center of the Americas (www.americas.org) is "devoted to the notion that every person in this world is entitled to the same fundamental human rights." According to the group's Web site, the Resource Center works to promote human rights by "learning and teaching about the peoples of the Americas—their history, culture and politics. We focus especially on the global economy, a system in which a minority flourishes while millions of people lack adequate food, shelter, and employment."

Located in Minneapolis, the Resource Center combines popular education with personal and community action. For example, their weekly "coffee hours" include a letter-writing table to make it easy for participants to contact corporate and government officials. Other activities include youth organizing on sweatshops and child labor, discussion circles for recent immigrants, and a labor solidarity campaign connecting U.S. and Latin American workers. They also earn income by developing materials and services for teachers, hosting community education workshops, and selling books and other items at their Bookstore of the Americas. In a recent year, 48 percent of the group's $1 million budget was earned from sales and program fees.

Learning to think and behave like entrepreneurs, says executive director Pam Costain, took several years, since many key staff and board members were concerned that earning money would somehow corrupt their mission. "We'd work twelve hours a day and give away everything. We were so grateful that anyone was interested, we wouldn't charge. Then we looked at our paychecks and realized, we can't keep giving it away." For an organization that focuses on fair wages overseas, this was a revelation. "We have a right to be paid," Costain says.

To address this reality, they set out to increase the budget through sales. "Some people feel that we've abandoned our principles to make money," she says, noting occasional criticism from outside the group, but she offers no apologies—and with good reason. All of their products and services advance the mission, educate the community, build the organization's credibility, and generate income.

Since one of the best ways to appreciate a different culture is by sampling its food, the Resource Center also runs the Café of the Americas. Their menu spans the culinary hemisphere from tamales and Caribbean vegetable stew to latte and homemade cinnamon rolls.

By keeping meal prices low, they hope to attract business from their working-class, increasingly Latino neighborhood. However, low prices mean smaller profit margins on each meal, making it harder to break even or show a profit. Given the relative costs and benefits, they're faced with a critical question: Do they keep the restaurant open or shut it down? Board and staff are debating the next move.

Sooner or later, all nonprofit business enterprises must address the balance between mission and money. Some organizations decide to subsidize unprofitable ventures because they meet the "mission test." Others bail out because they fail the "money test." While there is no easy answer to this puzzle, it would be wise to ask yourself and your colleagues two questions: Are we in this venture primarily to meet our mission or to make money? Can we continue to subsidize this venture if it keeps losing money?

If the first question doesn't solve the problem, the second one will.

Beyond T-shirts and coffee mugs

Nonprofits can sell almost anything. "For assorted charities," writes Joan Flanagan, "I have sold baseball caps, books, bumper stickers, candles, catnip toys, coffee mugs, cookbooks, cutting boards shaped like pigs, designer scarves, golf shirts, grapefruits, greeting cards, herbed vinegars, mouse pads, photographs, personalized letters from Santa, poodles crafted out of golf balls, salted nuts, tote bags, water bottles, wrapping paper, and enough T-shirts to outfit an army of teenagers." Among her discoveries: "It is easiest to sell a good product that is chocolate."[15]

While it's possible to use the same justification as the Girl Scouts—sales skills translate into leadership development—I would wager that few of the products Flanagan sold had any relationship to the mission or programs of the sponsoring organizations. Chocolate sells, in part, because candy is a low-priced item; however, you need to move a lot of product to make a significant profit. If your primary interest is generating revenue for your organization, there are more efficient options.

This book addresses a more ambitious question: How can you develop earned income strategies that actually support and extend your mission? In other words, how can you combine mission and money into something bigger and more effective? As we investigate this question, consider the following continuum of ways that nonprofits approach earned income.[16]

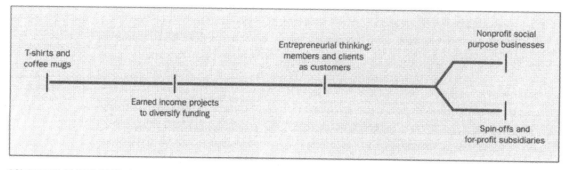

CONTINUUM OF HOW NONPROFITS APPROACH EARNED INCOME

At each point along the continuum, organizations have certain characteristics:

• *T-shirts and coffee mugs.* This stage includes your typical garden-variety grassroots group. The volunteers and staff members (if the organization has staff) sell a few products, but don't have any sales targets, marketing plan, marketing budget, or income projections. Their stock is piled in a closet and pulled out for sale at community events. Every year or two, the board engages in a long debate about whether to spend money printing more T-shirts, since they don't seem to sell very well. No one has particular responsibility for sales, so not much gets done. These groups raise a very small fraction of their income through enterprise.

• *Earned income projects to diversify funding.* These nonprofits are better organized. They offer a wider range of goods and services for sale. Somebody's job description (perhaps a volunteer) mentions marketing, promotion, or sales. These groups see earned income as a way to supplement other funding streams, usually grants and individual donors. They're always looking for ways to diversify but don't view themselves as "being in business," since enterprise is not their primary fundraising or outreach strategy. Organizations in this category are earning perhaps 5-20 percent of their budgets from sales.

• *Entrepreneurial thinking: members and clients as customers.* Groups at this stage think and behave a little differently. They ask themselves, "Do we have assets—goods, services, 'intellectual property'—that someone might buy? If so, who? How much would they be willing to pay?" They examine their free or low-cost services to learn if potential customers can pay and what price the market will bear. Many of these organizations have found ways to repackage their knowledge or programs to reach different audiences that are more likely paying customers. Earned income is an important line item in the budget, and several staff members are involved in product or service development, promotion, and keeping track of the income. They may also have an informal brainstorm group or "venture committee" made up of board, staff, and community volunteers. These groups usually generate 10 to 50 percent of their revenue through the sales of goods and services.

After this stage, the line diverges (as Yogi Berra once said, "When you reach the fork in the road, take it"). One fork leads to nonprofit "social purpose businesses"; the other leads to for-profit businesses "spun off" from their nonprofit hosts.

• *Nonprofit social purpose businesses.* These organizations have been set up (or evolved) to rely primarily on earned income. They have strong social missions but function as businesses in nearly all respects. They are attuned to the needs of the marketplace, since they survive and prosper by meeting the needs of their customers. By necessity, they tend to have more sophisticated accounting systems and the expertise to use them. Everyone on staff is involved in sales or customer service in some way. Grants and donations supplement earned income, rather than the other way around. These organizations typically earn 50 to 100 percent of their budgets.

• *Spin-offs and for-profit subsidiaries.* In some cases, a nonprofit will create or "spin off" a program and run it as a for-profit venture to avoid legal conflicts with the organization's charitable purpose. In other cases, the skills and requirements needed for running the business are so different from the primary culture of the organization that it created internal controversy. Although they are legally distinct, subsidiaries and their nonprofit hosts can have overlapping boards. They are taxed like any other business, receiving no tax benefits from their association with a nonprofit.

This subsidiary structure is fairly common; many thrift stores are managed in this fashion. One of the best-known and most lucrative spin-offs occurred in 1998, when Minnesota Public Radio—the folks who bring you "Prairie Home Companion"—sold their direct marketing subsidiary, Riverton Trading Company, for *$120 million* to retail giant Dayton Hudson. Most of the money was placed in the nonprofit's endowment fund.[17]

Minnesota Public Radio began selling T-shirts and tapes (and probably coffee mugs) in the early 1980s, which demonstrates the potential for moving along the continuum. However, don't assume that one end of this spectrum is somehow better or more desirable than the other end. Each organization needs to find its own place.

If placed beside the continuum, the nonprofits profiled in this book might look something like the illustration here. I hasten to add that this is my best estimate; the organizations themselves may not agree with my assessment or design. However, I believe they are *all* role models in devising strategies to earn money, which is why they've been included in this project.

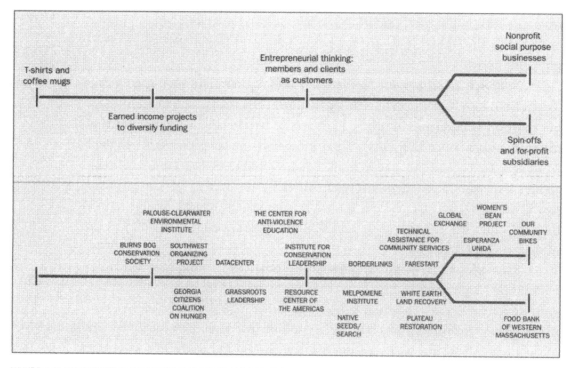

WHERE THE NONPROFITS IN THIS BOOK FALL ON THE EARNED INCOME CONTINUUM

In reality, the majority of nonprofits will never get involved in enterprise in any significant way.

- They don't have the time or energy or ready cash.

- They don't have the self-discipline.

- They don't have anything to sell that the market wants.

This book will help you decide if your organization can generate substantial earned income. You may ultimately decide that enterprise isn't an appropriate choice. If so, you'll be making your decision based on real information, rather than speculation, fears, or fantasies.

Now that you understand the history and context of earned income ventures, and the range of available approaches, it's time to consider your own strengths and weaknesses. Are you ready for the marketplace? Chapter Three, "Creating an Enterprising Nonprofit," will help you determine if you have the necessary tools, systems, and talents.

Flavors of the Desert

NATIVE SEEDS/SEARCH

TUCSON, ARIZONA

WWW.NATIVESEEDS.ORG

ANNUAL BUDGET: $806,000

EARNED INCOME: 33%

EARNED INCOME STRATEGIES

- CONSUMER GOODS: RETAIL
- CONSUMER SERVICES
- PUBLICATIONS

When Padre Ignaz Pfeffercorn ate his first chiltepine, or wild chile pepper, he described the experience as "hellfire in my mouth." Pfeffercorn, an eighteenth-century missionary, was posted to the region now known as Arizona and Sonora, Mexico. In the course of his travels, he became familiar with many traditional desert foods, ranging from posole and beans to nopalites (prickly pear cactus) and mesquite meal. He developed a sophisticated palate. "One becomes accustomed to it after bold victories," he wrote of the chiltepine, "so that with time the dish becomes tolerable and finally very agreeable."[1]

Flash forward two centuries. Mahina Drees and Gary Paul Nabhan were working on the Tohono O'odham reservation west of Tucson, promoting gardening for better nutrition. "What we found," says Drees, "was that nobody wanted broccoli. They'd say, 'Can you get me seeds for that *ha:l* squash my grandmother used to grow?'" Drees and Nabhan began an informal seed exchange, shuttling seeds from town to town across the sprawling reservation. In 1983, they and their spouses founded Native Seeds/SEARCH, which works to conserve the traditional crops, seeds, and farming methods that have sustained native peoples throughout the U.S. Southwest and northern Mexico.

Native Seeds/SEARCH manages a seed bank with 1,800 crop varieties, including corn, beans, squash, chiles, sunflowers, melons, and gourds. More than 250 varieties are offered for sale to gardeners, free to Native Americans living in the region. Since many of these crops are rare or endangered, one of the organization's goals is to ensure their survival through wide distribution By selling seeds, they support and promote their mission. They also tap a huge market: 40 percent of Americans identify themselves as gardeners. It's the number one hobby in the country.

Native Seeds/SEARCH uses four strategies to promote sales:

1. *Catalogs.* Every January, a sixty-page *Seedlisting* is mailed to 21,000 households. Winter is when gardeners, especially serious gardeners, select their crops and buy seeds, so timing is critical. To educate readers and place the sale of seeds in the proper context, the *Seedlisting* also describes indigenous agriculture in the Southwest. Several pages are devoted to other mission-related products: traditional foods, gardening books, native crafts, regional cookbooks, and gift baskets. A holiday catalog, mailed in October, emphasizes gift items. From time to time, postcards or brochures are sent to announce new products or promote perishables that need to be sold quickly. Catalog sales by mail, phone, and Web site net about $90,000.

NATIVE SEEDS/SEARCH ANNUAL CATALOG GOES TO 21,000 HOUSEHOLDS

In deciding which items to include, former executive director and board member Angelo Joaquin, Jr., says, "If it helps indigenous farmers to stay on the land and keep farming, we should sell it." Joaquin, a member of the Tohono O'odham Nation, adds, "We educate the public about how native people think about life in this region. In that sense, we promote cultural diversity through the products we choose."

Long-time distribution manager Junie Hostetler offers three more criteria: quality, sales potential, and origin. "A few years ago we added soup mixes and dried tomatoes from San Juan Pueblo in New Mexico," says Hostetler, who recently retired. "Whenever we buy directly from a Native American community, we're helping to fulfill our mission."

2. *Retail store.* Native Seeds/SEARCH operates a store in a lively historic shopping district in Tucson. Their 1,200-square-foot shop includes an exposed adobe wall (staff and volunteers spent weeks scraping off the plaster), racks of seed jars used as room dividers, and a counter that opens on the mail-order area behind the store. While shopping, customers can watch staff and volunteers filling orders and packaging seeds. This design also reduces costs—distribution staff can keep an eye on the store while processing orders. Retail items, including several not offered in the catalog, range in price from prickly pear lollipops (75 cents) to hand-woven Mayo rugs ($480).

To increase traffic, Native Seeds/SEARCH promotes the store in its newsletter, the *Seedhead News;* distributes flyers to local members; works with local and regional media on feature articles; and solicits free or discounted advertising from newspapers and magazines. The group also joined the local merchants' association, which buys a series of ads, purchased at a bulk rate to save everyone money, featuring local stores and restaurants. Retail sales from the store and seasonal events total $90,000 annually.

3. *Seasonal events.* Native Seeds maintains a busy calendar of public programs throughout the year. Many are free; workshops cost a nominal fee (for only $25, for example, you can learn how to harvest and prepare cholla cactus buds, a traditional delicacy). Staff and volunteers set up sales tables at every program. The biggest events are the annual La Fiesta de Los Chiles at the Tucson Botanical Gardens, and the twice-annual Fourth Avenue street fair, which brings hundreds of thousands of visitors to the district. A typical December street fair, which lasts three days, generates $5,000 to $6,000 in retail sales.

In recent years, Native Seeds/SEARCH launched an annual fundraising event called "Flavors of the Desert." Building on the chef-participation theme pioneered by Share Our Strength and other organizations, Native Seeds recruits local restaurants to help with a food sampling event. The hook is that participating chefs must use traditional desert foods in their recipes.

This event creates new business in at least three ways: attendees can buy recipes and special ingredients at the on-site sales table, publicity and word of mouth bring new customers to the store, and the organization builds relationships with local restaurants. Many chefs incorporate these recipes into their regular menus and shop at Native Seeds/SEARCH for their chipotles (smoked chiles), posole (hominy), chiltepines (wild peppers), cholla cactus buds, mesquite meal, four varieties of corn meal, sixteen varieties of beans, and other hard-to-find foods.

Chef Janos Wilder, owner of Janos restaurant, is a big fan, customer, and new board member. "Some of these crops have been grown and harvested for more than 2,000 years," he says. "As a chef, these products ground me, literally, in the culture and foods of the region. Our menus are informed by these foods. It's a unique selling point for our customers." Each October, Janos features a "chile harvest menu" based on chile products from Native Seeds/SEARCH. A percentage of the proceeds from these meals is donated to the organization.

In 1998, the organization purchased property for a conservation farm. While the primary purpose was to rejuvenate the seed stock, the acreage allows for bigger grow-outs, which means more seeds for sale. The farm is also being used for public education events and will eventually host a fall harvest celebration.

4. *Internet sales.* Native Seeds has been offering products on-line for more than two years, though until recently customers had to print out an order form and mail it in. When they added a secure credit card section, orders jumped. Internet business now accounts for about 30 percent of catalog income, says Julie Kornmeyer, the new distribution manager. Overall, sales are flat, she says, "but the mix is changing. Sales from the paper catalog are down, Internet is way up, walk-in business is increasing gradually."

Native Seeds/SEARCH serves more than 4,000 customers each year. Thirty percent are members of the organization, paying annual dues of at least $25 per year. (Native Americans living in the Southwest may join for free.) It's evident that these people are also the most committed: the average member customer spends 60 percent more on purchases than the average non-member customer. The organization encourages all shoppers to join through a special annual appeal. Each year, about 10 percent are converted to members.

Joaquin, the former executive director, is excited about the increasingly diverse mix of products, but he remains cautious about what goes into the store and the catalog. "We could probably make a lot of money selling tourist-type things," he says, "but we're not driven by money. We have to convey respect for these seeds and the people who grow them. We are simply caretakers."

THINGS TO THINK ABOUT

- *Watch the timing.* Some products are time-sensitive. In most parts of North America, you'll sell more seeds in February than September. As you develop goods and services, consider *when* people are likely to want them and plan accordingly.
- *If you can't predict cash flow, your business will falter.* At Native Seeds/SEARCH, holiday shoppers provide half the annual sales income in the final quarter of the year. As a result, staff and board learned to build up the bank balance in the winter and reduce expenses during the slow summer months. A detailed cash-flow projection can help you figure out when to spend money, when to save it, and when you'll need an outside subsidy, such as a grant or a loan.
- *The timing of your fiscal year can have an impact on your business and your budget.* For more than a decade, Native Seeds/SEARCH kept accounts on a calendar year. Because such a high percentage of their income is earned in the final quarter, however, preparing a timely, accurate budget for the following year was

always difficult. To address this problem, they switched fiscal years; for accounting purposes, the new year now begins October 1. The change also saved money on the annual audit, since their accounting firm offered the nonprofit an off-season discount price for work in their slower fall season.

• *Co-op advertising can save you money and increase your business.* Can you identify like-minded local businesses that will work together on joint advertisements or promotions?

• *If appropriate, involve local businesses as both customers and promoters of your products and programs.* Native Seeds/SEARCH spotlights local chefs at their "Flavors of the Desert" benefit. These chefs then promote the organization through restaurant events and patronize the business by buying ingredients. Everyone wins.

• *Incentives help members become better customers and help recruit customers as members.* To encourage members to shop, and to encourage shoppers to join, Native Seeds/SEARCH offers a 10 percent discount for members. Other organizations, such as Global Exchange, go even further, offering a 30 percent discount on the day's purchases when customers join in their store. What extra benefits do your donors or members enjoy in exchange for supporting your work? How will you promote those benefits to customers to encourage them to contribute?

Chapter 3

Creating an
enterprising nonprofit

▪   ▪   ▪

After working as a fundraiser for a succession of social change groups, including several entrepreneurial organizations, I launched my own consulting business in 1994. I did it gradually, working out of my home while I tested the market. With no formal business training, I was operating on instinct, a bit of practical experience, and common sense.

Despite my limited business background, I was confident of success. First of all, I had done my homework. I talked with other consultants and trainers, contacted prospective clients, figured out how much I could charge, made some informal financial projections, and began to get referrals. Second, to reduce the risk, I held on to my old job while building up my practice. I was working the plan, and the plan was working. Third, I had a contract to write a book, which I expected would generate income, credibility, and new consulting clients. (That book, *Grassroots Grants,* is available from Jossey-Bass.)

Most important, I was prepared to invest huge amounts of time and effort, as well as some savings, to make the business succeed. I was passionate about it. My new business was a means to an end. It allowed me to pursue my life's work: creating social change by helping nonprofits become more effective.

"If your vision is based on a deep-seated need of your own," Bill Shore writes, "you will not fail. Your need will not let you."[1] His book, *Revolution of the Heart,* isn't a self-help treatise; it's about nonprofit enterprise.

Without passionate people doing the work, your venture will fail. Without a strong sense of commitment spread through the whole organization—if you have one or two passionate people surrounded by a sea of skeptics—your unfortunate venture will sputter along in low gear. To make this work, you need to bring everyone along for the ride.

In this chapter, we discuss staff and board roles and issues of organizational culture in an entrepreneurial nonprofit. In case your group lacks any suggested knowledge or skills, a resource list is provided.

The enterprise advocate

Given the usual state of grassroots groups—overworked, underpaid, carrying the fate of the world on their collective shoulders—it's a wonder that earned income projects are launched at all. Faced with the daily crises, who has time to plan, finance, and run a business?

Everyone who has ever written, taught, spoken, trained, or thought seriously about this subject has come to the same conclusion: for the business to function, someone has to take responsibility. Organizations that stumble into sales reach a similar conclusion through trial and error. It's simple. You cannot manage a business off the corner of somebody's desk. You cannot run a successful venture when product development, financing, management, marketing, and customer service are shoehorned into someone's overflowing job description. It doesn't work. The person who assumes responsibility for the business might be called the "enterprise advocate."

The role of enterprise advocate is not defined by the number of hours assigned, although in most cases this person will invest a lot of time. In addition to business skills, the job requires focus, commitment, and a willingness to assume responsibility for the venture. Like an able community organizer, the enterprise advocate must have a knack for getting other people to help. She lines up her allies within the organization and beyond. At staff meetings, board meetings, and other venues where decisions are made, she advocates for the needs and interests of the venture. Even if she has other job responsibilities, she's always thinking about the business, and a substantial portion of her workday is dedicated to managing the business. She keeps pen, paper, and flashlight near her pillow to capture that crucial marketing idea when it arrives in the middle of the night.

Where can you find this person? You have two options: inside or outside the organization. Take a hard look at your current talent pool (staff, board, members, volunteers) to see if you can identify someone with appropriate business skills and interests, and train that person to do the job. William A. Duncan, in a booklet written for the Center for Community Change, suggests the opposite approach. "There are many feasible venture ideas," he writes, "but few people who can actually make them work. So although it might seem backward at first, you're wise to begin by finding those people," even if you have to look outside your group, "and building the business around their skills and interests."[2] Says Kirsten Moller of Global Exchange, "We've hired managers for their politics and not their business skills. They need both."

If you choose to go outside your organization, however, beware: hire someone who loves your mission as much as he enjoys building a business. "It's a sales job," says Judy Mahle Lutter of Melpomene Institute, "but what you're really selling is your mission, not your stuff."

Every organization profiled in this book includes an entrepreneur on staff or board, and many groups have different people in charge of different earned income projects. However, no one has the official title "enterprise advocate." Their job titles are executive director, distribution manager, development director, bookstore manager, board member, "the guy who handles marketing and distribution," president, associate director, communications director, fundraising committee chair, tour director, and—my personal favorite—farmer. They all share one trait: when they look at the world, they see opportunities for earning income.

The venture committee, the board, and the staff

To build an entrepreneurial organization, you'll need a "brain trust" or venture committee to help brainstorm, plan, implement, manage, and evaluate your ventures. Ideally, this team should include a couple of staff members (including the enterprise advocate or business manager), a few board members, and perhaps a sympathetic business person from the community. You might also include a member or client who is also a prospective customer. The ideal planning group has five to eight people. If the committee is too small, it won't spark enough ideas; if it's too big, you'll have a hard time reaching consensus. (You'll find tips on brainstorming and evaluating your venture ideas in Chapter Four.)

The venture committee brainstorms prospective earned income projects, assesses their feasibility, and plans the ones deemed most appropriate. Initially, it's an ad hoc team. If your organization ultimately decides against all of the potential earned income strategies (remember, enterprise won't work for every group), the committee disbands. If you choose to move forward, these folks can function as a standing committee of advisers to the business.

Board members participating on this committee play a crucial role because they carry the entrepreneurial message back to the full board. When they arrive, they are bound to meet resistance. Boards are designed to provide detached oversight. The inspired idea that carried the venture committee into fantasies of wealth and well-being might not survive a stiff cross-examination from the board. This is a good thing, as many marginal ideas will be screened out. However, if the board stonewalls from the beginning—"We've never done things that way," or "Running a business will compromise our integrity," or "What do you mean, charge people for our services?"—you'll probably need a new board.

"First and foremost," writes Richard Steckel, "don't do enterprise if your board doesn't agree. They will kill it—and most likely you—in the process.... Wait until a majority of the board members—including the most influential ones—approve the concept before undertaking it. Even after your board approves, you will need to continue educating them."[3]

Engaging and involving staff members raises a different but related set of challenges. As mentioned in Chapter One, many activists, organizers, social workers, artists, troublemakers, and nonconformists—the kinds of folks who are attracted to social change work—are suspicious of business and anything that smells like business. Some joined nonprofits after becoming fed up with the corporate world. Others are escaping bad experiences in retail sales. Still others distrust capitalism for all the reasons outlined in the first chapter. If they don't embrace commerce as an important part of your work, chaos will ensue.

Bringing the staff around involves several strategies, best used in combination.

- *Put them on the venture committee.* Participating staff members fill two crucial roles. First, they have the most knowledge about programs and day-to-day operations, so can best judge barriers and opportunities. Second, their enthusiasm will help allay the suspicions and concerns of other staff members.

- *Emphasize the ways that earned income can increase your organization's independence.* When staff positions are underwritten through grants, those jobs are at risk. If the group can become more self-sufficient, everyone benefits. "With [our] businesses," says Cindy Bowman formerly of Esperanza Unida, "we have the ability to make decisions and go in directions on our own, without being funded for it first."[4]

- *Explore a salary structure that includes incentives and bonuses based on business performance.* Bonuses can be used to reward the enterprise managers (see case study on Global Exchange following this chapter), or structured as an organization-wide "profit sharing plan." Earned income can also underwrite extra benefits for *all* staff, including professional training, tuition for further education, travel, mental health days, sabbaticals, and pensions.

- *Create a flexible workplace.* Bureaucracy is the enemy of innovation and, by extension, the death of enterprise. Business managers require a certain amount of freedom to try new ideas and, from time to time, to stumble and fall. You may need different standards of job performance and accountability for different types of jobs. In organizations that strive to be equitable, this can generate conflict.

David Sharken of The Food Bank of Western Massachusetts reports that running a farm "wreaked havoc on our personnel policies." Farmers work long hours during the growing season, he explains, and can't always attend staff meetings and file written reports. They require lots of autonomy to respond to the needs of their customers, who in this instance were both the anti-poverty agencies that distribute produce to their clients and the more affluent "subscribers" who pay the costs of running the farm. After years of trying to accommodate the various needs of the agency staff and the farmers, the farm was spun off and became a for-profit business working under contract to The Food Bank. This creative solution made everyone happier.

Recruiting for Enterprise: Grassroots Leadership

Grassroots Leadership (www.grassrootsleadership.org) was founded in 1980 to develop the community organizers, leaders, organizations, networks, and coalitions that will make long-term progressive change inevitable across the South. What makes the group unusual, says co-founder Si Kahn, is an emphasis on culture—music, drama, poetry, oral history, visual arts, preaching, storytelling, dance, and so forth— and how cultural work strengthens organizing. This focus also provides lots of earned income opportunities, since most people are willing to pay—indeed, expect to pay— for artistic goods, services, and experiences.

Grassroots Leadership has excelled at recruiting board members who understand enterprise and can help with earned income projects. Kahn points out that many "cultural workers"—artists, musicians, actors, designers, and so forth—fit the profile, so he invites them to participate. As he told *The Progressive*, "A surprising number of cultural workers are very successful self-managing business people. To make a living as artists, they have to learn small business skills," including financial management, cash flow projections, marketing, and promotion.[6]

Kahn, a well-known singer and songwriter, performs at about twenty events per year to benefit his organization. He's often joined by former board members Jane Sapp, Cathy Fink, and John McCutcheon, musicians who help out by donating performances, recruiting other artists, and organizing concerts.

McCutcheon took his board involvement a step further. Working with Rounder Records (www.rounder.com), which Kahn describes as "the largest small record company in the U.S.," McCutcheon donated his time to produce a series of multicultural CDs and cassettes for children.

SOME OF GRASSROOTS LEADERSHIP'S CULTURAL PRODUCTS

These include *Rainbow Sign,* which features music from around the world, with selections from Beausoleil, Sweet Honey in the Rock, Yellowman, and HARP (Holly Near, Arlo Guthrie, Ronnie Gilbert, Pete Seeger). *Rainbow Tales* and *Rainbow Tales, Too* collect spoken stories from Brenda Wong Aoki, Garrison Keillor, Jay Silverheels, and other storytellers. Sales have generated more than $12,000 (and lots of great publicity) for Grassroots Leadership. Without McCutcheon's skills and key relationships—his contacts with the record label and many of the artists—plus his willingness to put in the work, these albums would never have been created.

The moral of the story: when recruiting board members, seek wisdom, passion, energy, good politics—and self-employed people who understand how busness works and can bring useful relationships to the table. Don't automatically look for corporate officers; a small business owner or working artist may prove a better choice.

Finding and using outside help

One of the most important steps in launching an enterprise is figuring out what you don't know. Maybe you don't understand how to price your goods or services. Or you'd like to know if your income generation idea has been tried before. Or your accounting system needs an upgrade. Perhaps the idea of writing a business plan scares the sense out of you.

Take heart, help is on the way. Solicit an outside perspective to help you see past your assumptions about who you serve and what you can offer a paying customer. On the other hand—this is important—many consultants and "outside helpers" won't understand the culture of your organization; in some cases they won't have experience in the nonprofit world. You will need to educate them as much as they educate you.

Here are a few places to begin your search:

- *Your local business college.* Business professors are always looking for hands-on student projects. If you want help with brainstorming or testing venture ideas, market research, or business planning, ask a class to adopt your organization. If your local or regional business school offers a specialty in nonprofit enterprise, so much the better. You might even locate your next enterprise advocate in the classroom, nearing graduation and looking for a challenging, socially relevant job.

- *Your local nonprofit resource center.* In several hundred communities across the U.S, nonprofit resource centers provide training and technical assistance. Many are affiliated with the Foundation Center (800/424-9836, www.fdncenter.org) and house resource libraries. To find your nearest nonprofit resource center, check the Foundation Center affiliate list on their

Web site and talk with other nonprofits. If such a center is located nearby, someone will know.

- *Your local or regional community loan fund.* Community loan funds support mall businesses and nonprofit ventures in economically disadvantaged communities by offering low-interest loans. Many also provide technical assistance and training for entrepreneurs. For instance, the Northern California Community Loan Fund (www.ncclf.org) offers a "Fiscal Fitness" program to help nonprofits improve their financial management systems. You can learn more about community loan funds through the National Community Capital Association (215/923-4754, www.communitycapital.org).

- *Local businesspeople.* You and your organization conduct business daily: you buy food, rent space, use electricity, have the copy machine repaired, and so forth. Your vendors (and other local business owners) can be drafted to serve on the venture committee or simply provide informal advice. BorderLinks asked a supportive businessman to help with a growth plan, then put his advice to work. In five years, their annual budget has increased from $75,000 to $550,000.

- *Your local economic development agency or chamber of commerce.* Most of these folks are operating at a much higher financial level than your group—trying to lure multi-million dollar employers to town—but in some cases they can provide practical suggestions. And, as Eliza Olson of the Burns Bog Conservation Society points out, you may gain political clout by joining your local chamber of commerce.

- *Consultants.* Dozens of consultants—individuals, private firms, and nonprofits—specialize in nonprofit enterprise. Unfortunately, at this time there is no professional association or master list of practitioners, so you'll need to ask around. Four good places to start are the National Center for Social Entrepreneurs (800/696-4066, www.socialentrepreneurs.org), the Institute for Social Entrepreneurs (952/942-7715, www.socialent.org), Community Wealth Ventures (202/478-6570, www.communitywealth.com), and the Social Entrepreneurs Alliance for Change, or SEA Change (415/291-9900, www.sea-change.org). Your local nonprofit resource center may also offer referrals.

Remember, advice from an outside consultant is just that: advice. It's not a commandment or a guarantee. No amount of outside expertise can make up for a lack of internal understanding of enterprise, or limited follow-through with the advice provided. For this reason, the experts recommend that you do as much planning as possible within the organization, if only to educate yourselves. Don't hire someone to write your business plan; if necessary, hire someone to teach you how to write your own.

Knowing what your work costs

"Most small nonprofits," writes Nancy Haycock in *The Nonprofit Entrepreneur,* "do not have a realistic notion of what their internal costs are, and when they try to project the costs of their earned income venture, they have a lot of trouble. Often their estimates are too low. In many cases they don't include overhead or the value of their own time."[6]

The next chapter covers pricing, but since we're listing the components of an enterprising organization, let's talk about management systems. Sophisticated nonprofits embrace accounting. The people who work there are not afraid of math; indeed, some of them actually enjoy working with numbers. They also have systems in place (often, informal ones) to track everyone's time and productivity. Many food banks, for example, keep logs of how many people they serve, how many staff and volunteer hours are needed to provide that service, and what it costs to serve each person, including the value of the hours.

Commerce is based on a simple premise: The money you bring in must be of greater value than the time and money you spend. If we include the "second bottom line" of meeting your mission while you earn income, the equation looks something like this: The money you bring in and the mission-related benefits you create must be of greater value than the time and money you spend.

If you subsidize a failing venture with cash, you will lose money and eventually go bankrupt. If you subsidize it with time (in other words, paying people poorly and working them to death), you and your organization will crash and burn. If you don't have control of the numbers—both time and money—you can't project what it will take to break even and earn a profit. Under these circumstances, it's impossible to make a realistic plan.

Before you think seriously about starting a business, get control of the numbers. If you need help with accounting and time management systems, take another look at the resources listed above in the section on finding and using outside help.

Are you prepared to enter the marketplace? Do you have the right people, the right systems, the right attitude? To answer these questions, fill out Worksheet 3.1. Once you've completed this self-evaluation, it's time to start thinking about possible ventures. The process of generating earned income ideas, then sorting out and selecting the most workable options, is outlined in Chapter Four.

Are you ready for enterprise?

Use this worksheet to determine your "venture potential." Do you have the talent and infrastructure you'll need to build an enterprising nonprofit?

1. **TALENT POOL.** List anyone involved with your group—board, former board, staff, active member, key volunteer—with skills in the following areas:

   - Sales: _____

   _____

   _____

   - Provision of services/customer relations: _____

   _____

   _____

   - Marketing, including communications, media, advertising: _____

   _____

   _____

   - Graphic design: _____

   _____

   _____

   - Financial management: _____

   _____

   _____

   - Business planning: _____

   _____

   _____

   - Fundraising, including grants and individual gifts: _____

   _____

   _____

   Who are the best candidates to be your "enterprise advocate"? _____

   _____

   _____

   _____

2. **LEADERSHIP.** Rate your board on its leadership capacity for developing earned income ventures. Does your board have entrepreneurial skills or inclinations? Do you have a plan for recruiting more board members with useful expertise or relationships?

Excellent				Poor
5	4	3	2	1

Strengths of board for working on earned income strategies: _____

_____

_____

_____

Areas needing improvement: _____

_____

_____

_____

3. **OUTSIDE HELP.** List any external resources available to help with your venture. The list could include books, libraries, other nonprofits, consultants, college classes, training programs, and so on.

_____

_____

_____

4. **INFRASTRUCTURE.** Rate your management systems, using the questions in each category to guide your thinking.

- *Financial systems.* Can you keep accurate track of your finances? Do you produce monthly reports? If you were to start a venture, could your accounting system handle the billing, and keep track of payables and receivables?

Excellent				Poor
5	4	3	2	1

Strengths of financial system: _____

_____

_____

_____

Areas needing improvement: _____

_____

_____

_____

- *Time management.* Do you have a system for tracking people's time? How do you evaluate whether you're using staff and volunteer time effectively?

Excellent				Poor
5	4	3	2	1

Strengths of time management system: _____

_____

_____

_____

Areas needing improvement: _____

_____

_____

_____

- *Data management.* Does your database meet your needs? Do you schedule consistent staff or volunteer time to update the database? If you were to start a venture, is the database designed to keep track of customers, prospective customers, ordering, and inventory?

Excellent				Poor
5	4	3	2	1

Strengths of data management system: _____

_____

_____

_____

Areas needing improvement: _____

_____

_____

_____

5. **CURRENT EARNED INCOME PROJECTS.** What, if anything, are you selling now? List all goods and services that you currently offer for a fee.

_____

_____

_____

_____

Which ones are most popular? Why? _____

_____

_____

_____

Which ones *net* the most money? _____

_____

_____

_____

How much money do you generate each year from earned income? $ _____

What percentage of your budget is earned?   _____ %

What lessons have you learned from your sales program? _____

_____

_____

_____

_____

How have you applied those lessons to other aspects of your work? _____

_____

_____

_____

_____

Capitalism with a Conscience

GLOBAL EXCHANGE

SAN FRANCISCO, CALIFORNIA

WWW.GLOBALEXCHANGE.ORG

ANNUAL BUDGET: $3,160,000

EARNED INCOME: 63%

EARNED INCOME STRATEGIES

• TRAVEL AND TOURISM

• CONSUMER GOODS: RETAIL

• PUBLICATIONS

Ever consider a vacation tour of a prison? How about a meeting in the jungle with a group of armed freedom fighters? Would you prefer to spend your holiday in a shantytown, talking with employees of the local sweatshop? Or perhaps you'd like to learn first-hand what the words "economic embargo" mean to the people who've been embargoed?

If you think this sounds like a dumb idea for a travel agency, think again. Since 1989, more than 10,000 people have participated in "Reality Tours" organized by the human rights group Global Exchange. From South Africa to the north of Ireland, from Chiapas, Mexico, to Iran, from Palestine to Israel and back again, Global Exchange travelers learn about international conflict from a local perspective. A few years ago, the group launched an "Exploring California" program to provide similarly enlightening travel opportunities closer to home. Overall, their travel program grosses nearly $1.9 million per year.

Medea Benjamin and Kirsten Moller, who served as co-directors, founded Global Exchange in 1988 as a spin-off from Food First, an international hunger relief group. Their goal, in Moller's words, was to create "the Greenpeace of human rights" through public education, community organizing, and direct action on issues of corporate responsibility. They also set out to combine moral principles with successful business practices in their day-to-day operations. "Part of what we do," Benjamin told the *Los Angeles Times*, "is expose conditions at these companies and, on our own small scale, show how you can run a good business."[1]

Global Exchange has three business components:

1. *Overseas tourism.* From the beginning, both their community organizing and business strategies emphasized face-to-face contact between U.S. activists

and their counterparts in other countries. The organization has both built upon and helped to create an "alternative travel" movement that includes ecotourism and a wide variety of experiential education programs.

In reality, most Global Exchange tours are a lot more uplifting than visits to prisons and sweatshops. During a recent year, titles of their tours included Haiti: A Culture of Resistance; India: The Gandhian Legacy; Iran: History, Culture, and Revolution in Persia; and Ireland: St. Patrick's Day in the North of Ireland.

More than half of their scheduled tours go to Cuba, where participants can attend the International Latin American Film Festival and la Fiesta del Caribe; follow Che Guevara's footsteps; learn about sustainable agriculture and revolutionary culture; study Cuba's African roots, rhythms, and religion; and participate in women's, veterans, and youth delegations. Indeed, the organization is practically a Cuban travel agency—for every scheduled excursion to the island, they organize three customized tours for schools, churches, family reunions, and other groups. Despite the long-standing U.S. embargo against trade with Cuba, most educational trips to Cuba are allowed under U.S. law—a fact made clear in the group's promotional materials.

Prices for Global Exchange tours, which last a week or two, range from $750 to $2,850 plus travel to the host country, and include meals, accommodations, local travel, and educational programs. These prices are sometimes higher than those of other nonprofit travel groups, but lower than most university alumni study tours. "Our prices allow us to pay our workers a decent wage," Moller says. At the same time, the organization nets $350 per person per trip. This "surplus" is then plowed back into the program to develop future tours, since it takes several years for a new destination to break even.

Since the goal of these trips is to educate and activate, Global Exchange follows up with travelers once they return home. Moller estimates that more than half report back to their own communities with slide shows, church presentations, letters to their friends, and so forth. The Mexico trip alumni have an "action alert" e-mail list to help them respond to human rights developments in the region.

In some cases, individuals are so moved by the experience that they become citizen-diplomats. Malia Everette, who coordinates the Reality Tours, tells of a photojournalist who was appalled by the effects of the embargo against Cuba. When the journalist returned to the United States from a Global Exchange tour, he began raising money to buy better equipment for young Cuban athletes. Traveler Carol Press and her family brought three duffel bags of medical supplies to a dispensary run by a group of Cuban nuns. At her encouragement, a friend traveling to the island has recently done the same.

2. *U.S. tourism.* In 1996, Global Exchange launched the Exploring California program to offer educational tours of their home state. Recent trips have focused on the prison industry, forestry and sustainable development, environmental justice issues, changes in welfare law, the local garment industry, Mexico–U.S. border issues, and agricultural labor, including "Getting the Dirt on Lettuce." As former program director Lisa Russ told *Orange Coast* magazine, "I lived in agricultural Ventura County and always wondered who these workers were in the fields. But I couldn't just pull over, roll down the windows, and ask. Global Exchange trips are a way to pull over together and have conversations you could never have on your own."[2]

While Global Exchange has a clear political agenda, these trips are designed to include a wide variety of voices and opinions. "Their perspective was put on the table at the beginning," Julio Leboy told *Orange Coast* after visiting San Diego and Tijuana with the group. "But great effort was made to expose participants to a range of viewpoints."[3]

While U.S. travel expenses are often higher than those overseas, the domestic trips are priced to sell. Day trips cost $30 to $100 on a sliding scale; weekend excursion, $120 to $150; longer trips, up to $550.

"People are willing to pay more to go overseas," Moller says. "We can't charge enough to cover our costs in California." Indeed, participant fees cover only 10 percent of the expenses, which include staff time, insurance, promotion, and the like. The balance comes from foundation grants and membership donations. "This program will always require a subsidy," she sighs. "It's a part of our mission, so we'll raise the money to do it."

Global Exchange actively promotes their programs through mailings to their 12,000 members and aggressive outreach to travel writers and publications. They also work to build cooperative relationships with travel agents. The best source of new business is always word of mouth: at least 50 percent of their travelers are friends and family of past participants.

GLOBAL EXCHANGE PROMOTES ITS REALITY TOURS THROUGH MAILINGS TO ITS 12,000 MEMBERS AND OUTREACH TO THE TRAVEL INDUSTRY

3. *Retail sales.* To promote human rights and generate income for their programs, Global Exchange also sells crafts and other items from overseas. Their "Fair Trade" program grosses $600,000 per year through retail stores in Berkeley and San Francisco, plus a gift basket catalogue. Worker-owned cooperatives in sixty countries provide goods for the program, which includes a screening process to ensure fair wages and working conditions. When you "buy a basket from a typical crafts importer," their Web site states, "the peasant artisan receives a tiny fraction of what you pay. At Global Exchange Fair Trade Craft Stores, you know the producer gets her or his fair share, around 15–30% of the retail price."[4]

The San Francisco store, in fashionable Noe Valley, is a great place to experience sensory overload. The yellow walls are covered with weavings and hand-crafted mirrors. Mobiles and brightly colored Indonesian kites—birds, butterflies, and dragonflies—hang from the ceiling. The merchandise includes cloth hats from Nepal, papier-mâché animals from South Africa, coffee from Costa Rica and El Salvador, tea from Tibet, and hanging bamboo paintings from Vietnam. Prices range from fifty cents to $800, with the average item costing about $30.

To encourage sales, Global Exchange members receive a 10 percent discount on their purchases. When new members join at the shop, they get 30 percent off their current purchase. The first year's membership fee is then credited to the store's income line, which provides an incentive for store staff to solicit memberships.

Most years, Global Exchange strives to increase net profits by 7 percent. If the stores meet projections, retail employees receive a salary bonus, dividing 10 percent of the net profit. If they exceed it, employees share 25 percent of net profits above projections. In a recent year, one store met its target and the other exceeded it, so this is not merely a hypothetical bonus plan. While a typical part-time employee might receive a few hundred dollars, a successful store manager once pulled in a $1,600 bonus.

This policy was controversial, Moller says, because office and travel employees were not eligible for bonuses. With discussion and debate, everyone came to understand that retail employees have no flex time—when the store opens, the job begins—and fewer opportunities to participate in political work and organizational decision-making. The bonus plan is seen as a way to address that inequity. The program has worked so well, Global Exchange is considering bonus incentives for Reality Tour managers.

The Noe Valley store broke even in its first year—a remarkable achievement—and has made money every year since. The Berkeley store, on the other hand, took four years to cover its expenses, which is typical for a small business. A third store in Marin County was closed after losing money for two years because of a poor location.

For Benjamin and her colleagues, the bottom line is measured in more than dollars. After years of visiting overseas businesses where workers suffer through lousy working conditions, minimal pay, and "daily abuse," she's proud to have created a different kind of workplace. As she told the *Los Angeles Times,* "You can run a good, successful business *and* care about the world."[5]

THINGS TO THINK ABOUT

- *You're only as effective as your staff.* If you want to build a successful nonprofit venture, you'll need talented, committed, enthusiastic, well-trained staff. To attract and keep those people, as Global Exchange has done, you must offer fair wages, good benefits, appropriate training, and enough autonomy to allow them to do their jobs well.
- *Worker incentives can increase sales.* By giving retail employees a role in setting sales targets and then rewarding them for meeting and exceeding those targets, Global Exchange has made a conscious commitment to share both power and profits. The result: happier staff members (who are more enthusiastic sales people), less turnover, and more net income for the organization.
- *Maintain control of expenses.* "It's easy enough to get sales if you spend a lot of money," Kirsten Moller says. Her advice: take control of your budget and keep those expenses in line.
- *Even anticorporate campaigners need business skills, so get appropriate training.* Medea Benjamin offers standard advice to aspiring human rights activists: get an M.B.A. Young people "want to go work in poor communities overseas," she told the *Los Angeles Times.* "They ask, 'What should I do? Study health?' I say, study accounting, to help people operate their own businesses and cooperatives. I think the greatest need is for business skills—but business skills for people who don't want to get rich."[6]

Chapter 4

Choosing your new venture

▪   ▪   ▪

Nonprofit enterprise is about figuring out what you do well and selling it to people or institutions that want it. It's about power. When you're selling goods and services, you're negotiating from a position of strength. You've got something valuable that people want. You're in control. As Lucy Grugett of The Center for Anti-Violence Education says, "We like the control that fee-for-service gives us."

Thinking this way—imagining yourself dealing from a position of strength—may require a shift in perspective. If you're a community organizer, activist, social service provider, nonprofit manager, advocate, artist, or hell-raiser, you probably view yourself as the underdog, at least in the political arena. Once you identify what you have that others want, the equation changes. By developing products and services, you work to engage and satisfy prospective customers, who will likely become allies, members, and supporters. Through your sales program, you broaden your constituency. By raising unrestricted dollars and reaching new audiences, you gain more leverage over your future.

The first step in taking control—in seizing the power—is to think big. This chapter outlines a hands-on strategy for identifying and evaluating earned income ideas, then provides market research tools to help you test the feasibility of your ideas.

The brainstorming process

To begin, convene your venture committee and put them to work.[1] The committee needs a quiet place to work, a few uninterrupted hours, and something big to write on. (I like to use easels and chart paper, because it's easy to tape the notes to the walls.) The team should include a few people who are not at the center of the organization—a sympathetic local business person, perhaps, or a member who hasn't been deeply involved. If you provide services to the community, invite someone who has benefited from your services: a customer. As with any meeting, refreshments help to make everyone feel welcome.

Ask for a volunteer from the committee to facilitate the meeting, and another to write down all the ideas that will soon come tumbling forth. There's only one rule in a brainstorm: anything goes. In other words, all dreams are viable and nothing is too outlandish. Later, you'll sort through and evaluate all the options and many will be left behind, but for now, anything goes. The more outrageous, the better. If people say, "We can't do that," remind everyone of the rule. Be friendly but firm.

The purpose of the meeting is to answer the following questions, which you will also find on Worksheet 4.1:

Question 1: What do you do well? Write down three things about your organization—accomplishments, structure, the people involved, and so on—that you're most proud of. If you can come up with more than three items, write them down, too.

Question 2: What makes your group unique? What do you *have* or what do you *do* that no on else has or does? Like the first question, this one is designed to shift your mind into bragging mode. If you have trouble coming up with answers, move on to the next question.

Question 3: What assets do you have that someone might want? In the traditional sense, "assets" are physical property (your computer, your copy machine, your office) plus any investments or money in the bank. However, you must dig deeper. What is your expertise? Even better, what is your *unique* expertise? Any special skills? Sometimes we use the phrase *intellectual property*, which means, "What do you know that no one else knows?"

What products or services do you currently offer? Do you publish a newsletter? Who can you reach and influence: Your constituency? Your members? (Yes, I'm talking about the value of your mailing list.) Your funders? What about your track record, your credibility? How about the skills of professionals who help and support your organization? If a lot of people visit your facility—let's say you run a health clinic or a nature center—your "traffic" is an asset.

Our Community Bikes has access to lots of bike riders, so businesses that want to reach cyclists buy advertisements in their newsletter. FareStart runs a lovely restaurant serving good food at reasonable prices, but what makes the group unusual is their mission: they use the facility to provide job training for homeless men and women. The Georgia Citizens Coalition on Hunger connects African American farmers with an underserved market: residents of Atlanta's public housing projects. The organization is uniquely positioned to bring these two constituencies together for mutual support, and that's an asset.

The success of this process hinges on how creatively you answer the first question, so let yourself go. As Jed Emerson writes, "The New Social Entrepreneur...

can not only make lemonade from lemons, but lemonade and marmalade and scented shampoos and housecleaning sprays."[2]

If you have a hard time itemizing your assets, review your answers to the first two questions. You might find some ideas there.

Question 4: Given your mission and expertise, what additional goods and services could you develop? Another way of asking this question is, How can you repackage what you already do and what you already know to serve more people or provide new benefits to the people you already serve?

SouthWest Organizing Project turned their Chicano history book into an English-language video, a Spanish-language video, and a curriculum guide for teachers. Same research, same content, different formats. Technical Assistance for Community Services drew on decades of consulting experience to write and publish a handbook for new nonprofit organizations. Capitalizing on their relationships with musicians and record company staff, Grassroots Leadership produced a music CD.

Question 5: Who might want what you have to offer? Who are your prospective customers? Review all the ideas you've just generated and identify possible customers for current and potential products and services. You can create a master prospect list or, if you prefer lots of detail, separate lists for each product or service. Don't ignore your current constituents, but don't limit yourself—think as broadly as possible.

The Resource Center of the Americas offers community classes on language proficiency and cultural sensitivity. With a little repackaging, they were able to provide training to some unusual customers, including judges and other officers of the court and a large local newspaper. DataCenter sells research services to a wide range of clients, including immigration lawyers and brokers who specialize in socially responsible investments. In addition to their public tours, Global Exchange organizes customized trips for families and educational institutions.

Question 6: How can you reach your prospective customers? Once you've identified your customers, it's time to think about marketing. (For a whole lot of marketing ideas, see Chapter Seven.) As ever, ingenuity pays off in brainstorming and beyond. Include the obvious stuff, but go further.

The Women's Bean Project inaugurated a recipe contest that was written up in the *Denver Post*. The contest resulted in new food products to sell and new clientele to buy them. The Institute for Conservation Leadership solicits questions about nonprofit management from prospective clients, then publishes the answers in their newsletter and on their Web site. The Palouse-Clearwater Environmental Institute finds new customers for their commuter van service in the simplest way possible: they put their name, logo, and telephone number all over the van. It's a rolling billboard.

Question 7: Who are your potential partners? Who can help you develop or market these goods and services? By now, the walls will be covered with paper and some of the same constituencies will appear in several places. Prospective customers can also be partners: you sell them a service and, as part of the deal, they help you identify new customers or promote your work in other ways.

Our Community Bikes provides an interesting example. Through workplace training programs, they meet prospects who later patronize their bicycle shop for repairs and accessories. The corporations and government agencies that sponsor their workshops serve as promotional partners.

One-quarter of the organizations profiled in this book have created significant partnerships with businesses of all sizes—local, regional, and national. Don't assume that, because of your size or your politics, doing business with a corporation is impossible or inappropriate. Jennifer Lehman provides the details in Chapter Eight.

WORKSHEET 4.1

Brainstorming your new venture

Guide your venture committee through a structured brainstorm using this worksheet. Your goal: identify as many potential earned income projects as you can. After you've completed this exercise—and taken a few days off to gain perspective—use Worksheet 4.2 to evaluate your ideas and select the projects with the best odds for success.

1. **What do you do well?** Write three things about your organization—accomplishments, structure, the people involved, and so on—that you're most proud of.

    _____

    _____

    _____

    _____

    _____

    _____

    _____

2. **What makes your group unique?** What do you have or what do you do that no one else has or does?

    _____

    _____

    _____

    _____

    _____

    _____

    _____

3. **What assets do you have—products, services, expertise, intellectual property—that someone might want?** For ideas, look at your answers to the first two questions.

_____

_____

_____

_____

_____

_____

_____

4. **Given your mission and expertise, what additional goods and services could you develop?** (Another way of asking this question: How can you repackage what you already do and what you already know to serve more people or provide new benefits to the people you already serve?)

_____

_____

_____

_____

_____

_____

_____

5. **Who might want what you have to offer?** Who are you trying to reach? List all current and potential audiences, customers, clients, and so on.

_____

_____

_____

_____

_____

_____

6. **How can you reach your prospective customers?** Brainstorm as many promotional strategies as you can.

_____

_____

_____

_____

7. **Who are your potential partners?** Who can help you develop or market these goods and services?

_____

_____

_____

_____

_____

Location, Location, Location: Burns Bog
Conservation Society and Plateau Restoration

■　　■　　■　　■　　■　　■　　■　　■　　■　　■　　■　　■　　■

Just a half-hour from downtown Vancouver lies a unique landscape that is home to carnivorous plants, sphagnum moss, bears, water lilies, foxes, wild rosemary, sandhill cranes, Pacific tree frogs, black-tailed deer, a "bonsai forest" of shoulder-high lodgepole pine, patches of ground that quake and shiver when you walk—and the biggest city dump west of Toronto.

At 4,000 hectares (10,000 acres), Burns Bog is the largest urban wilderness in North America. In addition to providing high-quality habitat, the bog can store two to three times more carbon dioxide than a rainforest, which helps to clean the air of pollution and reduce the threat of global warming. It functions as the "lungs" of metropolitan Vancouver.

Two million people live in the area surrounding Burns Bog, and development pressures on the landscape are intense. The city landfill, which handles 500,000 tons of trash per year, already covers 10 percent of the bog. Faced with these threats, the Burns Bog Conservation Society (www.burnsbog.org) was formed in 1988 to protect the area through community education and conservation purchases. "We won the battle but not the war," says founder Eliza Olson, referring to a development plan they helped to defeat, "and we wanted to be ready when the war came."

Clearly, the group's primary asset is the bog itself, and they make the most of it through the following activities:

- Building boardwalks in a small nature reserve in the bog for walking, jogging, and educational tours.
- Sponsoring the International Bog Day festival.
- Publishing materials for visitors in English, Punjabi, and Mandarin Chinese.
- Selling bog-related merchandise, including teas and soaps made with bog herbs.
- Organizing tours and workshops for community members, scientists, and educators.
- "Bringing the bog to the students" with classroom programs.
- Creating and distributing environmental education materials. Local teacher Annette LeBox calls their curriculum "one of the best tools I've ever used."

In a far different environment, the threats and opportunities are much the same. The landscape of Southern Utah—well known for its national parks and other public lands—is austere, beautiful, remote, and heavily used. Nearly two million visitors per year hike, paddle, bicycle, backpack, swim, camp, and ride around in all-terrain vehicles that damage the fragile desert ecosystem. Even the more benign activities, such as walking, leave a profound mark on the land by damaging fragile soils, crushing vegetation, and reducing the food and shelter used by wildlife.

Former river guide and government resource manager Michael Dean Smith founded Plateau Restoration (www.plateaurestoration.org) to mitigate these human impacts with hands-on research, education, and ecological restoration. The work is accomplished through conservation service projects, where teams of visitors and locals volunteer to repair and redirect trails, control exotic weeds, plant native vegetation, and fence off replanted "recovery zones."

Through his years in the government, Smith knew that most federal agencies don't have the staff to organize restoration field trips, so he designed the nonprofit as a bridge between land managers and prospective volunteers. In this sense, Plateau Restoration has two sets of customers: agency employees want the landscape restored and maintained, and volunteers want a meaningful, productive experience in the wilderness.

From a business perspective, here's the best part: both sets of customers—the Feds and the volunteers—are willing to pay to have the same work done. Many of Plateau Restoration's volunteer workers—who haul rocks, plant seedlings, pull weeds, and swing pickaxes in the desert sun—provide money to help cover the costs of the projects, typically $100 to $150 per day per group. "When they're done," says Smith, "they can see a positive change in the landscape."

For many volunteers, including college students on "alternative spring break," the big draw is the location. The group's Web site touts the program as "a way for visitors to the Canyon Country of southeastern Utah to be a part of the long-term care of the Colorado Plateau." Not surprisingly, the pitch includes photos of volunteers working in the spectacular landscape. Like the Burns Bog Conservation Society, Plateau Restoration's biggest asset is its location.

What makes your community or local environment unique? How does your work contribute to that special sense of place? How can you take advantage of local pride or the unique aspects of your environment to create earned income opportunities?

Selecting the right venture

Look around you. The opportunities are endless. The room crackles with possibility. With the possible exception of your first big sale, this is perhaps the most satisfying moment in the process.

Enjoy the feeling, because things are about to change. It's time to take off the rose-colored glasses and put a skeptical look on your face. If the group has time and energy you can press on, but it might be better to let everyone go home, dream about all these wonderful opportunities, and come back another day prepared to throw most of them out.

"Assessing opportunities," writes Jerry Kitzi in *Enterprising Nonprofits*, "is a blended process of data collection and gut instinct. It is both a science and an art. Too much dependence on one or the other can lead to failure."[3] Try to use both when you take the next step and winnow the list. Consider the following criteria presented in Worksheet 4.2:

- *Passion.* Are most of the participants excited about a particular idea? Is *anyone* excited about it? If not, forget it. Even if it looks like your most profitable option, cross it off. Without a critical mass of enthusiasm—several enthusiastic people—it will fail, regardless of the financial benefits.

- **Relation to mission.** How does it fit with your current goals, programs, and skills? Does it build on something you already do well? (If you meet this test you'll have fewer problems with the tax collector, as you'll see in Chapter Nine.)

- **Appropriate management skills.** Does anyone within your group have the necessary skills to manage this type of venture? If not, can you recruit the right person?

- **Reasonable expectations.** "Having too many goals for a business is the biggest obstacle to making it work," writes William A. Duncan, citing groups that try to accomplish several of the following at once: "democratic ownership, jobs for low-income people, the use of renewable energy sources or recycled products, or fostering social equity."[4] Your immediate goal is to advance your mission and net a profit. Keep your expectations in check.

- **Market considerations.** Will anyone buy this product or service? How do you know? How will you reach them? Tips on market research are given later in this chapter.

- **Uniqueness and specialization.** For new businesses, another common mistake is attempting to be all things to all consumers. In creating goods and services, how will you build on your unique assets? What *one or two things* can you do that no one else can do?

- **Serves current customers.** As Edward Skloot points out in *The Nonprofit Entrepreneur,* your easiest option is to improve what you already do. In order of increasing difficulty, you can also "create a new product or service for an old market, find a new market for an old product or service, or create a new product or service for an entirely new market."[5] For most small businesses, 80 percent of their trade comes from 20 percent of their customers. According to marketing maven Jay Conrad Levinson, it costs one-sixth as much to sell the same product to an existing customer as to a new one.[6] Focus on finding ways to provide more services to the people who already know and support your work.

- **Capital needs.** How much money will you need? When? Will it come from within the organization or will you need to apply for grants or loans? (For more information on funding sources, see Chapter Six.) For obvious reasons, inexpensive options will enjoy a distinct advantage as you sort through the list.

- **Profitability.** Finally, if the venture succeeds, how much money do you stand to make? Will your net income justify the time and effort? Use market research to develop your best estimate.

The first and last points—passion and profitability—are the most important. If your idea can't generate much enthusiasm or income, it's not worth the trouble.

Evaluating your earned income ideas

Use a copy of this worksheet to rate each earned income idea for your organization, then compare scores to help you choose the most realistic option. This exercise will help you sort through the options, but it is not intended to take the place of a formal feasibility study for two important reasons: first, it's highly subjective, and second, the first and last criteria—passion and profitability—trump the others. If no one is passionate about the idea, or your research indicates that it's unlikely to be profitable, don't do it.

1. EARNED INCOME IDEA: _____

   Brief description: _____

   _____

   _____

   _____

2. PASSION. Rate the level of passion for this idea. Are most of the participants excited about it? Is anyone excited?

Excellent				Poor
5	4	3	2	1

   Notes: _____

   _____

   _____

3. RELATION TO MISSION. Rate how well this idea fits with your current goals, programs, and skills. Does it build on something you already do well?

Excellent				Poor
5	4	3	2	1

   Notes: _____

   _____

   _____

4. APPROPRIATE MANAGEMENT SKILLS. To what extent does anyone within your group have the necessary skills to manage this type of venture? If not, can you recruit the right person?

Excellent				Poor
5	4	3	2	1

   Notes: _____

   _____

   _____

5. REASONABLE EXPECTATIONS. Your immediate goal is to advance your mission and net a profit— how well will this project do that? Is it loaded down with too many other political and program goals?

Excellent				Poor
5	4	3	2	1

   Notes: _____

   _____

   _____

6. MARKET CONSIDERATIONS. Rate the likelihood that anyone will buy this product or service. (You may want to answer this question after you have completed Worksheet 4.3).

Excellent				Poor
5	4	3	2	1

Notes: _____

_____

_____

7. UNIQUENESS AND SPECIALIZATION. Rate to what extent this project builds on your unique organizational assets.

Excellent				Poor
5	4	3	2	1

Notes: _____

_____

_____

8. SERVES CURRENT CUSTOMERS. Rate how well this project will help you better serve the people who already know and support your work. (These folks are the easiest to reach and engage, and the most likely to buy.)

Excellent				Poor
5	4	3	2	1

Notes: _____

_____

_____

9. CAPITAL NEEDS. How much money will you need? Rate the likelihood that you can raise the required amount. (For obvious reasons, inexpensive options will enjoy a distinct advantage as you sort through the list.)

Excellent				Poor
5	4	3	2	1

Notes: _____

_____

_____

10. PROFITABILITY. How much money do you stand to make? Will the net income justify your time and effort? The greater the potential profit is, the higher the score will be. To begin to answer this question, do your market research; see Worksheet 4.3.

Excellent				Poor
5	4	3	2	1

Notes: _____

_____

_____

Total score: _____   Passion + Profitability only: _____

By comparing scores and paying particular attention to the Profit + Profitability score, your most viable ideas should emerge. This is only a comparison. There is no objective way to define a "good" score. Use what you learn in this book, do your market research, and trust your instincts.

Powerful Publications

Nearly half the groups profiled in this book create or distribute publications as a way of fulfilling their missions and earning revenue. Their product mix is extremely diverse, as the following list shows.

- Technical Assistance for Community Services publishes the *Oregon Nonprofit Corporation Handbook,* a 700-page guide for creating, managing, and funding a nonprofit. Now in its third edition, the book retails for $65, with discounts for bulk purchases. More than 4,000 copies have been sold. A new Washington State version was created in 2001.

- The SouthWest Organizing Project (SWOP) publishes a bilingual text book, *500 Años del Pueblo Chicano/ 500 Years of Chicano History.* The retail price is $38.50 for hardback, $18 for paperback. Since SWOP took over the project in 1991 (another nonprofit had published an earlier edition), more than 23,000 copies have been distributed.

- The Resource Center of the Americas creates teaching materials featuring the many cultures of this hemisphere and how they are affected by globalization. Their curriculum packets feature lesson plans,

A BROCHURE FOR A RESOURCE CENTER OF THE AMERICAS CURRICULUM PACKET

bibliographies, Web site suggestions, posters, maps, videos, and reproducible handouts. While teachers are the primary audience, the Resource Center also markets to distributors, who resell the materials to schools, libraries, and individual educators. Curricula sales—retail and wholesale combined—total $20,000 per year.

- FareStart, which runs a culinary job training and placement program for the homeless, teamed with another organization to produce a calendar ($20) and a cookbook, *Savoring Seattle* ($25). Both publications include full-color food photos—the kind you see in gourmet magazines—and recipes donated by local chefs.

- A number of organizations, including the Burns Bog Conservation Society, Melpomene Institute, Native Seeds/SEARCH, and the Resource Center of the Americas, also purchase books from publishers and distributors and resell them to their customers and members.

If you're interested in publications as an earned income option, consider the following points:

- ***How much front money will you need, and where will it come from?*** When publishing books or other printed materials, most of the expenses—development, writing, design, printing, and a portion of the promotional costs—are incurred before you sell the product. Without sufficient financing (grants, loans, gifts, money you've saved specifically for the project), you'll have a big cash flow problem. (For suggestions on financing your venture, see Chapter Six.)

- **Keep your expenses down by soliciting in-kind donations.** For FareStart's cookbook, all film and processing was donated and the photographer and designer worked at discounted rates.

- **Can you pre-sell the project?** One option is to pre-sell the publication to an institutional buyer, typically a corporation, that distributes it to customers. The Sporting Goods Manufacturers Association paid the Melpomene Institute $14,000 to research, write, and produce *Let's Get Moving*, outlining the benefits of physical activity for women over age 50. Fifteen thousand copies of the booklet (featuring the SGMA logo) were distributed.

- **If you're preparing a book with broad appeal, sell it to a commercial publisher.** Melpomene's best-known and best-selling title is *The Bodywise Woman*, written by founder Judy Mahle Lutter and her colleague Lynn Jaffee. Initially published by Prentice Hall, the first printing sold 15,000 copies and generated a $10,000 advance for the Institute. When Prentice Hall chose not to republish the book, Melpomene switched to another publisher—Human Kinetics—and negotiated a royalty agreement for 10 percent of sales plus a 50 percent discount on wholesale purchases. Between royalty payments and sales to members and customers, the second edition produced more than $16,000 in earned income. Nearly 22,000 copies have been sold in ten years—far more than the nonprofit could have distributed on its own.

- **To move larger quantities, work with distributors and retailers.** The SouthWest Organizing Project sells its Chicano history textbook to distributors (Baker & Taylor), major bookstore chains (Borders, Barnes & Noble), online retailers (Amazon.com) and independent bookstores throughout the region. If you plan to wholesale books, be aware that bookstores typically receive a 40 percent discount off the retail price; distributors, as much as 60 percent off. They also expect to return unsold copies for a full refund or credit.

- **Institutional buyers can be a lucrative market.** The St. Paul Public Library recently placed a $9,000 order with the Resource Center of the Americas, which demonstrates the high demand for multicultural materials. Can your publications benefit libraries, universities, government agencies, and other institutions? If so, how will you reach and service them?

- **Sell to educators.** The U.S. education market includes 200,000 institutions and nearly 4 million teachers. In many school districts, educators are required to cover specific subjects, such as social studies, geography, health, economics, and environmental studies. They're always looking for relevant, entertaining, up-to-date materials. According to consultants Ellen Arrick and Mary Virtue, teachers are exceptionally loyal customers, purchasing from publishers they know and trust. Their suggestion: "Gear your product development to established curriculum guidelines."[7]

- **If relevant, use public records to identify prospects.** Technical Assistance for Community Services (TACS) finds newly incorporated nonprofits by requesting contact information from government agencies—in this case, the Oregon Corporation Commission. TACS then sends these groups a brochure and order form for their *Oregon Nonprofit Corporation Handbook*. They mail to 400 groups twice per year, generating 50 sales at $65 each.

- **Where will you store the leftovers?** Before you get stuck with a big pile of books, test the market first.

Think retail last

"When citizen's groups decide to earn income," writes Charles Cagnon, "the first idea they usually have is to open a store." He suggests "extreme caution with this approach" for several reasons, including the fact that "small businesses earn small profits."[8]

Let's say your retail operation nets 5 to 10 percent of gross receipts, which is typical for some types of stores. (In other words, you get to keep 5 to 10 percent of the store's income after all direct and indirect expenses, including staff and supervisory salaries, rent, utilities, cost of goods, insurance, advertising, financial management, and so on, are subtracted.) Under this equation, you would need to generate $100,000 in retail sales to earn $5,000 to $10,000 in profits. That's a lot of work for a modest result, especially if the retail sales operation has no relation to your mission or programs.

Twelve groups profiled in this book sell products to the public, but only half of them manage retail stores. The rest serve their customers through mail order catalogs, Web site sales, community events, and walk-in sales at their offices. Some groups, such as the Women's Bean Project, sell most of their products wholesale, letting others with more experience and bigger marketing budgets interact with consumers. You net less money selling wholesale, but you sell more volume, which makes up for the smaller profit per unit sold. Generally speaking, it's worth it.

Before you go into retail sales, investigate other opportunities to earn income.

How to do market research

In selecting a venture, market research is a critical—perhaps the most critical—step. Good research helps you solve two common problems.

1. *Products chasing a market, instead of the other way around.* When nonprofits go into business, this is their most common blind spot. Just because you think somebody *should* want your goods or services doesn't mean they actually *do*. Sales are driven by demand, so find out what people want. If you have the capacity to provide it, sell it to them. If you don't, find other ways to bring money into your organization.

2. *Inappropriate financial goals.* "Most times you cannot accurately guess what will, or will not, generate your earned income goal," says consultant Jan Cohen. "It takes real market research. I stress this because most groups may not see the need for this in-depth work." Your financial projections will be based, in part, on what you learn about your prospective customers.

If you've ever researched a prospective donor or tracked down information about a foundation, you'll find that market research isn't all that different from these activities. Begin with *secondary market research,* which includes information gathered from preexisting sources: the library, the Web, trade associations, your local chamber of commerce or economic development agency.

Let's pretend that FareStart, which is based in Seattle, is interested in opening a second restaurant and chef training program in Portland. Here are ways they could start conducting market research on this idea:

- Gather information about the Portland restaurant market: how many, what specialties, how many opened and closed in the past year, who provides catering services, price ranges, and so forth. Is demand for restaurant meals growing, shrinking, or stable? Where are the restaurants clustered—where is the business traffic? How much of the trade comes from locals and how much from visitors? Most of this information is available from the local restaurant association, economic development agency, or visitors' bureau.

- Search the Web for cost and availability of commercial real estate. The Internet also provides information on the local job market, wage rates, and the like.

- Because they're planning to run a job training program, they can learn about Portland social service providers by contacting the United Way or another organization that offers social service referrals. Who provides job training? Are any agencies training kitchen workers? How many people want job training and how many are currently being served? (This is the supply-versus-demand question.)

This work would be followed by *primary market research,* which typically includes personal interviews, surveys, focus groups and site visits. The FareStart staff might take these two steps:

1. Travel to Portland to check out the restaurant scene, meet with chefs and restaurant owners, brainstorm with social service agencies, talk to realtors, look at prospective sites, and ask the same types of questions listed above. In many cases, these personal contacts will yield the most useful information and initiate relationships that are bound to prove helpful later.

2. Come up with a way to survey prospective restaurant patrons, perhaps by developing a joint survey with other established restaurants in the city. A local business college class could be enlisted to design, distribute, and tabulate the survey. To boost the response rate, respondents might be given the chance to enter a drawing, with meals donated by partner restaurants as prizes.

As mentioned, one goal in doing market research is to gather financial information: pricing, income, expenses, and profits. The simplest strategy is to ask other proprietors in the same field what their numbers look like. Believe it or not, many will share this information, at least informally. If you're concerned about tipping your hand to local competitors (remember, many competitors are potential allies and partners), contact business owners in another city and ask them. People love to talk about themselves and they really love to give advice, so ask away.

Here's an example: to learn if my rates are fair, I sometimes call other consultants and trainers and ask what they charge. From there, the questions fly back and forth: What are your clients asking for? Have your services changed in response? What percentage of your work time can you bill? (Based on my very unscientific poll, the record is 50 percent.) How do you market yourself? How much of your work comes from referrals? Are you looking for more work? I've always received straightforward answers. We often discover ways to help each other, which means that two potential competitors have become cooperators.

Use Worksheet 4.3 to begin your own market research efforts.

WORKSHEET 4.3

Market research

Use this worksheet to outline your market research strategy.

1. **EARNED INCOME IDEA:**_____

   Brief description: _____

   _____

   _____

   _____

   _____

   What specific questions will you answer by using market research? (Hint: one of them should be, "How much will this project cost and how much profit can we expect to earn after expenses?")

   _____

   _____

   _____

   _____

   _____

2. **SECONDARY RESEARCH SOURCES.** Secondary market research involves lots of reading, so list any library resources, Web sites, magazines, and so on, that you plan to use. Trade association materials are particularly useful.

   _____

   _____

   _____

   _____

   _____

3. **PRIMARY MARKET RESEARCH.** Primary market research involves getting feedback on your idea from a range of people in the community. Research techniques include interviews, surveys, and focus groups.

Personal interviews. Who will you discuss your idea with?

- *Business owners.* List here nonprofit and for-profit business managers who have experience with your proposed venture.

_____

_____

_____

_____

_____

_____

- *Members and clients.* Talk with people who already benefit from your work. List some of these people here.

_____

_____

_____

_____

_____

_____

- *Potential customers.* Whom do you want to serve?

_____

_____

_____

_____

_____

_____

- *Potential partners, including other nonprofits and prospective suppliers.*

_____

_____

_____

_____

_____

Surveys. Would you benefit from surveying your prospective customers? If so, will you do it by mail, e-mail, telephone, or in person at your place of business? Who will prepare and administer the questionnaire? How many people will you survey?

_____

_____

_____

_____

_____

Focus groups. Would focus groups be helpful? How many? If so, who will be responsible? Can you manage this in-house or will you need to hire a consultant?

_____

_____

_____

_____

_____

Site visits. In some cases—let's say you're planning to open a retail store—you will need to visit prospective locations, talk with neighboring businesses, check out the foot traffic, and so on. Would you benefit from a site visit? If so, who will do it? When?

_____

_____

_____

_____

_____

How to think about pricing

Nonprofit entrepreneurs fall into a lot of traps, and here's one of the biggest: they don't charge enough for their work. This problem is actually three interrelated problems:

• _Problem 1: They haven't calculated the true costs of the venture._ When pricing goods or services, factor in three components: direct costs, indirect costs, and a profit. _Direct costs_ include materials, manufacturing expenses, cost of goods for resale, advertising, customer service, travel, rent and utilities for any facility devoted to the venture, staff time to manage the enterprise, and so forth. _Indirect costs_ include an appropriate portion of the organization's general expenses, including accounting, insurance, employee benefits, and so on. _Profit_ is what remains after you've paid all direct and indirect costs. (If you can't cover the costs, you have a _loss_ or a _deficit._) Your goal in setting prices is to generate enough profit to justify the time, expense, and emotional energy required to run the business.

As business consultants Linda Pinson and Jerry Jinnett write, "The market determines the price ceiling....The price floor is the lowest amount at which you can offer a product or service, meet all your costs, and still make your desired profit....The viable business operates between the price ceiling and the price floor. The difference allows for discounts, bad debt, and returns."[9]

As discussed in the previous chapter, most grassroots organizations don't have a clue about how much it really costs to do their work. When it comes to setting prices for their goods and services, they don't know where to begin. Here's the first step: get your accounting and time-tracking systems in place. Once you've done that, you can begin to think rationally about how much to charge.

• *Problem 2: They undervalue their worth.* Are you feeling uncomfortable about charging for your work? Here's a hint from Dianne Russell of the Institute for Conservation Leadership: "If people pay, they take it more seriously." Kay Sohl of Technical Assistance for Community Services concurs. "Free is not a good price," she says—not for you, and not for your members, clients, or customers. Once you start asking the people who benefit to help pay for your work, you may discover that you're making a bigger impact. Your participants will begin to value what you do.

• *Problem 3: They haven't done their marketing homework, so they don't know how much money prospective clients will pay.* Your prices will be determined in large measure by your market research. What are your competitors charging? What's the relationship between demand and price? How much are your prospective customers willing to pay? Without good research, it's all guesswork, which is a dangerous way to start a business. If market prices won't cover your costs—not to mention a profit—you're looking at the wrong venture.

If you've decided to pursue retail sales, here's a hint: the typical mark-up is twice the wholesale price, which is sometimes called the *keystone price.* Keystone plus 25 percent or 50 percent—in other words, doubling the wholesale price and then adding an additional mark-up of 25 to 50 percent—is common practice with handmade or custom items. The inverse is also true: with the exception of books and a few other items, the wholesale price is usually half the retail price. In *The Museum Shop Workbook,* Mary Virtue and Jane Delgado write, "Be sure that you have a big enough markup that you will still have a profit even after you discount an item for members or put it on sale."[10]

For a detailed description of pricing strategy, take a look at "Understanding and Attracting Your 'Customers'" by Kristin Majeska in *Enterprising Nonprofits* (see Resources).

Conducting a feasibility study

Let's assume that you've brainstormed lots of intriguing ideas for earning income; tossed most of them out because they didn't meet the criteria listed above; conducted preliminary market research on the ones that remained and jettisoned a few more, due to insufficient "market interest"; estimated costs, pricing, and profits, and threw away a couple more candidates based on dubious numbers.

Congratulations! You've just completed an informal feasibility study. If none of your income-generating ideas can navigate this obstacle course, your organization is not a good candidate for enterprise (see the next section, "Getting to 'No'"). The committee should write up its findings, make a presentation to the board and staff, answer questions about its conclusions, and disband—having buried the fantasy of easy money, at least for the time being.

On the other hand, if any of your proposed ventures survive this kind of informal review, you might consider a more rigorous feasibility study. A feasibility study addresses a lot of hard questions, such as: How did you conduct your market research and was it thorough enough? What's the nature of your competition? What are your financial assumptions and how do you know they are valid? Who will staff the operation and what are their qualifications? Does your organization have the right mix of resources to accomplish its entrepreneurial goals? What internal barriers do you face? Is everyone committed to the task at hand?

This is a good moment to consider using outside help. Ideally, you want an unbiased professional with relevant business experience. If you can find someone connected to the organization who has the time and requisite skills, terrific—just be sure that person is objective. The process can take several months, depending on the size of the venture, and will conclude with a written report and a presentation to the decision makers (usually the board).

In determining whether you need a formal feasibility study, consider the size of the project. If you're planning a modest earned income project that requires a small initial investment of money and time, you can probably get by with the informal process outlined above. If you're considering a more ambitious and expensive opportunity, however, it's worth the time and money to complete a thorough feasibility study.

Getting to "no"

As mentioned earlier, a majority of nonprofits are not good candidates to earn substantial income. They lack the time, money, staff, or self-discipline to run a business. Many don't have a marketable product or service. Others are simply overwhelmed by current programs. These groups have survived reasonably well with other funding, and most will continue to survive.

Your choice to *investigate* enterprise should not be confused with a decision to *begin* one. Indeed, if the result is determined in advance, you can't get an honest assessment. Even if the process results in a "no go" decision, it will reveal useful information about your organization, your participants—board, staff, volunteers, members, supporters, customers—and their dreams for fulfilling the mission. Whatever you learn can be used to strengthen your group and renew everyone's collective commitment to the work.

On the other hand, says consultant Jerr Boschee of the Institute for Social Entrepreneurs, "don't wait for the perfect opportunity," because it rarely appears. Keep your eye open for the "pretty good opportunity," and when you see it, grab it.[11]

Having completed this chapter, you've worked your way through the process of brainstorming, winnowing, market research, and preliminary number-crunching. Most of your earned income ideas failed the test. The ones that remain—exciting, unique, potentially profitable—have the best chance of success. To further refine these ideas, you'll need a business plan. The basics of business planning are covered in Chapter Five.

The Power of the Footnote

DATACENTER

OAKLAND, CALIFORNIA

WWW.DATACENTER.ORG

ANNUAL BUDGET: $686,000

EARNED INCOME: 22%

EARNED INCOME STRATEGIES

- SERVICES FOR NONPROFITS AND OTHER INSTITUTIONAL CUSTOMERS
- TRAINING AND CONSULTING FOR NONPROFITS AND OTHER INSTITUTIONAL CUSTOMERS

One day the phone rang in Fred Goff's office. "The man on the line was one of our business clients," says Goff, co-founder and president of DataCenter. "He liked our work so much, he wanted to buy us out." Goff's eyes open wide. "He wanted to buy the whole operation. He didn't realize we were a nonprofit."

If imitation is the sincerest form of flattery, then how do you rate a customer who's so happy with the work he wants to take over the business?

DataCenter was created in 1977 as a spin-off from the North American Congress on Latin America, which promotes human rights across the region. In studying U.S. government and corporate complicity in human rights violations throughout the region, Goff and his colleagues had discovered what he calls "the power of the footnote"—the ways that documented research could be used as a tool for social activism. DataCenter was founded "to give activists a strategic advantage through the power of information," he says.

Through their Impact Research program, the organization provides research services to community organizations, labor unions, investigative journalists, lawyers, elected officials, scholars, foundation officers, socially responsible investment firms, and others. DataCenter also has a "current awareness" program featuring a customized electronic news clipping service. The group, which serves hundreds of clients per year, includes staff members with degrees in library science, journalism, and law, plus community organizing experience, so they know their stuff.

To learn whether activist organizations use research and how they pay for it, the group teamed up with the National Organizers Alliance, the professional association of community organizers, to survey the Alliance's members. Only 10 percent of the respondents had research budgets for their organizations, most had no investigative staff, and only 1 percent had ever paid to have research done. More than 80 percent of the groups used volunteers to conduct research. The bottom line: for most small organizations with limited budgets, professional research is a luxury.

What this means, in terms of business planning, is that DataCenter divides its clientele into two categories: mission-fulfilling and mission-related clients.

Mission-fulfilling clients include grassroots groups involved in community organizing and activism on a wide range of progressive issues. Since many smaller organizations pay a reduced rate or nothing at all for DataCenter's services, DataCenter subsidizes this work with grants, individual donations, and donated staff time. Former executive director Catherine Powell explains, "We made a conscious decision to focus less on revenue generation and put more staff time into supporting grassroots organizing." Here's a sampling of these kinds of projects:

- Two groups in Silicon Valley successfully stopped a local cement factory from burning discarded tires—and increasing the risk of toxic emissions—in its furnaces. DataCenter staff learned that the factory was owned by a multinational corporation rather than a locally respected firm, which helped to rally public opinion against the plant.

- The Nevada Interfaith Council for Worker Justice incorporated DataCenter research into a campaign and lawsuit against a construction company that takes advantage of immigrant workers.

- Health Care Without Harm used DataCenter research to convince a major manufacturer to phase out the use of PVC, a suspected carcinogen, in its intravenous fluid bags.

DataCenter also solicits contracts from national and regional organizations, since many of these groups have research budgets. Their client list reads like a "Who's Who" of the progressive movement: American Civil Liberties Union, Communities for a Better Environment, Fairness and Accuracy in Reporting, Greenpeace, International Campaign to Ban Land Mines, Public Media Center, Rainforest Action Network, Sierra Club, United Farm Workers, and many other groups.

An emerging market includes progressive foundations that hire DataCenter to provide on-call research and training to their grantee organizations. These contracts often last a year or more. For staff member Celia Davis, long-term client relationships "make us better researchers, because we learn how people really use information."

The final mission-fulfilling activity is training activists to do their own research. This is accomplished through one-on-one consulting and seminars at conferences and activist events. DataCenter is collaborating with other training organizations, such as the SPIN Project (media) and the Center for Third World Organizing (community organizing), to develop comprehensive training programs.

On the other hand, many paying customers would be considered *mission related*. This broad category includes the following types of clientele:

- Immigration attorneys needing human rights documentation. To serve these clients, staff members have developed a targeted brochure and rate sheet. Rates are $80 to $145 per hour—the quicker the turnaround needed, the higher the cost.

- Investment firms specializing in socially responsible investments. These companies contract with DataCenter to research corporate records on worker justice, diversity, worker safety, environmental policies, and so on.

- Journalists occasionally hire DataCenter to help with investigative work, though this is a tough market. As Powell points out, "Reporters aren't used to paying for information. If they won't pay, we ask to be credited in the story."

As a result of this split clientele, staff members find themselves "switching back and forth from entrepreneurial work to mission work," says researcher Leon Sompolinsky, "which sometimes requires a different set of skills." This approach also requires a clear client acceptance policy. Nike once approached DataCenter for marketing information on Latin America, but staff turned down this potentially lucrative contract because they don't support Nike's corporate anti-union behavior. In another instance, lawyers representing generals from the regime of Nicaraguan dictator Anastasio Somoza asked the organization for asylum assistance. Decisions about controversial clients are made after consultation with the staff. Even when DataCenter accepts controversial work, says Powell, "we have a policy that individual staff can opt out if they don't feel good about the specific job."

The other portion of DataCenter's work involves "current awareness" services. Clients can work with the staff to create a customized service to track electronic news coverage of a particular subject. Andrew Hagelshaw of the Center for Commercial-Free Public Education, a national clearinghouse, uses this service. "We're looking to spot developing trends in different parts of the United States," he says. DataCenter helped to find a new trend—student identification being used as a corporate marketing tool—when their researchers found a story about a Honolulu school that incorporates a "Coca Cola loyalty program" into their student I.D. cards. Thanks to the research, says Hagelshaw,

"We got an early start, and we're working to counter it." He adds, "DataCenter's work was invaluable. We can't get this information any other way."

With the continuing expansion of what he calls "predatory capitalism," Goff sees an increasing demand for DataCenter's services. "People doing social change need information. Organizers don't have the time, training, money, or equipment to do this work. When we started DataCenter, we looked at the need and said, 'We can do that.' I don't see the need going away any time soon."

THINGS TO THINK ABOUT

- *Specialize—do a few things well.* For many years, DataCenter had a walk-in library for activists, students, and community members, but it proved a big drain on the budget, staff time, and limited office space. With the advent of powerful on-line databases and with the goal of increasing its impact, the group became electronic-based, narrowed its focus, closed the walk-in library, and now primarily serves organizations rather than individuals.
- *Know your market—do market research.* In this case, the research confirmed what staff already knew: the groups they most want to work with are the ones who can least afford to pay. As a result, they revised their fee structure and increased outreach to charitable foundations and individual donors to subsidize the work. If your prospective clients can't pay, perhaps you can identify third parties that can.
- *Repackage your know-how as many ways as possible.* As Catherine Powell asks, "How many different ways can you slice the same data to reach different markets?" DataCenter offers customized research services, training, and a Web site.
- *Use client testimonials.* Staff members sent a promotional letter and brochure to the mailing list of the American Association of Immigration Attorneys, featuring testimonials from three happy customers. The result: inquiries more than doubled. "We invigorated old business" from lawyers who hadn't used the service in a while, says Powell.
- *Consider anyone who uses your goods or services a potential donor.* For DataCenter's twentieth anniversary dinner, dozens of clients "bought tables" and purchased ads in the program to show solidarity and to thank the organization for a job well done. The event netted more than $40,000. Think creatively about how to use special occasions—anniversaries, the retirement of a long-time staff or board member, a move to a new location, the launch of a new program—to ask your customers to become contributors.

Chapter 5

Developing a business plan for social change

■   ■   ■

When it comes to business plans, I am of two minds. On the one hand, no one with any sort of business training would consider starting an enterprise without a full-blown business plan, complete with every sort of financial document. On the other hand, thousands of businesses are launched every day with little planning or forethought. The ones that survive make it on sweat, prayer, and intuition. Some of them grow and prosper by learning the lessons of hard experience. It might be heresy to suggest that you can earn a profit without a business plan, but it's true.

Only a handful of organizations profiled in this book went to the trouble of creating an official, by-the-numbers business plan. "We've done little market analysis: who are our members and what are they likely to buy?" says Judy Mahle Lutter of Melpomene Institute. "We're just working on instinct," says Pam Costain of the Resource Center of the Americas, describing their publications program. Indeed, most of these groups are working on instinct, and their improvisational skills are exceptional.

Entrepreneurs are defined by their instincts—their intuitive answers to questions such as, "What does the market need?"—and their enthusiasm to fill that need. If you don't have a nose for business—if you can't smell an opportunity when it walks up and breathes in your face—even the best planning process in the world will not compensate. (Of course, it's always smart to use market research to test and confirm your instincts.)

That's one side of the argument. Here's the other: even though these non-profits did not have formal business plans, *they still knew where they were going and how to get there.* Sometimes the plan took the form of a grant proposal or a detailed letter to a donor soliciting start-up funding. At other times, the plan was hashed out during long discussion; the decision makers had a common understanding, though perhaps not a paper trail. Sometimes it was folded into a larger strategic plan for the organization. Other groups calculated their financial projections with pencil, paper, and a big eraser, then filed the notes in a drawer.

Cynthia Massarsky makes a strong case for business planning. In *The Nonprofit Entrepreneur* she writes, "Emerging businesses need a written plan to force careful thinking, encourage discipline, forge internal communication, and enhance coordination and clarity of purpose among their managers and investors. They need a business plan to determine the amount of capital required, and to help raise it. And, once the business is operating, they need a yardstick against which to define and measure their progress."[1]

At some point, intuition becomes inadequate for the job at hand. You need a strategy to help you shape and apply your best instincts. That's when it's useful to have a plan. Furthermore, planning will give you a competitive advantage, since it forces you to think ahead, which will help you avoid some pitfalls. This chapter will teach you the "whys" and "hows" of planning and provide tools to help you outline a rough draft of your business plan.

A matter of scale

Do you need to prepare a *formal* business plan? Your decision will depend on two factors: First, the size of your proposed project. How much time and effort will it take, and how many people will it employ? How much money is required? Second, whether you can raise the initial funding from internal sources—current income, cash reserves, gifts from members and donors—or you will have to go outside the organization for capital.

If you're considering a relatively small or inexpensive venture or you expect to generate the money internally, you may not need a complete business plan—though a less formal planning document is still an excellent idea. If you're looking at a big project, however, or you hope to pursue outside funding from a bank or "social lender" (see Chapter Six), a formal business plan is in your future. Investors don't like risk, and the process of preparing a business plan helps you to identify and address the risks associated with your enterprise. By writing a comprehensive plan, you'll improve your odds of securing the funds you need.

How big is "big?" The Food Bank of Western Massachusetts prepared a business plan to create and market microwave popcorn—start-up expenses, $20,000. The SouthWest Organizing Project wrote one for the publication and distribution of its textbook, *500 Años del Pueblo Chicano/500 Years of Chicano History*—up-front costs, $25,000. Esperanza Unida created a business plan for its bookstore, ¿Qué Pasa? Coffee and Books—initial investment, $65,000. These are substantial sums, and with that much money on the line, thorough preparation is essential.

No matter the scope of your venture, it always helps to organize your ideas, and especially the financial projections, by writing them down. If you can't make your project work on paper, you'll have a much harder time making it work in the real world.

How to use a business plan

An effective business plan does two jobs. By laying out your strategies and benchmarks, it assists you in running and evaluating your venture, month by month. By outlining your financial goals and your design for achieving them, it helps to attract outside funding, specifically grants or loans.

Employing the first use is sometimes called "managing against the plan." The staff members of White Earth Land Recovery Project (see the profile following this chapter) refer to their plan from time to time as way of checking their expectations against reality and adapting accordingly. Here's what they've learned: the business plan includes a lot more work than they can accomplish, given the limitations of available funding and staffing. As an idealized picture of the enterprise, it reminds them of their ultimate goals and helps to guide choices about marketing strategy.

As mentioned, outside investors—foundations, banks, "social lenders"—will require some form of business plan to justify the use of their money. In fact, they will often review your plan and suggest changes before seriously considering a loan or a grant. Even if you're not seeking external funds, you might approach an appropriate organization—perhaps your local community loan fund—and request an informal review of the document. An outsider is bound to raise questions no one in the group would ever think to ask. In this way, you can use the business plan to evaluate your project before you look for financing.

Who writes the plan?

"The three most important considerations in determining who writes the business plan," says Cynthia Massarsky, "are the requisite skills, the available time, and a clear understanding of the relationship and interplay between the business and the exempt mission of the organization."[2] This mix creates a tricky problem. Your staff members are most knowledgeable about the mission, but may not have the time or technical business skills to prepare the plan. (Expect to spend 50 to 100 hours on the process, including research, writing, rewriting, and producing the financials.) You can hire an outside consultant, but that person will probably have less understanding of, and commitment to, your work. You run the risk of buying a boilerplate document that doesn't reflect the values of your group.

For example, the White Earth Land Recovery Project used consultants from a local university to create a business plan for Native Harvest, their retail business. The consultants' suggestions, says Donna Cahill of Native Harvest, were more appropriate for mainstream farmers than for a nonprofit working to protect and restore traditional cultural practices. In the end, the nonprofit staff wrote their own plan, using some of the consultants' ideas and ignoring others.

For most nonprofits, especially grassroots organizations, the best solution combines both approaches: using outside help to supplement the staff (especially the enterprise advocate or business manager) and the venture committee. Creating the business plan is yet another stage in the brainstorming and feasibility testing process. By wrestling with the details, especially the financial projections, staff and board will gain crucial insights about how best to run the business.

Components of a business plan

During a recent visit to my local bookstore, I found nine books detailing how to prepare a business plan. This indicates two things: first, there's a big market, and second, many other people know more about this topic than I do. What follows is a brief outline of the components. If you determine that you'll need a formal business plan for your venture, I encourage you to do more reading and recruit appropriate help. Several books are included in the Resources section, along with a list of Web sites.

The following summary is adapted from a booklet written specifically for small nonprofits by William A. Duncan.[3] Like grant proposals, business plans follow a more-or-less standard format, though experts tend to use different phrases or put the sections in a different sequence. In fact, a business plan is not unlike a grant application. If you've prepared a proposal for your venture, you may already have a good start. A typical business plan, including financials and supporting documents, is forty to fifty pages long and has the following elements:

- *Executive summary.* A one-page summary of everything to follow.

- *Definition of the business.* What business activities will you engage in? What goods and services will you sell, and to whom? How do these sales activities relate to the mission, goals, and programs of your organization?

- *Management and leadership.* Who's in charge? What skills and relevant expertise do they bring to the job? How many people will be employed in the enterprise? This is also the place to discuss support staff—for example, your bookkeeper—and the role of the board and outside consultants.

- *The market.* What's your niche? What makes your products or services unique? This section includes both a *market analysis*—likely customers, pricing, growth potential, your market share—and a *marketing plan*—how you will reach your prospective customers. For more information on marketing, see Chapter Seven.

- *Competition.* Who are they and what can you learn from them? Richard Andrews of Our Community Bikes credits his competitors for teaching him about quality control: "Doing our work consistently and well. Having knowledgeable people who can answer questions." Do you see potential for mutual support through referrals or joint marketing?

- *Technical operations.* What are your space requirements? Who will be your suppliers? How will you manufacture and package your products? How will services be delivered to customers? Detail the nuts-and-bolts of how you will create your goods and services and get them to market.

- *Financials.* The financial section outlines available assets to be applied to the business and describes how loans or other outside capital, if needed, would be used. It also lists external sources of financing. The financial statements—the pages covered with numbers—include the following:

  - *Projected profit and loss statements* for three years (a monthly, quarterly, and annual accounting of how much money you expect to net or lose)

  - *Projected balance sheets* (your assets and liabilities at the end of each year)

  - *Projected cash flow* (your estimate of how much money you will earn and spend, month by month).

  Attach a page of *financial assumptions* detailing how you developed these numbers. In *Anatomy of a Business Plan,* Linda Pinson and Jerry Jinnett write, "One of the most frequent errors made by people writing a business plan is that what they say in the text portion of the plan does not correlate with the numbers they use in their financial documents....This is a fatal error." Their suggestion: prepare the narrative first, keeping in mind the costs and revenues associated with each section. (What will it cost to implement each marketing strategy? How many staff members will you need, and how much will you pay them? How many customers will you serve each month, and how much will you charge them?) As you write, note any financial assumptions on a separate piece of paper. Once the narrative is finished, use your notes to complete the financial sections of your business plan. For clarity, attach a page to the financials explaining your assumptions.[4]

- *Supporting documents* can include résumés of key staff, board member biographies, copies of contracts and agreements, press clippings, letters of reference, charts and graphs, and any other items needed to tell a compelling story about your venture.

When writing the plan, you may also want to describe your *exit strategy;* in other words, under what circumstances you will spin off, sell, or close the business. As Pinson and Jinnett write, "An exit strategy is not a plan for failure. It is a plan for success.... Before you begin the race, you need to know where you expect to finish."[5]

For nonprofits, potential exit strategies might include creating or "spinning off" a for-profit subsidiary, selling or giving the business to an entrepreneur, handing it off to another nonprofit, or solving a specific community need via the venture, declaring victory, and shutting it down. For example, Minnesota Public Radio sold its subsidiary, Riverton Trading Company, to a major retailer, while Esperanza Unida transferred asbestos removal and restaurant ventures to training program alumni, who turned them into successful for-profit businesses.

For many grassroots groups, creating the financial statements is the most challenging and frustrating part of the process. Many books, Web sites, and computer programs are available to help you complete the job; see the Resources section for recommendations. Invest the time to prepare your own financial statements—especially your cash flow projections. You can write wonderful, uplifting sentences about your enterprise, but the numbers reveal a different kind of truth, and that truth is often sobering. Make sure the math matches your vision. If it doesn't, you'll need to adjust your vision, your financial projections, or both. Sophisticated organizations create two or three sets of projections based on optimistic and pessimistic scenarios, then base their operations and expenses on *the most pessimistic* income estimates.

WORKSHEET 5.1

Preparing a business plan

This worksheet will help you begin the planning process by evaluating available skills and resources, then creating a rough outline of a business plan. Many books and software programs are available to help you further with business planning, including how to prepare your financial documents (see the Resources section).

1. **Evaluate your current resources.** List all staff, board, and key volunteers with business planning experience, including how much time each of these people can dedicate to this project:

    _____

    _____

    _____

    _____

    _____

    _____

    _____

    _____

List local resources for business planning—training programs, colleges, government agencies, consultants, and so on. (For ideas, see "Finding and Using Outside Help" in Chapter Three.)

_____

_____

_____

_____

_____

2. **Draft an outline of your business plan.** Start by answering the following questions. Don't worry about creating perfect sentences. Use phrases and numbers, where relevant, to address the main points.

Definition of the business. What business activities will you engage in? What goods and services will you sell, and to whom? How do these sales activities relate to the mission, goals, and programs of your organization?

_____

_____

_____

_____

_____

Management and leadership. Who's in charge? What skills and relevant expertise do they bring to the job? How many people will be employed in the enterprise?

_____

_____

_____

_____

_____

The market. What's your niche? What makes your products or services unique? This section includes both a market analysis—likely customers, pricing, growth potential, your market share—and a marketing plan—how you will reach your prospective customers.

_____

_____

_____

_____

_____

Competition. Who are they and what can you learn from them? Do you see potential for mutual support through referrals or joint marketing?

_____

_____

_____

_____

_____

Technical operations. This includes space requirements, suppliers, manufacturing, packaging, how services will be delivered to customers, and so on. Detail the nuts-and-bolts of how you will create your goods and services and get them to market.

_____
_____
_____
_____
_____
_____
_____
_____
_____

Financials. The financial section outlines available assets to be applied to the business and describes how loans or other outside capital, if needed, would be used. It also lists external sources of financing. This exercise is designed to focus your thinking on financial matters, but *it cannot and should not take the place of a more thorough financial analysis.*

- *Expenses.* Based on your market research—talking with other entrepreneurs, suppliers, prospective customers, and the like—determine how much it will cost to launch and manage this venture for each of the first three years. Start by listing all categories of likely expenses on a separate sheet (salaries, benefits, rent, utilities, marketing, and so on), then estimate an annual cost for each. Don't forget indirect expenses, such as supervisory time and accounting fees. When in doubt, always overestimate your expenses.

Total expenses: Year 1 $ _____

                    Year 2 $ _____

                    Year 3 $ _____

Total expenses for three years (add the numbers above): $ _____

- *Revenue.* Use your market research to estimate all sources of earned income from fees, sales, and so on. Once again, prepare a list on a separate piece of paper. For example:

Year 1:

        5 workshops with 20 participants @ $75 per person $7,500
        300 workbooks @ $20 6,000
        50 training videos @ $50 2,500
        Total: $16,000

When in doubt, underestimate income. In fact, always underestimate income.

To test your assumptions, share your projected expenses and revenue with two or three knowledgeable people who are not involved with your group and ask for their feedback.

Total revenue: Year 1 $ _____

                    Year 2 $ _____

                    Year 3 $ _____

Total revenue for three years (add the numbers above): $ _____

Revenue minus expenses = estimated profit or (loss) after three years: $ _____

3. **Now ask yourself, is it worth it?** If not, this is an opportune moment to abandon the project.

4. **If you plan to proceed, consider the working capital you will need.** In preparing your financial statements, you will create a cash flow analysis that projects income and expenses, month by month. This will help you determine how much seed money you'll need to get started. To estimate quickly the amount of start-up funding required to launch your grassroots venture, do the following exercise.

Review all expenses for Year 1:

- Highlight any one-time expenses to be paid during the first year, such as design and printing fees for a new book, capital improvements to a building, extra marketing costs for launching a new retail business, and so on.

- Total the remaining expenses—the ones you pay regularly, such as salary and rent—and divide by two. In other words, include six months' worth of these costs. Write this number in the margin and highlight it, too.

- Add the highlighted numbers. Since it's safe to assume that new ventures will earn no income for at least six months, this is the minimum amount you'll need to get started.

Warning: This rough estimate cannot and should not replace a formal cash flow projection. When you do the math in detail, you will likely discover that you'll need even more working capital than you thought.

Writing the Plan: White Earth Land Recovery Project—Native Harvest

Every September, at the time of the wild rice moon, the Anishinaabeg Ojibwe people launch their canoes on the lakes of northern Minnesota. Working in pairs, they move through the reed-filled waters—one poling the canoe, the other using two long sticks to bend the reeds over and knock *Manoomin,* or wild rice, into the boat.

"*Manoomin* is a centerpiece of the nutrition and sustenance for our community," writes Winona LaDuke in *Whole Earth* magazine, "a gift given to the Anishinaabeg from the Creator. It is a food uniquely ours, a food used in our daily lives, our ceremonies, and in our thanksgiving feasts." In addition, she continues, wild rice is a cash crop for community members, who go ricing "to feed their families, to buy school clothes and fix cars, and to get ready for the ever-returning winter."[6]

LaDuke, a well-known indigenous rights activist, author, and political figure—she was Ralph Nader's Green Party running mate in 1996 and 2000—founded the White Earth Land Recovery Project (www.welrp.org) to protect and restore the land and culture of the Anishinaabeg people. Since only 7 percent of the reservation is controlled by Indians, the organization raises money to buy back privately owned parcels (1,200 acres to date) and works to have federal, state, and county lands returned to the White Earth Band.

Native Harvest (www.nativeharvest.com), one of the group's programs, was begun in the mid–1990s to get a fair price for the work and the products of the land, while also helping to fill the organization's funding gap as start-up grants ran out. This enterprise gathers, grows, processes, packages, and markets several traditional foods to generate income for the local community, while honoring and preserving traditional harvest practices. In addition to *manoomin,* their homegrown product line includes *Aninaatig zhiiwaagamizigan,* or maple syrup, harvested from their 380 acres of sugar bush; *Miskomin*, or raspberries, grown on their farm; and *Gijikonayezigan*, or hominy corn. Native Harvest also buys and resells products from other indigenous entrepreneurs, including buffalo sausage (*mashkodebizhiki wiiyaas*), birch bark baskets, and homemade quilts.

A SAMPLING OF
PRODUCTS FROM
THE NATIVE HARVEST
CATALOG

LaDuke and her colleagues prepared a business plan to guide the expansion of the enterprise and help secure funding. With attachments, the document contains more than 70 pages. To give you a sense of what went into the plan, the table of contents and executive summary are reproduced here:

Table of Contents

Executive Summary

Native Harvest, over the past two years, has distinguished itself by providing a quality product in a timely manner to mail order and other customers regionally, nationally, and internationally. Through the diligence and hard work of Native Harvest and White Earth Land Recovery Project staff, the organization has developed the capacity to begin reaching for those objectives outlined...by the Board and staff of WELRP. Through this work, we have also developed a line of products that have a number of unique characteristics:

- Native American-produced products
- Ecologically produced products using, for instance, horse-drawn equipment
- Natural products; at some point in the future, certifiable organically by MOGBA, OCIA, or a Native American certifying agency
- Benefits a community effort to recover land and cultural practices, i.e. is tied to a broader set of goals
- Provides a source of employment and revitalization of cultural practices in the Ojibwe community
- Excellent quality products and crafts
- Competitive pricing, timely delivery

All of the above enhance the marketability of the Native Harvest brand of products. Previous market studies—completed by Ann Potter and Associates, Tammy Hinman, and updated data prepared by staff and interns of the White Earth Land Recovery Project—indicate that all the above factors weigh heavily in the decision of customers to purchase Native Harvest and WELRP products. Most direct mail consumers—representing the bulk of the business—support Native Harvest for the political and socially responsible reasons they support the WELRP. Similarly, the "niche" of food, Native American, and other stores presently outlined in the marketing plan, and interviewed, indicate that product loyalty to Native Harvest was related to many of the above characteristics.

This strength of our products needs to be augmented in our publicity, advertising, and labeling (i.e., photos of our people and horses, and a listing that we have honey-based preserves for sale, will augment our ability to sell our products.)...

There are two options ahead of us in expanding Native Harvest as discussed previously in our market studies of wild rice, maple syrup, and raspberry preserves. Both of these show promise in the coming months. They are:

1. Further penetration of present markets, and

2. Expansion and broadening of product lines.

It is recommended that we pursue both of these options.

This excerpt works for several reasons.

1. It outlines Native Harvest's track record of producing and selling goods. Because they're not starting from scratch, this inspires confidence.

2. The author identifies the unique attributes of Native Harvest products and makes a strong case for why these qualities matter to their customers.

3. It shows, albeit briefly, how the sales program supports the mission of the organization.

4. Both the table of contents and the executive summary mention hands-on market research.

5. The document appears to be thorough. (We don't have the whole thing to review, but the table of contents is exhaustive.)

6. It hints at specific next steps for building the business, which is the function of the plan.

The inclusion of numbers—current sales and net profits, projected sales and net profits, the amount of capital needed to expand the business—would have made this summary even stronger.

With a plan in hand, you're ready to raise money. Strategies for locating seed money to begin your project—where to look and whom to ask—are covered in Chapter Six.

How to Build a
Working Neighborhood

ESPERANZA UNIDA

MILWAUKEE, WISCONSIN

WWW.ESPERANZAUNIDA.ORG

ANNUAL BUDGET: $3,250,000

EARNED INCOME: 63%

EARNED INCOME STRATEGIES

- EMPLOYMENT TRAINING AND JOB DEVELOPMENT
- SERVICES FOR NONPROFITS AND OTHER INSTITUTIONAL CUSTOMERS
- CONSUMER SERVICES
- CONSUMER GOODS: RETAIL

When she enrolled at Esperanza Unida, an employment training program, Cheryl Rogers was a single mother with six children. Her earlier jobs had offered low pay, no benefits, and little inspiration. She'd spent the previous year on welfare and was worn down from the stress of raising her kids on a limited budget. "I had a real bad attitude," she told the *Milwaukee Journal Sentinel,* "a nasty attitude. I just felt like I wasn't getting anywhere." Richard Oulahan, executive director of the nonprofit, concurred. "Cheryl came in here an angry woman," he told the newspaper. "And that's where someone with her intelligence should have been."[1]

Rogers was accepted into the metal fabrication training program, where she learned welding skills by repairing and building waste containers. Her instructor was Bernie Flood. "When I couldn't get a sitter or my kids were sick," she says, "Bernie would come and pick us all up to come to class. He'd put them in his office and find things for them to do so I could get my work done." Two Americorps volunteers preparing a replication manual for Esperanza Unida captured Rogers's words and her gratitude: "There wasn't a problem that I had that Bernie wouldn't help me with."[2]

"If you do a cost-benefit analysis," Oulahan told the *Journal,* "Bernie's done more to turn welfare around than the governor."[3]

Within two years, Rogers took over for Flood as the chief welding instructor. Her "family-supporting job" has enabled her to provide for her children, buy a car, and look to the future with confidence. More important, she's trained dozens of welfare recipients, both women and men, and helped them to land secure jobs. "I'll tell you what I know from experience," she says. "Work is necessary for building strong neighborhoods."[4]

Esperanza Unida—Spanish for "united hope"—was founded in 1971 to assist Latino workers with employment and worker's compensation hearings, and gradually expanded its mission to encompass other aspects of worker justice. In response to a series of plant closures in Milwaukee, they launched their first "Training Business Model" in 1984—a program to teach auto repair to laid-off factory workers by creating and running a car repair business.

Since then, Esperanza Unida has launched several other training and job placement ventures. These programs are built on two premises: first, they must prepare the participants for family-supporting jobs that actually exist. Second, they must generate a substantial portion of their revenue from sales.

Over the past decade, Esperanza Unida has earned an average of 50 to 60 percent of its operating revenue while graduating more than 2,000 students. During a recent year, 77 percent of graduates landed family-supporting jobs. Eighty percent were still working after ninety days. They earned, on average, $3 per hour above the minimum wage. Year after year, the group's success rates exceed Wisconsin and national averages for employment training programs. "The Training Business Model," says Oulahan, "is our answer to the question, 'How do you level the playing field in a capitalist society?'"[5]

The organization now operates eight enterprises and has "spun off" several others. When Esperanza Unida closed its restaurant, a former employee opened his own café at the same location. An asbestos abatement program was handed off to another worker, who continues to run it as a for-profit business. Currently the group runs the following programs:

1. *Welding and metal fabrication.* In 1990, as it was shutting down its waste container manufacturing shop in Milwaukee, Waste Management of North America gave Esperanza Unida the contract to take over the fabrication business. The corporation also offered to serve as business adviser and customer, buying everything the nonprofit could produce.

Like all of Esperanza Unida's training programs, the nonprofit welding business was designed to create two "products": skilled welders, and fabricated metal materials for the marketplace. Training welders and finding them jobs, while demanding, turned out to be the easier part of the equation. More than 400 students have graduated, learning relevant math and blueprint-reading skills to complement hands-on metal fabrication techniques.

Marketing the finished materials remains a lot more challenging. Within two years of start-up, Waste Management bought another manufacturing operation and ended their business relationship with Esperanza Unida. "It turned out to be a blessing in disguise," says Flood. "It forced us to expand our production and repair services and customer base. I just got out the Yellow Pages and started calling all the waste companies.... I got some nice new customers out of it."[6] Today, property owners and managers make up most of the customer base, and the City of Milwaukee is also a big client.

2. *Construction.* Esperanza Unida's construction program took off when the organization purchased the International Building, an abandoned department store in their largely Latino neighborhood, and converted it into a community training center. Financing for the $5.5 million project came from a combination of federal, state, local, and private grants, in-kind donations, and a $1.7 million bank loan. The contractors hired to rehabilitate the building were required to take on apprentices from the community. "We had eleven kids trained in the skills trade as a result of the renovation," Oulahan told the *Milwaukee Sentinel.* "Now they've left with the contractors and are learning the trade."[7]

Today, through the Esperanza Unida Construction Company, the organization is instructing its own apprentices while fixing up inner-city homes and handling other contracting projects.

3. *Home sales.* The group also purchases old homes slated for condemnation, renovates them with trainee labor, and sells them at cost to the working poor, including program graduates. "In vocational school, they build a wall and tear it down," Oulahan told journalist Robin Garr of the Web site GRASS-ROOTS.ORG. "That doesn't make any sense. We build houses."[8]

4. *Customer service training.* With support from Ameritech, a regional telecommunications company, Esperanza Unida created a twelve-week training program for the booming tele-services industry. "Ameritech funded the whole start-up," former development director Paula Gokey told the *Milwaukee Journal Sentinel,* citing a $75,000 donation. "They paid for the classroom, helped hire the instructor, and worked with us on a curriculum."[9]

Students learn conflict resolution strategies, database and word processing, sales skills, and also receive assistance with personal and family issues. Since its inception, more than 100 people have completed the training program and 81 percent have been placed into customer service jobs.

5. *Printing and graphic design.* The printing and graphic arts training center offers a full range of design, printing, photocopying, and finishing services. Their best clients are other nonprofit agencies, says Flood. They market themselves the old-fashioned, time-tested way: "By banging on the doors of nonprofits and businesses," he says.

6. *Auto repair and used car sales.* Esperanza Unida solicits donated vehicles, then teaches students to repair them and offers the cars for sale. Graduates from

any of the training programs can buy vehicles at a deep discount, providing them with flexible, reliable transportation.

7. *Child care.* The lack of affordable child care is a huge barrier preventing low-income families, especially single-parent families, from finding and keeping jobs. To address this problem, the organization opened a day care center, Esperanza del Futuro (Hope for the Future) to train and certify child care workers and to provide affordable day care for its staff. Pick-n-Save Mega Mart, a regional grocery chain, provided a site at a local shopping center. The store renovated the space specifically for the child care center and furnished the facility at no charge. Employees of both the nonprofit and the shopping center receive a popular benefit: preference in enrolling their children. The day care center operates in the black, with a surplus being used to underwrite other training programs.

8. *Coffee and book shop.* ¿Qué Pasa? Coffee and Books is the only bookstore in Milwaukee specializing in Spanish-language materials. Launched with a $65,000 gift from a private donor, the bookstore also serves as a bilingual cultural center, providing refreshments and space for community events. Students from the El Puente alternative high school, which is located in the building, market ¿Qué Pasa? products through their entrepreneurship training program.

"I'm certainly learning a lot about running a business," Simon Martinez told *The Business Journal.* The former manager of a fast-food restaurant served as the bookstore's first manager. "I know right now I'm probably not getting the best deals on these books. But that kind of knowledge comes with time, and that's what the store is here for."[10]

"It doesn't bother me if, at times, we've wasted money or made a mistake," says Oulahan, backing up his employee. "Perfection is unattainable. The mere idea of it stops people from getting in there and just doing it."[11]

The final word on Esperanza Unida comes from Cheryl Rogers, as quoted in the organization's replication manual. "Almost every week, graduates come back to the shop to get extra help with their welding skills, or just to tell us how they're doing. And you know, most of the time, they're making more money in their new jobs than I am! It doesn't bug me, because I'm not in this for the money. I believe in what this place is doing. Look what it did for me. The students remind me of that."[12]

THINGS TO THINK ABOUT

• *Most commerce is conducted business-to-business, not business-to-consumer. How can you best serve businesses (and nonprofits and government agencies) in your area?* Esperanza Unida fabricates and repairs waste containers, provides printing and graphic design services, manages a child care center in partnership with a local retailer, and works with a regional communications company to train customer service employees. Their primary customers are other businesses, not individual consumers.

- *Successful corporate partnerships are built on mutual self-interest.* Esperanza Unida's mission is to develop training programs and place their students in "family-supporting" jobs. Ameritech, a regional telecommunications company, wanted employees who were better prepared for the workplace. Combine these two needs and what do you get? The Ameritech Customer Service Training Center, funded by the corporation and managed by the nonprofit. Ameritech screens graduates for possible employment.

- *How many different ways can you slice the same idea and use it to earn money?* All of Esperanza Unida's programs are based on a single, powerful idea: job training works best in the context of real businesses that need to cover a substantial portion of their own costs. Over the years, they've used this model to create a dozen different ventures, most of them successful.

- *Good media outreach is good marketing.* Esperanza Unida has a compelling story to tell, and the group works effectively with the news media to get the story out. It takes time and energy to interact with reporters and editors, but it's time well spent, especially when you compare the costs of other promotional strategies. (For ideas on media outreach, see Chapter Seven.)

- *Your look is a big part of your identity. Once you've found the design elements that work, stick with them.* All of Esperanza Unida's materials use the same typefaces and color scheme, and their program brochures are created from a standard layout. For the customer, this means easy recognition and predictable quality. Consistency inspires confidence.

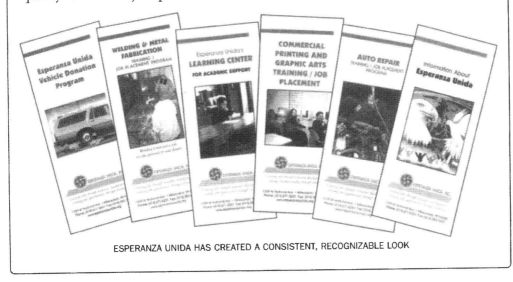

ESPERANZA UNIDA HAS CREATED A CONSISTENT, RECOGNIZABLE LOOK

Chapter 6

Finding capital to launch your venture

■   ▩   ▩

Lack of "operating capital"—money when you need it to purchase goods for resale, cover salaries, or pay the bills—is often listed as the primary cause of business failure. The typical successful small business takes three years to reach profitability. New ventures might be profitable during the busiest months (such as the holiday shopping season for retailers), but over the course of the year cash outlays exceed income. Without operating money to carry them through during the lean months, these enterprises won't have the opportunity to grow into self-sustaining businesses.

There are essentially three ways to subsidize a new enterprise: with time, with money, or with both. Grassroots organizations, despite being overworked, tend to view time as more obtainable than money, and therefore choose low-cost ventures that can be done with the talent on hand. As William A. Duncan writes, "The nonprofit itself may be able to put a portion of its staff time into a business activity which generates immediate cash income. Using this approach may not be all that different from what you do already....This 'greenhouse approach' demands creativity and a new point of view about what an opportunity looks like [and can be] grown incrementally out of available staff skills."[1] Most organizations profiled in this book relied to some degree on a "greenhouse approach" to generate income from their existing programs.

Time is a great asset, but it won't pay the phone bill, cover the postage for your promotional mailing, or put fuel in the gas tank. Even inexpensive earned income strategies require up-front cash, either in the form of gifts and grants (which don't have to be repaid) or loans (which do).

In this chapter, we discuss fundraising options for earned income projects. If you're looking for capital, here are places to start your search.

Internal and informal sources of funds

One advantage of using internal sources (defined, for our purposes, as money moving through your organization's bank account or provided by individuals close to your group) is that the decision makers already know your nonprofit, believe in your mission, and have demonstrated commitment to the work. For better or worse, they are more likely to view your proposal with optimism. There are a number of opportunities for securing internal funds:

• *Current income.* The vast majority of small nonprofits finance entrepreneurial projects from current income—unrestricted support from members, donors, and grants, or net income from other ventures. The simplest solution, if you can afford it, is to include a line item for enterprise expenses in your budget. Allocate that money to prevent it from being spent on other needs.

• *Cash reserves.* Sensible organizations strive to set aside a reserve fund to protect against the loss of grants or a decrease in donations. Ideally, your reserve will be large enough to cover three to six months of basic operations. If the payoff looks promising—in other words, if the potential reward justifies the risk—you might consider using a portion of the reserve fund to seed a new project. For example, The Food Bank of Western Massachusetts dipped into their reserves to enter the microwave popcorn business.

• *Windfalls.* "Take an unanticipated gift or bequest and earmark it for venture planning," suggests Edward Skloot.[2] As he points out, external funding is hardest to raise for the planning phase, so you'll probably need to find that money internally.

• *In-kind support.* Look for creative ways to reduce your cash needs by soliciting donated goods and services. At the Palouse-Clearwater Environmental Institute, volunteers drive the organization's commuter vans in exchange for a free ride to work. When FareStart renovated its restaurant, the group received $92,000 worth of professional services and construction materials.

• *Board members.* You can approach current and former board members for gifts or loans. As Ellen Arrick writes in *The Nonprofit Entrepreneur,* they are "patient sources and willing to accept high risk." A negative aspect, however, may be the resulting keen interest of investors. "This commitment," she writes, "implies a much more active involvement with day-to-day activities on the part of board members than most nonprofits are accustomed to."[3]

• *Major donors.* Individual supporters can be approached to designate a special contribution for the venture, perhaps as a challenge gift to spur other donations. Esperanza Unida launched their café and bookshop with $65,000 from a donor family. You can also negotiate low- or no-interest loans from contributors.

• *Members, friends, and family.* "The most likely source of startup capital is your local constituency, friends, and advisors," Duncan says. "I have been involved in several ventures that raised $5,000 to $20,000 in the form of numerous small loans from local supporters.…There were usually about 20 subscribers of all income levels…and in each case they were all repaid! That's probably because the ventures got pretty thoroughly analyzed in the course of obtaining 20 different loans from people who needed their money back."[4]

If you're borrowing money—especially from supporters—you must apprise them of the risk. If the donor loses the loan, you will likely lose the donor, so the risk cuts both ways. Before you borrow, do your homework. Make sure your project has a reasonable chance of success.

External sources

Of necessity, external funders and lenders are much more cautious and systematic about providing money. Foundation staff and loan officers tend to see your work in terms of *risk* and *return*: measuring the likelihood of success and the benefits it would bring against the potential costs of failure. In many cases, the "return" is the social benefit rather than (or in addition to) the financial reward. When seeking outside funding, would-be entrepreneurs must learn to think this way as well.

Some organizations use a combination approach: they start with internal funds, then seek outside money to expand the enterprise after it's up and running. This is known as "second-stage financing." It's much easier to interest an outside investor if you have customers, sales, financial reports—in other words, a track record. "Funders have given money to great ideas that never happened," says Richard Oulahan of Esperanza Unida. "The idea here is to show them that we can and will make it happen—because it is already happening."[5]

In the long run, the rigors of applying for grants and loans can work to your advantage. To secure capital, you must do your homework, including detailed financial projections. Many marginal ideas will fail the "investor test," and the ones that survive are more likely to succeed in the marketplace. As with internal sources, there are a number of places to look for external funding:

• *Fee-first contracts.* If you can identify a corporation or government agency to buy your work in advance, you won't need to borrow money or risk your own resources. "Don't use your money, use theirs," writes Richard Steckel in *Filthy Rich*. "Nonprofit ventures can be accomplished with corporate money."[6] His former employer, the Denver Children's Museum, pre-sells nearly all of its programs to corporate partners and then uses that money to produce the relevant goods and services. Melpomene Institute conducted health research under contract to CIGNA Corporation, while Plateau Restoration and The Center for Anti-Violence Education have negotiated contracts with government agencies. For more information about establishing corporate partnerships, see Chapter Eight.

• *Grants from foundations and other funding agencies.* A number of earned income projects have been launched or expanded with foundation money. The Georgia Citizens Coalition on Hunger was awarded a $60,000 grant from Oxfam, the international hunger relief group, to open a thrift store and farmer's market, and the Institute for Conservation Leadership received foundation grants to initiate a fee-based fundraising training program. BorderLinks solicited church funding to expand its experiential education offerings on the U.S.–Mexico border. In all cases, these "investors" provided capital in exchange for program results rather than a financial return.

• *Loans from "social lenders."* This category includes community loan funds and program-related investments from foundations. In some cases, non-commercial financial institutions, such as credit unions, also operate as social lenders.

Community loan funds are designed to assist small businesses in disadvantaged areas: inner-city neighborhoods, rural communities, Native American reservations, and so forth. In addition to capital, these funders also provide training and advice. For more information, contact the National Community Capital Association (215/923-4754, www.communitycapital.org).

Program-related investments (PRIs) are a form of foundation funding; these investments are sometimes called "recoverable grants." According to the Foundation Center, U.S. foundations provided $266 million in PRIs in 1999, nearly double the 1997 total. Most commonly, these funds support "community revitalization, low-income housing, micro-enterprise development, historic preservation, human services, education, church renovations, and many other types of projects."[7]

Program-related investments are granted on the condition that nonprofits repay the money over time, with interest. PRIs function like loans, but without collateral. Not many foundations advertise the availability of PRIs, but if you have a long-standing relationship with a funder, you might explore this option. Sometimes you can negotiate a package that includes both a grant and a program-related investment for the same project.

Revolving loan funds for nonprofits. This category covers a variety of loan pools set up to help nonprofits diversify income. Repayments replenish the funds, providing capital for other organizations. Examples include the Independent Press Association (www.indypress.org), which loans money to members for subscription development, and the Environmental Support Center (www.envsc.org), whose loan fund helps environmental groups build their membership or launch earned income ventures. Native Seeds/SEARCH received seed money from the Environmental Support Center to begin operations at their conservation farm. Seeds grown at the farm are sold through the Native Seeds/SEARCH catalog, with sales and fundraising income used to repay the loan.

Credit unions are membership-owned financial institutions. Some credit unions have progressive lending and investing policies. VanCity, for example, offers both grants and loans to entrepreneurial organizations in its home base of Vancouver, British Columbia. VanCity provided start-up and expansion funding for Our Community Bikes.

In many cases, social lenders offer lower interest rates than commercial banks. However, they require the same level of "due diligence," including a sophisticated business plan and financial projections. While seeking financing to publish their textbook on Chicano history, for example, the SouthWest Organizing Project approached the New Mexico Community Development Loan Fund. After a rigorous review of their business plan—which included sales targets, cash flow projections, and specific strategies for marketing and distribution—the fund approved a $25,000 loan.

• *Commercial lenders.* For nonprofits, banks are usually the financiers of last resort. The interest rates are higher, the repayment schedule is stricter, and you'll almost always need collateral—some sort of tangible, saleable asset—to back up your borrowing. (Without collateral, your chances of having a loan approved are greatly reduced.) Furthermore, the relatively small loans grassroots groups need don't generate enough profit to make them worthwhile for a commercial lender.

If you decide to approach a bank, start with the financial institution that handles your organization's checking account and holds any savings or reserve fund. Your pre-existing business relationship with the banker can make all the difference. As another option, ask a well-to-do member or supporter to co-sign (guarantee) the loan, with the understanding that this member or supporter will be responsible if your group can't repay the money. The Food Bank of Western Massachusetts found a generous donor to co-sign their loan from the Vermont National Bank, which helped to purchase their farm.

The coldly analytical cheerleader

"The nonprofit entrepreneur," writes Ellen Arrick, "has to wear two hats in going about the business of locating financing." On one hand, she has to be a "promotional cheerleader," enthusiastically talking up the venture, its benefits to the community, its potential to earn income for the organization, and so forth.

Creative Financing:
Palouse-Clearwater Environmental Institute

■   ■   ■   ■   ■   ■   ■   ■   ■   ■   ■   ■   ■   ■   ■   ■

Here's a riddle: What has four wheels, fifteen seats, a bunch of happy riders, and drives around rural Idaho saving 4,000 gallons of gasoline each year?

A VanPool Network van, that's what. On weekdays, three vans run between the towns of Moscow, Lewiston, and Lapwai, Idaho, shuttling commuters and students to jobs and school, then home again. The VanPool, sponsored by the Palouse-Clearwater Environmental Institute (PCEI), was developed to reduce air pollution, cut down on parking problems, and save money. It also builds a sense of community among the riders, who spend several hours together each week. "We call it our little village on wheels," says Tom Lamar, executive director of the institute.

The VanPool was developed in response to the Persian Gulf War, when local residents brainstormed ways to reduce the use of petroleum. Their strategy: create a subscription service for commuters that would pay for itself. After informal market research indicated a positive response, PCEI still faced a financial roadblock. Nice vans—equipped with individual seats and reading lights, much like airplanes—would attract business, but they cost a lot of money. How could a small, grassroots group finance the purchase?

PCEI (www.pcei.org) set a budget of $100,000 to purchase the three vans and underwrite enough staff time to launch and manage the service for one year. Their financing strategy had three components:

- **Grants.** A federal grant through the Intermodal Surface Transportation Efficiency Act, or ISTEA, provided $80,000 on a challenge basis. The application entailed a lot of work, Lamar says, but was worth the effort; unlike loans, grants don't have to be repaid. This allowed the van service to become self-sufficient in its second year.
- **Community support.** To receive federal funds, the remaining $20,000 had to be raised from the local community to complete the match. The University of Idaho, facing parking problems around campus and wanting to reduce the number of commuter cars, made a substantial commitment. The balance was contributed by more than twenty local businesses and individuals. This "community support" strategy offered another opportunity for market research and business planning, because the nonprofit had to test its idea with potential "investors." It was time-consuming—lots of phone calls, meetings, and questions—but it resulted in a clearer concept and more fully realized action plan. Once invested, all these backers were enlisted as boosters—informal promoters—of the project.
- **In-kind support.** To keep costs down, PCEI barters with their volunteer drivers. In exchange for being punctual and diligent, each driver gets a free ride to and from work plus a designated number of "personal miles."

When a fourth van is added soon, PCEI will be able to transport more than 50 commuters per day. The program is paying for itself and demand remains strong. "If people have options," Lamar says, "they will do the right thing."

On the other hand, "she has to be coldly analytical" while wrestling with the numbers and judging the financial risk and rewards of the project.[8]

Donors and investors need to see both sides of the equation. They want to feel your excitement, but they also need an honest assessment of the risks. Anything less would be unethical. Indeed, if you can't itemize the risks, your external prospects (and some internal ones, too) will do it for you, and you will look unprepared or unduly optimistic. Among the risks to consider and discuss are the following:

- If the project fails, your lenders and investors could lose their money. Of course, everyone understands that it's nearly impossible to loan money without risk. Your job is to minimize the risk through good market research and business planning.

- If you borrow money from donors or foundations and can't repay it, your relationship with these folks will be damaged, making it more difficult to receive further gifts and grants. As Shakespeare reminds us in *Hamlet,* "Neither a borrower, nor a lender be, for loan oft loses both itself and friend."

- If business growth takes longer than expected, repayment could be delayed.

- If you face any sort of community backlash against your program—"those alleged do-gooders are trying to make money off of poor people," or "that nonprofit is competing unfairly with legitimate small businesses"—your investors might get splattered with a little mud, too.

- You could be wildly successful, earn more than expected, and create an internal controversy about where your money comes from. This is known as a "good problem." Under this scenario, your investors are fully repaid and might even provide more money for second-stage financing, so their short-term risk is zero.

Before you go out in the world to ask for money, examine every potential enterprise with a ruthless eye. Use Worksheet 6.1 to create a full picture of your potential funding sources. As you do, keep in mind the need to be realistic.

All successful ventures generate their own money—through sales. The sooner you can find, reach, and engage your customers, the sooner you can begin earning income and the less start-up funding you will need. Now that you've drafted a financing plan, it's time to think about reaching those prospective customers. In the next chapter, you'll learn about marketing options and draft a customized marketing plan based on your organization's skills and resources.

Finding start-up funding

How much money will you need and when will you need it? After drafting your business plan, use this form to create your financing plan. Don't assume that all of your start-up funding will come from one source. More than likely, you'll need to piece it together from several sources.

Earned income project: _____

Up-front money required $_____   **By when?** _____

Use the following chart to plan your steps for developing your start-up funding.

1. **Do you have relationships with any people—funders, donors, bankers, or businesspeople—who could help you secure financing?** If so, list them:

   _____
   _____
   _____
   _____
   _____
   _____
   _____

2. **What *Internal and informal sources* can you identify for funding?** Note on the following grid how much you can ask them for, and how you will plan your next steps.

POTENTIAL SOURCE	AMOUNT SOUGHT	PERCENTAGE OF TOTAL NEEDED	STATUS OF REQUEST	NEXT STEPS	WHO DOES IT?
CURRENT INCOME					
CASH RESERVES					
WINDFALLS					
IN-KIND SUPPORT					
BOARD MEMBERS:					
a.					
b.					
c.					
d.					
MAJOR DONORS:					
a.					
b.					
c.					
MEMBERS, FRIENDS, FAMILY:					
a.					
b.					
c.					

3. Where will you look for *external funding*?

POTENTIAL SOURCE	AMOUNT SOUGHT	PERCENTAGE OF TOTAL NEEDED	STATUS OF REQUEST	NEXT STEPS	WHO DOES IT?
FEE-FIRST CONTRACTS:					
a.					
b.					
c.					
GRANTS:					
a.					
b.					
c.					
d.					
e.					
SOCIAL LENDERS:					
a.					
b.					
c.					
d.					
COMMERCIAL LENDERS:					
a.					
b.					
c.					
d.					

Reclaiming History/ Reclame La Historia

SOUTHWEST ORGANIZING PROJECT
ALBUQUERQUE, NEW MEXICO
WWW.SWOP.NET
ANNUAL BUDGET: $373,000
EARNED INCOME: 10%

EARNED INCOME STRATEGIES
- PUBLICATIONS
- CONSUMER GOODS: RETAIL
- CONSUMER GOODS: WHOLESALE

In 1997, two public schoolteachers were fired by the school board in the small town of Vaughn, New Mexico. Their crime? Teaching Chicano history in a largely Chicano community. Sisters Nadine and Patsy Córdova had 35 years of classroom experience between them and were popular with the students. Even the Anglo kids, they said, wanted to learn history from a Chicano perspective. The superintendent banned their textbook of choice, *500 Años del Pueblo Chicano/500 Years of Chicano History* because, among other things, it included the phrase "Anglo colonizers."

The story of the Córdova sisters became a national news event, covered in media ranging from National Public Radio to *Low Rider* magazine. The teachers eventually reached a legal settlement with the school system, marking a small but significant victory for the SouthWest Organizing Project, or SWOP, which publishes the book.

SWOP, founded in 1980, works to empower the disenfranchised in the Southwest to realize racial and gender equality, and social and economic justice. "We don't do advocacy or technical assistance," says co-director Michael Leon-Guerrero. "We empower our communities to stand up for themselves." Perhaps best known for helping to launch the environmental justice movement by building an international network of social justice groups, the organization is involved in many local and regional issues, including indigenous land rights, cultural survival, corporate accountability, immigrant organizing, and youth development.

As part of its community education strategy, the SouthWest Organizing Project has an active publications program featuring *500 Years of Chicano History,* which they first published in 1991. This bilingual textbook pulls no punches. While including names, dates, and hundreds of photos documenting oppression and exploitation, it also outlines the rise of the Chicano rights movement, the farm worker struggle, and other recent positive developments. *500 Years,* which has now been approved for schools by the state of New Mexico, builds on an earlier edition published in 1976 by the Chicano Communications Center of Albuquerque, New Mexico. The retail price is $38.50 for hardback, $18 for paperback. Since SWOP took over publication, more than 23,000 copies have been distributed.

Book production and printing costs were financed by a $25,000 loan (at 10 percent interest) from the New Mexico Community Development Loan Fund. As part of the application, SWOP wrote a "marketing, distribution, and fulfillment plan" for *500 Years,* which included a variety of outreach strategies, sales goals, and cash flow projections. The plan focuses on sales to schools, which looks like a good bet: the U.S. has 200,000 educational institutions and nearly four million teachers. (It's also a very competitive market, with 4,000 publishers trying to sell their materials.)[1] Latinos, the country's fastest-growing ethnic group, now make up 12.5 percent of the population nationwide; the percentage is much higher in the Southwest. The demand for Chicano history materials, especially in the region, is likely to increase.

To promote the book, SWOP sends brochures to principals and teachers, especially those who teach Spanish, social studies, or history. They sell directly to distributors (Baker & Taylor), major bookstore chains (Borders, Barnes & Noble), on-line retailers (Amazon.com) and independent bookstores throughout the Southwest. They also promote *500 Years* and other publications in their newsletter *Voces Unidas,* which has a circulation of 11,000 and a readership of perhaps twice that many.

"We're proud of our database," says Roberto Roibal, who handles marketing and distribution. Over the years, SWOP has collected names from "direct contact"—membership information, door-knocking, sign-in sheets at meetings and demonstrations, phone and mail inquiries, and customer purchases. Roibal emphasizes that they clean the list regularly by inputting new names, updating address changes, and removing bad addresses. "We never have to buy any lists," he says.

Perhaps their most unusual promotion has come through *Low Rider.* The magazine has a substantial, loyal readership among Chicano custom car aficionados. A regular column, "La Raza," reports on news of interest to the community. In 1992, the magazine announced publication of *500 Years.* Five years later, they reported on the Córdova sisters and included contact information for SWOP.

These articles, says Roibal, generated "a big response." Stories in *Low Rider* revealed another unexpected market: according to Roibal, "hundreds and hundreds of prisoners" have purchased books, asked for free copies (SWOP honors many of these requests), and sought information about the group's work. Because these magazines are collected, saved, and passed around for years—both inside prison and out—Roibal says, "I still get letters."

Most advertisers would pay big money for this kind of longevity. Indeed, the SouthWest Organizing Project saw the opportunity and purchased advertising in the magazine, but the results were disappointing. This echoes the experience of many nonprofit marketers, who've found that "free media"—news articles and other media coverage—generate more business than paid advertising.

According to Louis Head, SWOP's former development coordinator, Chicano youth—the group's number-one target market—are consistently good customers. SWOP put ordering information on the Internet to reach well-to-do progressives, Head says, "but the biggest response came from Chicano students." Their Web site includes a simple but well-designed *mercado* where visitors can buy SWOP publications and other products through secure credit card transactions. Internet sales and donations total $350 to $400 per month.

"[Being able to accept] Visa and MasterCard helps a lot," Roibal says. "It also tightens up credit with bookstores. We push them to pay with credit cards, because we've been burned." Over the past seven years, he says, they've written off about $5,000 in bad debt from non-paying customers, mostly retailers and nonprofits. Although that works out to less than 2 percent of sales per year, which is acceptable, it can certainly be improved. The new system seems to be helping.

To accompany the textbook, the SouthWest Organizing Project worked with Collision Course Productions to create an educational video, *¡Viva La Causa! 500 Years of Chicano History*. The one-hour video, available in Spanish or English, retails for $38.50 to individuals and $53.50 to schools, nonprofits and other institutions. The "Combo Special" ($45 to individuals and $60 for institutions) includes the video and the paperback; deeper discounts are offered for the year-end holidays.

This kind of two-tiered pricing is a common strategy, reflecting two facts: first, that schools and other organizations will use these materials many times, so they should theoretically pay more; and second, they tend to have bigger purchasing budgets than individuals.

Having repackaged the same content two different ways—book and video—SWOP looked at the market and said, "How else can we present this information?" The solution: the Chicano History Teaching Kit ($114), which includes a book, video, and curriculum guide for elementary and secondary schoolteachers.

More than 300 have been sold, which works out to $35,000 in income. They cost about $27.50 to produce and ship (not including staff time), so SWOP has netted almost $27,000 on this item. The teaching kit is a terrific example of how to augment successful products, and increase income, by creating new products that appeal to the same consumers.

The SouthWest Organizing Project also publishes a handbook for community organizers and others interested in social change. When Intel Corporation opened a plant in the Albuquerque area, it received large tax subsidies, simplified air emissions regulations, and a host of other concessions in exchange for the promise of local jobs. *Intel Inside New Mexico: A Case Study of Environmental and Economic Injustice* documents SWOP's long-running campaign to make the corporation more accountable to the public.

This report, which sells for $11.50, has been purchased by government agencies, city councils, community organizations, and socially responsible investors who monitor the high-tech industry in their own communities. "As the level of understanding about this industry starts to change," says Head, "more and more people are asking for our materials."

Finally, SWOP offers a small but creative array of gear and gifts, including logo berets and baseball caps; posters; note cards; Chile Harvest Fiesta T-shirts; coffee from Chiapas, Mexico; bilingual coloring books; and a cassette featuring original songs from SWOP's youth group, *Jóvenes Unidos*. All of these items can be purchased on the Web or by mail—indeed, the final two pages of *Voces Unidas* function as a mini sales catalog.

The SouthWest Organizing Project offers a great lesson in how to combine uncompromising politics with smart product development and sales promotion. Nadine Córdova told *Voces Unidas,* "If you're not teaching relevant education, then you're not teaching."[2] SWOP proves you can ask a similar question about your sales program —"If you're not selling relevant products, why sell them?"—and still earn substantial income.

THINGS TO THINK ABOUT

• *Your database is a great tool for both sales and fundraising.* Make it a priority to collect data on current and potential customers and donors, keep it current, test the list, and remove people who don't respond after several solicitations. Can you say, as Roberto Roibal does, "We're proud of our database"?

- *Community loan funds are a good source of capital.* SWOP received support from the New Mexico Community Development Loan Fund to help create and market their products. Other regions, states, and cities also have social purpose loan funds to launch small businesses, underwrite affordable housing, and provide capital to underserved communities. While more flexible than many banks, community loan funds will review your business plan rigorously, so don't expect easy money. Says Riobal, "We were an established group with a good track record. A new organization probably wouldn't have gotten the loan."
- *Once you've defined your market, figure out what those people like to read, watch, listen to, and so on.* Then try to reach them—preferably with free media coverage—through their favorite newspapers, magazines, radio stations, Web sites, and television stations.
- *Positive news coverage can help sell your goods and services.* This doesn't mean that you should reject all paid advertising, but use your advertising budget (if you have one) carefully.
- *If appropriate, combine products and sell them in sets.* The SouthWest Organizing Project has created a $114 product by combining three individual items—and it *sells*. Indeed, it might be under-priced. According to Roibal, "Some people say we should charge $200."
- *Think about how you can take the same material and repackage it for different markets.* The ¡Viva la Causa! video is available in both English and Spanish; same footage, same music, different narration. Adding a different voiceover opens up a huge new market, though the cost can be substantial. In this case, translation, narration, and production expenses totaled $13,000, which SWOP split with its video production partner.
- *Credit card capability will boost your business,* whether customers are shopping in person, over the phone, by mail, or on-line. Yes, the banks charge a set-up fee and a take a percentage of sales, but customers want the convenience and, as a result, most businesses net more money.

Chapter 7

Marketing your mission

For most people, "marketing" means advertising; for instance, the $2.3 million television ads that accompany football's Super Bowl. Marketing, however, is a much broader concept. It refers to everything you do to increase awareness of your organization, your programs, and the goods and services you offer. The best marketing strategies build "brand identity" by emphasizing the values and programs that make your nonprofit unique. When you see the words *Red Cross,* for instance, you undoubtedly think of blood banks, and people caring for victims of emergencies and natural disasters. You might recall their motto, which defines their mission: "When help can't wait." The organization's strong brand has been built with great care for more than a century.

When it comes to developing a brand identity for your group, you've got a lot of competition. According to the business magazine *Fast Company,* you're being bombarded by 3,000 commercial messages a day:[1] on television, radio, the Web, newspapers, magazines, direct mail, billboards, bus and taxi and subway ads, posters, flyers, logos on T-shirts and caps and jackets and underwear, even on tattoos—and, of course, on the products themselves. Face it, you're surrounded.

One of the gurus of modern marketing, Jay Conrad Levinson, offers a "Rule of 27" to explain this saturation strategy. Thanks to cognitive research, we know that the human brain only remembers a commercial message one out of every three times that message is presented. Furthermore, that message must be internalized nine times before someone will act on it. Since $9 \times 3 = 27$, you need to put your message (your logo, slogan, mission, product) in front of people 27 times before they know who you are, what you stand for, what you're selling— and before they're willing to buy.[2] Recognition is directly related to repetition.

If this sounds like brainwashing, well, it is. If this news depresses you, I sympathize. However, if you want your enterprise to actually earn money, you'll need to think and act like a marketer by figuring out how to reach your customers in multiple ways. Here's what marketing isn't: sending newsletters to people twice a year and expecting them to understand why you exist and what you do, not to mention what you sell.

In addition to outlining the rationale for marketing and helping you to create a marketing plan, this chapter provides a wide range of strategies for generating attention and promoting your venture. Please note that factors such as quality, service, and price are at the heart of the marketing mix. If you're selling poor-quality goods, providing lousy service, and offering non-competitive prices, all the advertising and publicity in the world won't create a sustainable enterprise. Before you enter the marketplace, make sure you have something of value to offer your customers.

Market segmentation

In developing a marketing program, one of your first tasks is to "segment your market": identify the specific characteristics of the customers you wish to serve and develop goods and services to meet their specific needs.

BorderLinks focuses on two distinct markets: the faith community, especially people of faith who care about social justice issues, and people in higher education. Their promotional materials are designed with these constituencies in mind, using different language and graphics to appeal to the needs of each group. For the religious community, a brochure features a *campesino* carrying a cross. The caption says, "Opening our eyes…Challenging our faith…Deepening our commitment…on the U.S./Mexico border." For the secular education market, the brochure shows a woman standing in her doorway in a poor Mexican neighborhood. It reads, "A program in experiential education on the U.S./Mexico border." One brochure is distributed in places of worship; the other, at educational institutions. This is a simple but effective use of niche marketing.

BORDERLINKS APPEALS TO TWO CONSTITUENCIES BY USING DISTINCT MARKETING DESIGNS

Segmentation really begins with product development; the promotion comes later. As you design your goods and services, think about how different types of customers will use them. When faith groups travel with BorderLinks, a substantial portion of the itinerary is devoted to prayer, reflection, and discussion of spiritual concerns. That program wouldn't work with a secular tour group.

When you brainstormed possible ventures in Chapter Four, you developed a list of potential customer groups. Once you've chosen a venture, revisit the list. Each of these constituencies is a different market segment. Which ones have priority? Why? (Hint: They are likely to be the most profitable.) What do they like to read, listen to, watch? Where do they hang out? How do they spend their money? How do they spend their time? How will you reach them?

Most novices start by thinking of big-time media—say, the *New York Times*—to reach a wide range of people with one strategy. Unfortunately, when you're chasing all your market segments at once, you can't customize the message. The tighter your target, the more effectively (and often, inexpensively) you can reach your prospects. An article in the *Times* is a fine thing—especially if it describes your goods and services—but one story in the newspaper does not equal a marketing plan. Don't forget the humbler strategies, such as the lowly flyer and the ubiquitous e-mail. Since successful marketing is based on repetition, you want to reach your customers and prospective customers through as many avenues as possible.

The Nonprofit Niche:
Institute for Conservation Leadership and Technical Assistance for Community Services

■   ■   ■   ■   ■   ■   ■   ■   ■   ■   ■   ■   ■

Imagine a movement with hundreds of thousands of organizations and millions of activists spread across the continent. They're busy revitalizing their neighborhoods, fighting poverty, promoting public health, educating their children, creating cultural opportunities for everyone, restoring wildlife habitat, dismantling racism, exposing injustice, cleaning up pollution, and advocating for the common good. Their work is their passion. It gives them energy and a sense of purpose.

Unfortunately, passion doesn't pay the bills or keep the office running. To build their organizations and create real change, these folks must master a wide range of skills: recruiting volunteers, motivating board members, developing new leaders, raising and managing money, getting good publicity, planning for the future. Acquiring these skills is generally a haphazard process, based on trial and error. As environmental activist Ann Hunt told the Institute for Conservation Leadership, "There is no other schooling that prepares a person for this work, only learning in the saddle."

With nearly 1 million nonprofits in the United States, the charitable sector is a huge market niche. In recent years, many organizations have sprung up to service this niche through training, consulting, and technical assistance. Two leading "capacity builders" are the Institute for Conservation Leadership, or ICL, and Technical Assistance for Community Services, known as TACS. Taken together, they deliver the following services:

- Strategic planning
- Board development
- Fundraising training and planning
- Financial management
- Volunteer recruitment
- Leadership training
- Diversity training

- Conflict management
- Coalition building
- Holding effective meetings
- Time management
- Training for trainers
- Meeting facilitation
- Organizational assessment

Rather than attempt to serve everyone, these providers work with specific target markets within the nonprofit world. The Institute for Conservation Leadership (www.icl.org) has defined its niche in three ways:

1. As its name implies, the group works exclusively on environmental and conservation issues—though the words "environmental" and "conservation" are interpreted broadly.

2. They emphasize experiential education: practicing a skill rather than listening to someone talk about how to do it. As a recent workshop participant wrote, "I've been on antibiotics for a week, I'm taking antihistamines, and I was still energized."

3. More and more, they focus on long-term training programs: working with particular individuals and organizations for a year or more. Current long-term programs cover executive director training, grassroots fundraising, building sustainable organizations and sustainable issue campaigns, and the Environmental Strategies Project, which focuses on statewide collaboration and political effectiveness.

When they began work in 1990, says executive director Dianne Russell, "We were concerned there wasn't a market. A lot of conservation groups are very small and have no money for staff, let alone consultants." Still, Russell and her colleagues were adamant about the value of paying customers. "If people have to pay," she says simply, "they take it more seriously." Today, ICL generates about 40 percent of its $1.2 million budget from fees and contracts with a variety of environmental groups, government agencies, and the occasional corporate client.

Founded in 1976, Technical Assistance for Community Services (www.tacs.org) serves the breadth of the nonprofit community, but limits its reach to a specific region: Oregon and Washington, and for some jobs, the greater Pacific Northwest. From the beginning, TACS was designed to charge and collect service fees, earning as much as 75 percent of its budget in some years. Given this entrepreneurial focus, why was the group created as a nonprofit and not a private business? "Our interest was nonprofits," says co-founder Kay Sohl. "We assumed that what we learned by managing our own organization would be useful to our clients."

In addition to training events, TACS offers an unusual mix of publications, programs, and consulting support, helping nonprofits in all stages of development—"from pre-start-up to ossified," says Sohl. Their goods and services include the following:

- Their free information and referral Helpline handles 2,000 callers per year.

- They publish *Nonprofit Corporation Handbooks* for both Oregon and Washington. These books retail for $65, with more than 4,000 copies in print.

- They run a leadership development program for women, people of color, the disabled, and others typically excluded from leadership roles.

- They sponsor professional networks serving executive directors, nonprofit fiscal managers, technology managers, and "diversity leaders." For an annual subscription fee, participants attend monthly workshops and share ideas on how to make their work more effective. "We emphasize, 'This is important, this is how we make a plan, this how we implement it,'" says staff member Guadalupe Guajardo.

- They offer individualized consulting to more than 250 organizations each year on all aspects of nonprofit management.

Some consulting and training relationships last a long time, which testifies to both the quality of the work and the potential for sustainable income. Bradley-Angle House, Portland's first domestic violence shelter, has been contracting with TACS for more than twenty years. "We started as consultants," says Sohl, "but now we're peers."

Several other groups featured in this book (BorderLinks, Grassroots Leadership, The Center for Anti-Violence Education, DataCenter, and the Resource Center of the Americas) provide training for nonprofits. There are endless opportunities to serve this market. Do you have anything to offer—goods, services, publications, skills, expertise, or a fresh perspective—that might be of use to other nonprofit organizations?

Creating and using a marketing plan

Your objective in creating a marketing plan is to reach the right people at the right time for the right price and the right amount of effort. As Gary J. Stern writes in the *Marketing Workbook for Nonprofit Organizations,* "Every marketing goal is an *action goal:* you want marketing to produce specific, measurable results…by a certain point in time."[3]

As should be clear by now, a marketing plan can be used *externally* for several purposes:

- To increase community awareness of, and appreciation for, your mission and programs

- To highlight the qualities that make your group unique (your "brand")

- To encourage supporters and customers to take specific actions: attend an event, participate in public debate about a current issue, purchase your goods and services, and so on

- To create and reinforce relationships with prospective partners, such as businesses (see Chapter Eight) and other nonprofits

Your marketing plan can also be used *internally* in several ways:

- To clarify program goals by asking questions such as, "Who are we trying to reach (serve, organize, involve)?" In this sense, it functions as a component of a broader strategic plan.

- To unify your message to ensure that all staff, board, and volunteers are using similar language and emphasizing the same aspects of your work.

- To set performance and evaluation goals for staff, board, and volunteers.

- To improve efficiency by breaking down your marketing program to specific tasks and assignments, and plotting them on a calendar.

Given your skills, your schedule, and your finances, how can you best select from all the promotional options? Here are some things to think about:

- *Know your target audience.* Which strategy, or combination of strategies, is likely to be most effective with your market or markets?

- *How big is your budget?* How much money is available, and when will it be available? Professionals suggest that you budget 7 to 12 percent of your gross receipts for advertising and marketing, though most nonprofits can probably get away with spending less. Research what it will cost to implement the most appropriate strategies and build that expense into your enterprise budget.

- *How big is your labor pool?* How many volunteers or staff members are available to help? Handing out leaflets can be a great attention getter if you have volunteers to hand out flyers. On the other hand, if you have to pay people to do it, it's probably not worth it. The same holds true for telephone banks and mailing parties.

- *What's your timeline?* How much time do you have to achieve your goal? If you're publicizing a workshop or an in-store program, how long until the event takes place? Some promotional strategies are only effective over the long run, while others work best if you need instant attention. As usual, it's best to plan ahead.

- *Do you have a newsworthy story?* If you expect to rely on news coverage to spread the word about your enterprise—always a dubious strategy—learn to think like a journalist and design your marketing plan accordingly. Read the newspaper analytically, watch the television news, and try to figure out why some stories get prominent play and others are buried. Sensationalism has a lot to do with it, so if you can build something sensational into your plan, great. Conflict is always good for getting media attention. Timeliness is vital: are you doing something that's important now? Can you "piggyback" on, or react to, a breaking news event? These are the main components of a "hard news" story.

An alternate approach is the "human interest" story—woman conquers disease, man carries on lone battle against city hall, artist paints murals of junkyards to protest garbage, and so on. If you've got an unusual or touching angle, use it. This provides a handle for the news media to grab. If you can design your earned income program to include several media handles, you are more likely to get coverage.

Sample Marketing Plan: Esperanza Unida

Esperanza Unida, profiled in the case study following Chapter Five, provides job training through a comprehensive program of nonprofit ventures, including welding and metal fabrication, construction and home sales, customer service training, printing and graphic design, auto repair and used car sales, child care, and a coffee and book store. All "training businesses" are built on two premises. First, they must prepare participants for family-supporting jobs that actually exist. Second, they must generate a significant portion of their revenue from sales.

Over the past 30 years, the group has become well known in their home town through a combination of uniquely effective programs and sophisticated marketing. Here's a brief summary of one of their marketing plans.

Esperanza Unida
Housing Rehabilitation and Construction Program
Community Outreach Campaign

Goals

To educate and connect Milwaukee's property owners with information on the benefits of house/property donation; to create awareness of Esperanza Unida's Construction Company and Training Program to generate business prospects and training candidates; and to increase capacity for program self-sufficiency.

Components

- 700 60-second radio spots for MARS (Milwaukee Area Radio Station) Campaign—September and October—Starting slowly on September 4, 2000 with most spots running in October—providing time for response, and response building as needed.

- ACHOICE/WUWM PSA Underwriting spots—dates to be determined.

- Based on results of Radio phase, may implement a 5,000 piece Letter/ Direct mail to non-owner occupied units and nonprofit organizations in Milwaukee County—November 2000 targeted mailing date. Letter drafted and database in place.

- Press Conferences/Releases at key benchmarks: house donation, rehab startup, student success profiles, house sale/family in a home, and so on.
- Possible Add-on Options: Print and Billboards—to be discussed as outcomes of initial campaign components progress.
- ACHOICE newsletter ads, distributed to 50 targeted Milwaukee nonprofits. (First wave: July 2000).

Summary

Esperanza Unida's Housing Rehabilitation and Construction Project helps Milwaukee's inner-city youth build skills and habits for a successful adulthood. This program combines hands-on construction and academic training with leadership skill building to give our kids a real chance at building a self-sustaining future. One of the program's key focus areas is on rehabbing houses into a safe, affordable homes while expanding relationships between adults and neighborhood youth.

We target youth from our community—those who are struggling with today's complicated issues of poverty, crime, racism, violence, and hopelessness—for training and learning opportunities. Through a 5-principle approach, the program uses construction work as a tool for providing personal development, along with academic and vocational training. This hands-on training plants positive seeds that provide area youth with academic and skill training—and a real chance at a family-supporting job in the construction industry. It also makes safe, affordable housing available to the community.

We are asking our audience to think about possible benefits of donating a house, rental property, or vacant land to this project. This type of donation can provide the donor with a tax write-off and a quick end to property ownership hassles, and will give our inner-city youth positive alternatives to hopelessness, crime, drugs, and violence.

Esperanza Unida, a nonprofit agency serving Milwaukee's low-income and minority populations, has a 30-year history of developing projects that build self-esteem and self-reliance in the youth and adults who enter our training programs. Our skill preparation and job placement efforts have been recognized across the nation for meeting youth and adult needs while reflecting our community's uniqueness and strengths.

The Campaign's Five Principles

1. Make productive use of work for personal growth, along with academic and vocational training, focusing on construction skills.

2. Expand supportive and working relationships between adults and neighborhood youth.

3. Create and enhance opportunities for our community's youth to be actively involved in decisions that affect them, and to interact positively with their peers.

4. Guide students to use non-school hours for constructive activities.

5. Provide support and continuity for successful transitions among institutions and activities for young people.

This is an effective summary for several reasons:

1. Esperanza Unida is targeting a specific market—property owners with a sense of social responsibility—rather than trying to reach everyone.

2. They combine several outreach strategies in a thoughtful sequence, with flexibility to add components as needed.

3. They have chosen media likely to connect with their target market. ACHOICE is Milwaukee's alternative workplace giving program, while WUWM is the local public radio station.

4. They know how to turn a newsworthy moment—"house donation, rehab startup," and so on—into a photo opportunity. Not to mention their "student success profiles," which make great human-interest stories. This adds up to a lot of positive news coverage.

5. They make a clear case for the benefits of the program.

An expanded marketing plan would also include the following items:

- A budget (what will each of these components cost?)
- An assignment sheet (who is responsible for following through with each strategy?)
- A list of media contacts with telephone and e-mail information
- A calendar of marketing activities, showing the sequence graphically, for easy reference.

Promotion options for grassroots groups

There are many ways to communicate with prospects. This is by no means a complete list, but everything that follows is feasible and affordable for small nonprofits.

Personal selling

The simplest way to make a sale is to ask for it, and the most effective way to ask is face-to-face. Describe your goods and services, ask questions, and respond to questions. Look people in the eye. Be friendly and passionate, but above all be responsive. You embody your organization, so make a good impression.

Where can you sell? If you operate a retail store, sell in the store. If you're hungry, take a prospect to lunch and talk about your work. If you're staffing a table for your group at a community event, come out from behind the table and greet people. If you're at a gathering and it's time for announcements, stand up, make an offer, and encourage people to talk with you individually.

If you're a Girl Scout, sell cookies to anyone anywhere. Be sure to wear your uniform. Get your friends and family and neighbors to sell, too. How do the Girl Scouts move 250 million boxes of cookies in six weeks? A lot of personal selling.

Your members: Your sales force

Enlist your membership to help promote your goods and services. For example, when Grassroots Leadership schedules an out-of-town concert, speech, or public workshop, they send postcards to their donors in the area asking them to publicize the event.

In the case of Melpomene Institute, 80 percent of the group's 1,450 members are also customers, buying books and other materials from the organization. Melpomene has attempted to deepen this relationship by asking customer-members to sell products for the organization in their respective states. Presumably, these people are committed to the mission and understand the products—so they meet the first two requirements of effective sales. Nothing beats good word of mouth in generating sales. By turning happy customer-members into sellers, Melpomene creates maximum impact from their testimonials.

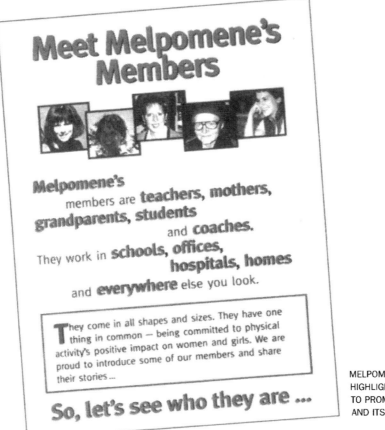

MELPOMENE INSTITUTE HIGHLIGHTS ITS MEMBERS TO PROMOTE ITS MISSION— AND ITS PRODUCTS

Show and tell

Demonstrations are an important aspect of personal selling. Sometimes these are called point-of-purchase promotional activities. At Native Seeds/SEARCH, people who wander into the store are encouraged to sample native foods. (The best way to test chili powder is with your nose, so take a big sniff.) When Grassroots Leadership hosts a public event, their "Rainbow Sign" CD plays in the background. At Our Community Bikes, you can watch the mechanic repair a bicycle—then you can rent the tools and repair your own, with or without the mechanic's help.

Telephone calls

When I first launched my consulting and training business, I spent a lot of time calling prospective clients and discussing their needs and my skills. In some cases, I was "cold-calling" strangers; in other cases, I was contacting referrals (see the next section). Perhaps one out of ten calls led directly to a job and another two or three yielded leads, so phoning turned out to be an efficient use of my time.

While I wouldn't recommend setting up a phone bank or hiring a tele-marketing firm to call a bunch of strangers, I definitely encourage phone contact with your best customers and prospects. Telephoning is cheap, flexible, and you can use it effectively if you're facing a deadline: trying to fill a community class or selling last-minute holiday items to your members. With the possible exception of e-mail, the phone is the easiest way to reach your most likely buyers: the people who already buy.

Soliciting referrals

Ask your customers and members for leads. There are dozens of ways to do this: in person, on the phone, through the mail, at events, and so on. Many nonprofits encourage their members to suggest other potential members. Looking for new customers is essentially the same process. When seeking a referral, request permission to "name drop." It makes a huge difference if you can say, "Hi, my name is Andy Robinson. Sally Jones is one of our customers. She suggested that I call you." (This works better if you use your own name, not mine.)

Dianne Russell of the Institute for Conservation Leadership tells an interesting story about referrals. Like any service business, the Institute bids on jobs that don't pan out. Perhaps the prospective client chose another provider, didn't want to pay the price, or decided the timing wasn't right. However, Russell makes a point of keeping these folks on the mailing list and checking in with them when time allows. The result: good word of mouth. "We get referrals from groups we first contacted five or ten years ago," she says, amazed. "Even groups that never hired us. That says something about the value of long-term relationships."

Personal letters and direct mail

Personal letters are written directly to the prospect, not "Dear Member" or "Dear Customer" or "Dear Friend." (Would you ever address a *real* friend that way?) They're signed by hand and include a personal note, perhaps thanking the recipient for past support. Direct mail, which is more impersonal, includes form letters, catalogs, newsletters, brochures, flyers, and postcards.

Nearly every group profiled in this book uses the postal system to promote its goods and services, often combining a personal letter with a catalog or brochure. In addition to your "house list," consider borrowing or renting lists that will reach your target market. To boost your results, wait a week and follow up with a phone call. Remember, effective marketing means reaching out to your prospects multiple times in multiple ways.

Newsletters

Most nonprofits publish a newsletter, and with good reason. It's a cheap, effective way to reach your best market: your members and donors. If you sell goods and services, feature them in your newsletter. The SouthWest Organizing Project includes a two-page spread in their newsletter *Voces Unidas* to promote their books, videos, organizing handbooks, and a variety of logo gear.

E-mail

The advantages of e-mail are numerous and obvious: it's instantaneous, cheap, easy to use, and easy to personalize. Like the telephone, it's great for last-minute offers and special deals. You can include photos or other graphics. Use e-mail to drive people to your Web site, where they can learn more about your work or make online purchases.

Collect e-mail addresses any way you can. Include an e-mail line on your donor response cards. When you pass around a registration form at events, ask for e-mail addresses. Offer visitors to your Web site the chance to sign up for action alerts, a free e-mail newsletter, or let them know you provide "discount alerts" via e-mail. If you're sponsoring a raffle or door prize, encourage people to write their e-mail address on their entry. These same strategies can and should be used to gather phone numbers, too.

Web site promotion and sales

Most nonprofits profiled in this book advertise their goods and services on their Web sites. Several also collect credit card information on-line for Web-based sales, yielding up to 30 percent of their sales income.

Having a Web site is no longer optional. It's an easy, essential reference point for donors, prospects, customers, volunteers, the news media, and other people who are curious about your work. Plan to invest some time and money to make it look good and keep it updated. While I doubt that the Web will ever replace a personal presentation or a friendly voice on the phone, online sales are likely to increase. If you offer products but don't yet handle credit card transactions online, investigate how to do so. It's an increasingly popular way to make donations, too.

Flyers and brochures

With the exception of a face or a voice, the best way to get a person's attention is to put something in his or her hands. If you've got the volunteers, handing out flyers or brochures at public events (concerts, trade shows, ball games, and the like) is an excellent way to promote your products and services—assuming that your target market is likely to attend concerts, trade shows, or ball games. Choose the right event. The White Earth Land Recovery Project might hand out flyers at a concert featuring Native American musicians, or the Burns Bog Conservation Society could give away leaflets at the local Earth Day celebration.

For some businesses, flyers double as coupons: customers who bring them in receive a discount or a free gift. (To make an impression, offer a 20 percent price break; deeper discounts are even better.) By counting the number of "coupon customers," you can easily track the effectiveness of the promotion. To save printing costs, set up your flyer-coupons so they can be printed two to four to a page, then slice with a paper cutter. And don't be discouraged if most of them end up on the ground. Even though you can't see it, most of your mailings also "end up on the ground," but you can still build a successful enterprise with support from the small fraction of people who respond.

Posters and signs

Keep the design simple, clear, and strong. Make sure the important information can be read at a distance. Brightly colored announcements will tend to attract more attention than black and white. When hanging posters, consider placement based on your target audience. If you have the money and want to blanket the town, commercial postering firms can help. (These companies tend to come and go, so get references.)

Community events

If you sell products, set up a table or booth at your local street fair, church bazaar, Fourth of July barbecue, and so on. If you offer services, go to events where likely prospects gather, such as conferences and trade shows. Even better, become a presenter at one of these events so you can demonstrate your expertise.

Workshops and seminars

Many nonprofits organize workshops as a way of fulfilling their missions: Technical Assistance for Community Services hosts a series on nonprofit management, and Native Seeds/SEARCH teaches people how gather and cook wild desert foods. For savvy nonprofits, these workshops double as marketing opportunities to sell products and promote future events.

Print advertisements

The key to advertising is (surprise!) repetition. If you plan to run display ads in newspapers or magazines, expect to spend money regularly. Running an ad once or twice will not have a significant impact. However, most publications don't sell all their ad space, so you can often negotiate big discounts and—since you're a nonprofit, community-service organization—free advertisements. I know of one weekly newspaper that "adopts" a few nonprofits each year, providing them with free advertising space as it becomes available. Call, visit, and negotiate. If you begin with an advertising budget—in other words, if you show up with some money to spend—you can negotiate from a stronger position.

GLOBAL EXCHANGE RUNS
A SUCCESSFUL HOLIDAY
ADVERTISING CAMPAIGN

Another option is cooperative advertising: joining together with other small businesses and nonprofits to purchase ad space at a bulk rate. In many communities, for example, independent bookstores pool their advertising dollars to take on the chain stores. By working together, they can afford larger, more frequent ads.

Once again, choose publications that reach likely customers. A free ad in the wrong newspaper or magazine is not worth the effort.

Classified advertisements

People who read the classified ads want something—a job, a house, a car—and whatever they want is listed by classification. Assuming that your goods or services fit any of the usual categories (and there are lots of categories), classified ads provide a cost-effective way to reach people who are looking to buy. If you sell to your local community and believe that your products might appeal to a wider audience, try running classified ads in regional or national publications. It's a relatively inexpensive way to test your instincts. If you use classifieds, budget enough money to run your ad several times before evaluating the results. With all advertising, words make a difference. Study the ads to see which ones jump out at you. Avoid using lots of abbreviations just to save a few dollars. Keep it simple.

Public service announcements

Radio and television stations offer a certain amount of free advertising (public service announcements, or PSAs) for nonprofits. Nonprofit organizations typically use PSAs to promote specific, time-limited community events: a holiday sale, a class or workshop, an open house or grand opening party. Radio tends to be the better choice, since it's easier to target specific demographic groups: youth, Spanish speakers, senior citizens, and so on.

For radio, you'll need a brief (10-, 20-, or 30-second) summary for the announcer to read on the air. Many radio stations prefer to receive your news release and write their own PSAs; check in advance. If you have access to professional video production equipment, television stations will sometimes air pre-produced 15- and 30-second video PSAs. Again, check with your local stations for specifications. Many cable TV services have "video bulletin boards" for which they accept PSA copy.

Radio advertisements

As mentioned, radio allows you to reach specific markets with relative ease—and radio ads can be more affordable than you think. As an example, many arts organizations advertise on their local public radio stations, since public radio listeners tend to be more affluent folks who are interested in the arts. Some non-profits buy ads on a regular basis, budgeting a certain amount each month, while others participate in "day sponsorship" programs or time their radio spots to coincide with upcoming performances or special events.

Publicity stunts

Be creative. You can use sandwich boards, murals, and the like. Ask your volunteers to hold signs or drape banners from street overpasses, or spell out messages along the highway, Burma Shave–style. Set up a human alphabet chain at a football game and, on cue, spell out your message one letter at a time. Hand out phony money with information about your upcoming sales event or grand opening. Once again, if you're clever enough and your timing is good, you can multiply your effectiveness by getting free media coverage of your promotional stunts.

Contests

The Women's Bean Project runs a job training program where women package and sell bean soup mixes and other food items. To generate new products *and* publicity, the group offered local chefs the opportunity to create recipes for their catalog. The contest resulted in two new mixes—focaccia roll and curried lentils—and a feature story in the *Denver Post*. A common variation is the poster or essay contest for youth ("Create a poster showing how our community will look when we end violence") which can lead to stories in the local media.

Reports and studies

By researching and releasing your own investigative reports, you can meet several objectives at once: educating the public about your issues, building credibility for your organization, and—if you do your homework—receiving significant news coverage. The Women's Foundation commissioned DataCenter to help produce a "report card" outlining the status of women in California. The release of the report, in which the state received an overall grade of D, was a major media event.

Columns (write your own)

Create your own media. If appropriate, write a column for a local or regional publication. The big daily papers are hard to break into, but smaller publications—weeklies, monthlies, local and specialty magazines, church newsletters, and so on—often need material. Don't expect to be paid much, but use the forum to promote your issue, your organization, and perhaps your goods and services.

Judy Mahle Lutter of Melpomene Institute has been a regular columnist for both the *St. Paul Pioneer-Press* and the *Minnesota Women's Press*. Brett Bakker of Native Seeds/SEARCH wrote a gardening column, "Itchy Green Thumb," for his local food cooperative in Albuquerque.

Media coverage

The groups you've been reading about in this book all receive substantial news coverage, and they all credit good publicity as an important factor in generating earned income. News coverage reaches a wide audience and provides instant credibility. When you photocopy a positive article and use it in your mailings and other solicitations, it conveys long-lasting credibility, too. Media coverage does have one drawback: unlike every other strategy listed here, you can't control the message. Regardless, you should make news media outreach a central part of your marketing plan. Here are some tips for working with the media:

NEWS RELEASES. Also known as press releases, even though they can (and should) be sent to the broadcast media as well. It might be helpful to mentally divide your releases into two categories: a "hard news" or "feature" release that describes your group's programs or activities (your goal: a detailed feature article), and a "calendar" release that promotes an upcoming event (goal: a feature story and/or calendar coverage). When DataCenter announces a new study on women's health, or the SouthWest Organizing Project puts out a report on pollution from local industrial plants, they tend to generate feature stories. On the other hand, speeches, workshops, book signings, and other events are usually covered in the community calendar.

Most news releases are limited to one page, double-spaced, although major stories might warrant more pages. Provide the basic information—who, what, where, when, and why—plus a relevant quote from someone involved in the project. If available, enclose an appropriate photo, preferably a black-and-white glossy print, although color photographs and slides can also be used. Newspapers and magazines are always looking for good photos.

Many groups now distribute their news releases by e-mail or fax. This is a useful strategy for late-breaking stories or if you're facing a deadline. If scanned properly, images can also be attached to e-mail. Check with your media contacts to find out which format works best for them.

When developing your list for where to send news releases, don't forget the "alternative" media: alumni magazines, community radio stations, newsletters from other nonprofits, church bulletins, community access cable TV, professional and specialty journals, weekly or suburban or rural newspapers, and so on. While it may be difficult to get a big feature story in your big daily paper, smaller news outlets are always looking for copy. If you choose carefully, you can use them to effectively reach your target markets.

After you send a release, always follow with a phone call. Be persistent. You may need to call three or four times before you actually talk with the reporter or editor. Phone calls make a huge difference in securing coverage, so pick up the phone.

MEDIA TOURS AND PHOTO OPPORTUNITIES. If your earned income strategy is site specific, with great photo opportunities, consider organizing a media tour. Plateau Restoration could invite a television crew to talk with volunteers on a trail repair project. BorderLinks could host a media tour of factories along the U.S.–Mexico border. The Georgia Citizens Coalition on Hunger could invite reporters to visit one of their outdoor farmer's markets. In fact, if you can find a good visual image that embodies your work, you've got a news story.

Provide press packets—a news release, organizational brochure or fact sheet, relevant documents—to all media personnel. Designate a spokesperson who can talk in clear, brief sentences about what your group does and why.

MEDIA RELATIONS. When working with journalists, let common sense and common courtesy guide your actions. The quality of their work is directly related to the quality of your preparation. Make life easy for reporters and you will receive lots of proactive, positive coverage.

- *Before approaching the media, sit down and write your ideal news article.* Use this language to sharpen your news releases and interviews. In fact, it's useful to write down your agenda before being interviewed. Anticipate likely questions and prepare your answers.

- *When writing a press release, use lots of quotes.* Some will find their way into the news.

- *Build your story around current news items.* React to a controversial issue or show how your organization's programs address a current community need.

- *Earn credibility by being accurate and reliable.* Be selective in what you present to the media as news. The fact that shoppers who visit your Web site receive a 25 percent discount is an advertisement, not a news story.

- *Journalists are busy, so respect their time.* Know their deadlines and try to call when it's likely to be slow, or request an appointment for a later time. Journalists face many of the same obstacles as activists—multiple deadlines, inadequate staffing, poor pay—so treat them with gentle respect.

- *Don't expect 100 percent accuracy.* Unless the reporter misses the entire point of your work, keep your criticism to yourself. Learn to live with small factual errors. (As I said, if you're marketing through news stories, you can't control the message.)

- *Thank journalists for their effort.* They rarely receive praise, only complaints. A note or phone call will do the job.

There is so much to say about news media strategy, it could fill a book. And it has—in fact, several books. For suggestions, see the Resources section.

Media Savvy: Melpomene Institute

The Melpomene Institute, a research and education organization, sends out a dozen news releases each year promoting their findings about physical activity and women's health, new Melpomene products, speeches by staff, public workshops, awards, fundraising events, and so on. A half-time staff member cultivates a core group of 35 to 50 media contacts, using letters and press advisories to plant story ideas.

In the past, editors and reporters received a pre-printed Rolodex card with Melpomene contact information. The card itemized a wide range of women's health issues and suggested that Melpomene staff could provide expertise or a good quote. The organization now finds e-mail to be the most effective way to reach the media.

"We were in the news more than 100 times last year," says CEO Judy Mahle Lutter. Their assertive, professional approach to media has a big impact on both sales and membership recruitment. Lutter estimates that half of all customers first find out about the Institute from news coverage. "When we get a major story," she says, "we get a hundred new members. And they're good members—most people who join from a news story seem to renew, because they're well-educated about what we do."

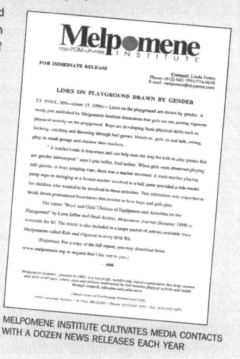

MELPOMENE INSTITUTE CULTIVATES MEDIA CONTACTS WITH A DOZEN NEWS RELEASES EACH YEAR

Effective marketing is neither quick nor easy. It requires forethought, patience, and at least a small investment of money. But remember:

- If you offer high-quality products and services at a fair price
- If you segment your market and try not to do everything for everybody
- If you develop multiple strategies for reaching your best prospects
- If you implement those strategies with persistence and commitment—

You will get results. Use Worksheets 7.1 and 7.2 to begin to create your marketing strategy.

In the next chapter, we'll discuss how to use corporate partnerships to expand your marketing efforts, reach new audiences, and generate more income.

WORKSHEET 7.1

Creating a marketing plan

Use this form to create a marketing and promotion plan for your venture.

1. **AUDIENCE/MARKET SEGMENTATION.** Who are you trying to reach? List all the different markets that would benefit from your goods or services.

_____

_____

_____

_____

_____

_____

_____

2. **BUDGET.** How much money is available to spend on promotion? $ _____

3. **LABOR POOL.** How many staff members and volunteers are available to help? _____

4. **WHAT'S YOUR SOUND BITE?** Given limited time, what words will you use to capture people's attention? Write down phrases or sentences that describe your product and provide an emotional appeal for the reader or listener. Tell a compelling story.

_____

_____

_____

_____

_____

_____

_____

_____

5. PROMOTIONAL OPTIONS. Consider your budget, time, and talent, and choose the options that best reach your intended audiences.

OPTION	PRIMARY AUDIENCES	COST	LEADER	SUPPORT TEAM
☐ PERSONAL SELLING				
☐ YOUR MEMBERS: YOUR SALES FORCE				
☐ SHOW AND TELL (DEMONSTRATIONS)				
☐ TELEPHONE CALLS				
☐ SOLICITING REFERRALS				
☐ PERSONAL LETTERS AND DIRECT MAIL				
☐ NEWSLETTERS				
☐ E-MAIL				
☐ WEB SITE PROMOTION AND SALES				
☐ FLYERS AND BROCHURES				
☐ POSTERS AND SIGNS				
☐ COMMUNITY EVENTS				
☐ WORKSHOPS AND SEMINARS				
☐ PRINT ADVERTISEMENTS				
☐ CLASSIFIED ADVERTISEMENTS				
☐ PUBLIC SERVICE ANNOUNCEMENTS				
☐ RADIO ADVERTISEMENTS				
☐ PUBLICITY STUNTS				
☐ CONTESTS				
☐ REPORTS AND STUDIES				
☐ COLUMNS (WRITE YOUR OWN)				
☐ MEDIA COVERAGE				

Marketing calendar

Once you've selected your marketing strategies, schedule your action steps to create an annual promotional calendar.

Year _____   Total marketing budget $_____

ACTION STEPS BY MONTH

STRATEGY	COST	JANUARY	FEBRUARY	MARCH	APRIL	MAY	JUNE	JULY	AUGUST	SEPTEMBER	OCTOBER	NOVEMBER	DECEMBER
	$												
	$												
	$												
	$												
	$												

continued on next page

continued from previous page

ACTION STEPS BY MONTH

STRATEGY	COST	JANUARY	FEBRUARY	MARCH	APRIL	MAY	JUNE	JULY	AUGUST	SEPTEMBER	OCTOBER	NOVEMBER	DECEMBER
	$												
	$												
	$												
	$												
	$												
TOTAL COST	$												

Crossing Borders

BORDERLINKS

TUCSON, ARIZONA, AND NOGALES, SONORA

WWW.BORDERLINKS.ORG

ANNUAL BUDGET: $550,000

EARNED INCOME: 60%

EARNED INCOME STRATEGIES

• TRAVEL AND TOURISM

• TRAINING AND CONSULTING FOR NONPROFITS AND OTHER INSTITUTIONAL CUSTOMERS

• PERFORMANCE AND PUBLIC SPEAKING

Nogales, Arizona, has what most U.S. residents take for granted, at least on the surface: solid houses, clean water and clean air regulations, utility services, on-the-job health protections, and a decent wage for some, if not all, workers.

Rick Ufford-Chase, program coordinator of BorderLinks, offers a comparison tour of Nogales, Sonora, just across the border in Mexico. "Look around you. Those homes are made of packing crates, cardboard, scrap lumber, and corrugated tin. The early morning air hangs thick…. Car exhaust and wood smoke conspire before moving slowly up the canyon and across the border. Do you see that raw sewage flowing through the streets and into Nogales Wash? During the next heavy rain, it will head north."[1]

North means Arizona, which is both downwind and downstream from Sonora. "Nogales, Arizona, has a higher particulate pollution count than Phoenix, a city 136 times its size," writes Ufford-Chase. "Residents have more cases of lupus per capita than in any other place in the world. Unemployment is also high. When the Mexican peso fell to half its former value, this small Arizona city lost more than a thousand jobs."[2] In other words, these two communities—two countries, two governments, two cultures—are completely interdependent, and both are hurting.

Ambos Nogales, or "both Nogaleses," as these combined communities are known locally, are typical of the border region. The North American Free Trade Agreement (NAFTA) expanded a subsidized manufacturing zone on the Mexican side. To take advantage of lower costs while maintaining easy access to the huge North American market, many international corporations closed down their U.S. and Canadian factories and opened *maquiladoras,* or assembly plants, in Mexico. "Lower costs" equals cheap labor—*maquila* workers earn $3 to $5 *per day*—no unions, limited workplace safety rules, and lax environmental laws. The American Medical Association called the border region a "cesspool" because of the persistent, dangerous levels of pollution.[3]

The border touches us all. If you use consumer electronics or appliances or car parts, there's a good chance your equipment was assembled in a *maquiladora.*

BorderLinks, founded in 1987, grew out of the Sanctuary Movement, at a time when hundreds of religious institutions opened their doors to refugees fleeing war and persecution in Central America. Through experiential education and face-to-face contact, BorderLinks "encourages a shared analysis of the implications of the global economy" by breaking down the barriers that separate North Americans and Latin Americans. The organization is incorporated in both the United States and Mexico, with thirty staff and intern positions split between Tucson, Arizona, and Nogales, Sonora.

BorderLinks maintains a strong religious orientation. "As people of faith," states the group's brochure, "we know that what we hold in common is more important than what differentiates us. Our commitment is to cross borders— national borders, religious borders and ideological borders—and to test our perceptions against the reality of what we experience."

For most BorderLinks customers, "experiential education" means a journey to the borderlands and a taste of life on the other side of the line. From day trips to semester-long immersion programs, participants see life on the border from a variety of perspectives. "Experience the U.S.–Mexico border firsthand," reads their Web site. "Stay with families in squatter communities."[4] A typical five-day trip, which costs $375 per person, includes the following activities:

- A meeting with U.S. immigration officials

- Dinner with a Guatemalan refugee now living and working in the United States

- Discussions with local church officials about the role of faith in addressing border issues

- A *maquiladora* tour and meeting with the plant manager

- An environmental tour led by a community health advocate

- Lunch with a Mexican union organizer

- Two nights in Colonia Las Torres, a squatter's settlement, staying in community homes

- Exercises and discussions to explore the questions, "What does this mean?" and "What do we do now?"

Spending the night in a Mexican *colonia,* while educational, isn't for every-one. Even so, the program has been very successful. "Early on," says Ufford-Chase, "there was a lot of resistance. Nobody believed that anyone would come to the border." Time has proved the skeptics wrong. In a typical year, more than one thousand people participate in BorderLinks programs, generating more than half the organization's budget through fees. A recent six-month schedule included thirty-six trips with a wide range of clients: the University of Arizona public health program, Chicago Center for Global Ministry, Niagara University, Center for Global Education, five seminaries, and several congregations from across the continent.

Not surprisingly, these programs don't draw upscale tourists. "Upscale is hard because of the contact with poverty. There are so many class issues," Ufford-Chase says. "We find that our time is better spent with college students who are more open to change." Given this reality, BorderLinks focuses on two primary markets: higher education (including seminaries) and church groups, which together account for 85 percent of their business.

These trips have a profound impact on everyone involved. "I learned more in two weeks than I've learned in the last two years of seminary," says Steve Austin of United Theological Seminary. Deborah McIlroy of the University of Arizona says, "In this time when I have heard the term 'business ethics' referred to as an oxymoron, this tour is definitely a necessary component of a business college student's education."

A new "semester on the border" program, priced at $5,500, includes hous-ing and a full course of study and service: history of the border, philosophy and culture, intensive Spanish, peace and justice studies, immigration policy, and bor-der theology. Students split their time between BorderLinks's Tucson campus and *Casa Misericordia,* their social service center in Sonora. Ufford-Chase estimates that, once ten students register, BorderLinks will net about $20,000 per semester after paying instructors, supervisory costs, and student living expenses.

For most trips, BorderLinks charges a basic rate of $75 per person per day—about half the daily cost of $130 to $140. The organization has made a conscious choice to keep prices low so more people can participate. The balance is underwritten through church collections, individual contributions, and foun-dation grants. After their tour, participants are mailed a thank-you note, then added to the database for three annual solicitations. All prospects receive person-alized fundraising letters with hand-written notes from the staff and board. About 20 percent of trip participants eventually contribute, though it takes up to two years for the first donation. The median donation is $75, indicating strong potential for future major gifts.

To raise awareness about border issues and promote their educational programs, BorderLinks staff and board travel extensively to conferences, seminaries, congregations, and colleges. They made twenty-five presentations during a recent quarter, including an interactive "debt skit" that demonstrates how local communities get squeezed by the global economy. The group charges $500 to $1,000 plus travel for weekend workshops on globalization, with discounts and free training sessions for some groups.

BorderLinks participant Youmna Chlala writes, "Walls and fences are built by hand, and they must be dismantled by hand—or by words. Only by combating the language of 'us and them' can we create a new reality. By remembering this and acting on it daily, we can spread awareness and break down the borders that divide us."[5] In this sense, Borderlinks's most important "products" are the many face-to-face relationships built across boundaries of language, culture, class, and nationality. "We won't change the world," says Ufford-Chase, "until people get to know each other."

THINGS TO THINK ABOUT

• *Know your niche.* For BorderLinks, focusing on the faith community "was the best move we ever made," says Ufford-Chase. "We can't be everything to everyone." As a result, most participants come from churches and seminaries and want to learn about globalization and social justice from a faith perspective. Some nonprofits (and small businesses) resist specialization because they fear it will limit their pool of customers. However, if you choose a large enough market, the opposite is likely to happen. For example, there are 375,000 churches, synagogues, mosques, and other houses of worship in the United States. Because faith-based institutions are such a huge market, and because BorderLinks is uniquely positioned to meet their needs, specialization should help the organization grow.

• *Higher education is a large and lucrative market.* The United States has more than 4,000 institutions of higher learning. Many colleges and universities hire outside contractors to augment their educational programs. If you provide public education programs, can you package them to meet the needs of faculty, students, and college staff?

• *Partnering with your group can help another organization or business stand out.* The international business program at Arizona State University West offers BorderLinks tours to its students, providing the kind of ground-level education they can't get at other business schools. "They're trying to make their name through creativity," says Ufford-Chase.

Think about what you have—knowledge, prestige, skills, access to a specific community—that another organization or business might want. How can you market that asset to advance your program and generate income?

• *Use talks and other presentations at churches, conferences, and community events to market your programs.* Word of mouth is the best form of advertising; given a captive audience, you can be that mouth. Speak from the heart about what your group does and how people can participate—then sign them up.

Chapter 8

Considering corporate partnerships

Jennifer Lehman

■   ▦   ▨

Like many American cities, Denver, Colorado has experienced an exponential level of growth in recent years. Despite public support for careful growth planning, suburban sprawl continues at a dramatic rate, raising concerns about a variety of consequences to the environment as well as to human quality of life. One effort to preserve and enhance the natural landscape is the Museum of Outdoor Arts (www.fine-art.com/museum/moa.html)—a haven of sanity and beauty in the midst of the Denver metropolitan area. Its large bronze statues, multi-media sculpture, and other artwork of steel and stone are a striking accent to the modern high-rise buildings that surround it.

The museum began as an idea formulated by developer John Madden and his family but, unlike typical landscaping strategies in office parks, this piece of land has become much more than just open space among office buildings. Today it is a respected venue for large sculpture exhibits and a place where powerful art experiences, such as outdoor labyrinths, can be enjoyed by local schoolchildren and residents as well as by the hundreds of people whose offices look out over the museum's acreage.

Since the inception of the museum, executive director Cynthia Madden Leitner has been involved in every aspect of its operations. Like many nonprofit executives, she is fundraiser, financial manager, program developer, and liaison to the arts and business communities. Her varied work has taught her a lot about how nonprofits can work best with corporations. Leitner and the museum staff have learned the lessons of savvy groups: be careful whom you partner with to advance the mission of your organization and the outcomes will be positive for all sides. This chapter will help you evaluate your organization's potential for corporate partnerships, then plan a strategy for outreach to—and negotiation with—prospective partners.

For decades, the idea of a partnership between a social change organization and a corporation was considered an oxymoron. Today, although fundamental differences in values often remain between the worlds of activism and corporate capitalism, a new generation of corporate leadership has come to power. Many of these leaders see a place for corporate support of social mission. In this context, creating alliances with corporations can be done with the highest standards of integrity. The challenge is to find the right fit by pursuing partnerships with corporations that benefit your organization, do not compromise your values, and do not contradict your mission in spirit or in practice.

In the case of the Museum of Outdoor Arts, the apparently logical choice of partners to raise income for programs and art acquisitions were the large corporations leasing offices near the museum's open space. Leitner learned, however, that proximity did not necessarily mean shared goals. "Some of the corporations represented in these buildings had virtually no interest in what we were doing," she says. Others had their own artistic agendas—for example, to replace current pieces with sculpture the corporate leadership thought was more "attractive" or "appropriate." Their financial support of the organization would be predicated on having access to fundamental artistic decision making. "We not only had to stick to our artistic principles, but we had to be ready to walk away from the offer of a lot of money if those principles were threatened with compromise," says Leitner. "At the same time, we were receiving unsolicited positive support for the museum from corporations that did not have offices in the Denver area at all."

The nuts and bolts of corporate relationships

There are many potential advantages to participating in nonprofit-corporate partnerships, including the following:

- Greater income and a more diverse funding stream

- Increased credibility

- A larger audience, thanks to the marketing muscle of your business partners

- Reduced cash flow problems

- Favorable media coverage

Use these prospective advantages to guide your thinking about what specific results you want from the alliance. For example, how much income do you want to earn? How many new members do you want to recruit? How much news coverage do you want? As we will discuss later, questions like these are at the heart of evaluating how well a corporate partnership is working.

As you think about what you want from the relationship, consider too what might motivate your prospective corporate partner:

- An incremental and measurable increase in sales from the sense of integrity and dependability your name lends them

- Greater customer loyalty based on a more positive image of their brand as a corporate citizen

- Expanded market share for existing products or brands through reaching your market as well as offering enhanced social value to consumers

- Access to innovative product and service ideas

- Favorable media coverage

Not surprisingly, the pursuit of corporate partnerships also poses a number of risks for nonprofits:

- Damage to your public image if you choose inappropriate businesses. (For example, consider the potential fallout from relationships with tobacco companies or weapons manufacturers.)

- Lots of effort for a relatively small financial return.

- "Opportunity costs"—the time invested in this approach is time you can't spend on other ways to raise money and advance your mission.

- As with any earned income strategy (or even grantseeking), the pursuit of funding can subtly alter your mission.

Corporations and nonprofits have at least three types of funding relationships:

- With *corporate sponsorship* or *underwriting,* you seek funds in exchange for promotional considerations: a business logo on your brochure, a corporate banner over the stage at your next event, and so on.

- *Cause-related marketing* pushes the relationship a step further: the business trumpets its alliance with you as a way of increasing sales and finding new customers, or perhaps you endorse (or help to create) a corporate product in exchange for a percentage of the sales.

- *Corporations can be customers* for goods and services produced by nonprofits.

Because these approaches often overlap, the lines between them can get a bit fuzzy. In this chapter we will emphasize the last two but touch on all three.

As discussed earlier in this book, your first step should be a thorough self-assessment. One of the most beneficial outcomes of pursuing marketing alliances with corporations is that the process forces nonprofit organizations to take a good, long look in the mirror. Before looking outside for partners, you must evaluate why you exist, what you offer, and what challenges you face. Having answered these questions, you're ready to begin researching potential partners.

Be wary

Being wary—even suspicious—of the corporate sector is a credible position. But it is also important to recognize that today's business executive is often sensitive to the social as well as financial bottom line. Businesses can expect investors to ask questions not only about financial risk and return, but also about social responsibility: "What does this corporation care about? Which causes matter to your directors and chief executives, and how do they prove it?"

The success of socially responsible investment firms—Domini, Citizen's Fund, Calvert, and the like—attests to the significant number of people who want no part of corporations that maintain little concern for how they generate profits or run their businesses. CEOs do not have the luxury of ignoring their role in the larger society and their place in making a difference for good in the world. Poor ratings from such groups can affect share price; a reputation for indifference to social causes can hurt the financial bottom line.

Beginning with caution, ask tough questions of corporations so you can define the boundaries of what your organization will and will not do. Tough questions establish a high standard of critical thinking about strategizing for partnerships. And, perhaps most important, they flush out the corporations that use social responsibility as a front. A healthy dose of suspicion can assure that you make alliances only with businesses that believe in what you stand for—and are willing to spend money to prove it.

Of course, what constitutes a "tough question" will vary from group to group and industry to industry. Here are a few to consider asking your prospective corporate partners:

- What percentage of your pre-tax profits do you give away to nonprofit organizations?

- What's the salary ratio between your highest- and lowest-paid staff?

- How do you demonstrate your commitment to worker rights and democracy? For example, do you support unionization of your workers?

- How do you demonstrate commitment to diversity? For example, what percentage of your leaders are women? People of color? People with disabilities?

- How do you demonstrate your commitment to a healthy environment?

Customize your marketing plan

As with other earned income strategies, corporations you seek to partner with will expect your nonprofit to operate like a business. Show your prospective partners that you can present a well-thought-out plan based on sound business principles and marketing realities.

How you start the process of seeking corporate partnerships will guide you in developing the best plan. Don't start by looking for the right company with which to do business. Identifying the best possible partner should, in fact, be the final stage of the marketing plan process.

The first stage should build from knowing who you are and what you're trying to accomplish. Identify themes that can serve as initiatives for a corporate partnership. Ultimately, these themes can be customized for presentations to particular companies, incorporating their brands and other established marketing strategies. Suggested initiatives should also include ideas for implementing the plan, such as new product ideas, promotions, and slogans or "tag lines."

This stage of the plan development process allows your organization to get philosophical, even sentimental, about what lessons your mission can teach the average consumer. It also aligns you with the way advertising agencies operate: they paint a picture for their corporate clients of what the marketing idea will look like, sound like, and how it will create an emotional pull for customers.

Don't limit yourself to catchy phrases. Back up your ideas with mechanisms to implement those themes. This is the most challenging and time-consuming part of marketing plan development. The process starts with brainstorming and plenty of research into potential products, services, special events, and advertising gimmicks you might offer. The themes and mechanisms suggested should be congruent with the values of the organization, while at the same time attractive to potential corporate partners. They should be simple and easy for consumers to understand. And because your goal is to reach as many consumers as possible, the themes should be creative but not too wild. Give your potential corporate partner several options.

For example, the nonprofit Share Our Strength teamed up with American Express for the "Charge Against Hunger" program. The mechanism: every time a consumer used the American Express card, a small donation was made to Share Our Strength. By promoting this cause-related marketing program in its advertisements and promotions, American Express boosted its business and improved its image while raising millions of dollars for hunger relief *and* increasing the profile of its nonprofit partner.

Conduct Internet searches on ideas you think are fresh and new; corporate marketing executives do a lot of reading on their industry and good ones will be familiar with cutting-edge ideas already in operation. Also, research your potential partner's marketing programs. See if you can incorporate variations on previous successes for the corporation.

Corporate Contracts and
Cause-Related Marketing: Melpomene Institute

∎ ∎ ∎ ∎ ∎ ∎ ∎ ∎ ∎ ∎ ∎ ∎ ∎ ∎ ∎

In 1896, at the first modern Olympic Games, a Greek athlete named Melpomene (pronounced mel-POM-uh-nee) made history. She became the first woman to enter (and finish) an Olympic marathon. While the historical details are sketchy, she apparently disguised herself as a man, since women were not allowed to compete. Her run created a big scandal. Decades before Title IX and other anti-discrimination laws, Melpomene demonstrated the inequalities faced by women who want to participate in athletics.

Nearly a century later, her story became the inspiration for the Melpomene Institute (www.melpomene.org). Founded in 1982, the organization fulfills its mission by conducting research on the relationship between women's health and physical activity, then translating that research into practical information for women and girls. From the beginning, the Melpomene Institute was designed to generate earned income. "We knew we couldn't survive on donations," co-founder Judy Mahle Lutter says, so staff and board created a product development and marketing plan that covers each of the organization's programs.

On occasion, they've solicited research projects on contract as a way to both generate new knowledge and earn income. CIGNA Corporation paid Melpomene Institute $15,000 to explore women's motivation for physical activity, because they wondered why female employees were not using the on-site fitness center. Based on the results of the survey, CIGNA renewed its commitment to providing "activity opportunities" at the workplace by reducing barriers identified in the study.

The CIGNA research led to a $20,000 grant from Blue Cross Blue Shield of Minnesota, enabling Melpomene staff to develop a curriculum, guidebook, and training program to help sedentary women increase their physical activity. "We'd love to franchise this program," says Lutter, who sees opportunities for contracts from the health care industry. Other research clients have included the national YWCA, World Games—Australia, and a host of magazines: *Self, Shape, Essence,* and *Runner's World.*

The Melpomene Institute excels at creating sales partnerships with business sponsors to generate profits and good publicity for everyone involved. Here are some examples:

- The Sporting Goods Manufacturers Association provided $14,000 for Institute staff to research, write, and produce *Let's Get Moving* ($4.50), a 32-page booklet about the benefits of physical activity for women over age 50. The exchange: 15,000 copies of the booklet prominently feature the SGMA logo.

- With support from 3M Foundation, Melpomene created an educational video on osteoporosis. For three years Melpomene sold the video to doctors and hospitals for $199. Having maximized their own distribution channels, the organization then sold distribution rights to a national company for a 35 percent royalty (percentage of sales income). Overall, they earned more than $25,000 from this project.

- 3M also purchased 2,000 copies of *Breast Cancer: A Handbook*—published by Melpomene—for distribution to employees. Says Jean O'Connell, director of corporate quality at 3M and a former Melpomene board member, "Our employees were interested in health education materials, so we made the books available in a variety of ways, and within a year they were gone. That was four years ago, and I'm still getting requests." By pre-selling such a large quantity, the Institute was able to pay the printer up front (solving a cash flow problem) and still make a profit.

- *Heroes: Growing Up Female and Strong* was co-produced by Melpomene and local television station KARE–11. Not coincidentally, the producer was also a Melpomene board member. The station kept the broadcast rights (the program was re-broadcast in several other cities) while the Institute retains distribution rights for the education market, including schools, colleges, churches, other non-profits, and individuals. Lutter emphasizes that, to extend its life span, the video was designed for long-term relevance. "It's not ageless," she says, "but it should be around for awhile." Sales income from *Heroes* totals $38,000 to date.

Do your homework on potential partners

When you do effective prospect research, you solve two important problems. First, you weed out inappropriate partners. You may uncover a labor practice (for example, union-busting) or an investment history that conflicts with your organization's values. You may develop suspicions when language in a company's annual report isn't straightforward about distribution of profits or environmental responsibility. You may learn the professional history of a CEO you don't respect; that's reason enough to avoid partnership with this company.

Second, and just as important, you enhance your credibility with prospective partners. When you've done your homework, you can speak with familiarity about the corporation's products, its competitors, and its future marketing challenges. When sleuthing for information on a corporation, imagine yourself a potential shareholder. Would you buy stock in this company? If you were considering buying a stake in this corporation, what would you want to know? With specific information about the company in hand, you can itemize the benefits of your proposed marketing relationship.

The do-your-homework process is based on the belief that information is power. The more you know about your partners, the more control you have. In addition to understanding your prospects, know your rights: the right to expect certain terms in the relationship, plus the right to back away from this marketing option, if that becomes necessary. The bottom line: your organization should not sell its soul to generate income through a corporate partnership.

Corporations do their homework, too

As you research potential corporate partners, you will be concerned about their reputation. You'll analyze how they're perceived by your constituents and what your supporters will think if you decide to do business with them. The same is true from the other side: corporations have to choose their nonprofit partners just as carefully.

Charitable organizations must be open to the same level of scrutiny as corporations. Several painful experiences have damaged the nonprofit sector, including widely reported stories of unprincipled executive directors who appear to be doing good while abusing clients or raiding the donations fund. Corporations are understandably gun-shy. They don't want to put their brand name next to that of an organization and then look foolish for not seeing the truth behind a compelling mission statement.

Wholesaling to Businesses: Women's Bean Project

In 1989, social worker Jossy Eyre grew frustrated while volunteering at a local day shelter for women. Her clients faced a wide range of troubles, including poverty, domestic violence, substance abuse, and chronic unemployment. The shelter, while providing an essential service, wasn't creating long-term solutions. She decided to tackle these problems with the best tool she could find: a bag of beans. Eyre set up an impromptu packaging plant in the shelter's lunchroom, hiring the women to make soup mixes. The Women's Bean Project was born.

Today, the organization employs thirteen to eighteen women at a time to create, package, market, and distribute a wide variety of food items, including bean soup, salsas, bread and cookie mixes, and gift baskets. The participants also manage a successful catering service. According to their mission statement, "The Women's Bean Project functions as a steppingstone toward outside employment and personal and economic self-sufficiency....Within the context of a viable business, the women earn a steady paycheck, develop solid, transferable work skills, and strengthen their sense of self-confidence and personal responsibility." About one hundred graduates are employed throughout the Denver area.

In addition to retail sales—through mail order, walk-ins, corporate gift baskets, and church fairs and other community events—the Women's Bean Project wholesales its products. Wholesale accounts generate 60 percent of their earned income, totaling about $375,000 per year. (Wholesalers also receive a deep discount, typically one-half off the retail price.) There are three main categories of wholesale customers:

• *Distributors.* "Selling through large grocery chains moves the most product quickly and reaches customers we otherwise wouldn't reach," says executive director Priscilla Yacovoni. In the cutthroat world of big supermarkets, where thousands of products compete for limited shelf space, the Women's Bean Project would normally have a hard time getting in the store. By selling through DPI Food Products, a local distributor, they gain access and clout. DPI has also hired graduates of the program to work in their warehouse, so this business relationship supports the group's mission in multiple ways.

- *Independent groceries.* The project sells directly to independents and small chains, such as Wild Oats, a natural foods grocery.
- *Boutiques and specialty stores.* A variety of retailers, ranging from gift shops to Denver's famous Tattered Cover bookstore, sell Women's Bean Project merchandise. "We solicit them just like anyone else," says Yacovoni. "Cold-calling and pounding the pavement."

To develop an effective sales strategy, the group recruits board members with entrepreneurial skills and business contacts. Todd Martin, who works for a national beverage company, has served on the board for several terms. "My entire professional career has been in the consumer packaged goods area," says Martin. "The things we need to do occasionally at the Women's Bean Project are activities I've done for years at work."

As part of the promotional plan, cardboard displays provide better placement in the stores. Using Martin's contacts and negotiating skills, five hundred displays were produced for $6 each, plus $250 for the design work. He points out that, in dealing with retailers, "A nonprofit might be treated a little better when it comes to consideration of their products, but the performance expectations are still there." As with any business relationship, professionalism and follow-through are essential.

From plan to action

When a corporation's marketing decision makers say, "Yes, we'd like to meet with you and discuss a partnership with your organization," are you ready to proceed?

The first step in the selling process is psychological. Are you ready for them to say yes? Inexperienced nonprofits put a great deal of energy into generating ideas for a public purpose marketing plan, but they have two defensive positions: Either they don't really want a corporate relationship and haven't been honest about it, or they don't have confidence in their ideas and can't imagine that the corporation will be interested. You had better believe in your plan—marketing executives are skilled at detecting cold feet.

Next, be sure to see the right person or people—typically the CEO or marketing director, *not* the person who handles corporate philanthropy. Don't get shuttled off to someone without the power to make a decision. Be assertive in your request for specific individuals to participate in the meeting. Ask nicely, but ask: "Are you the decision maker?" Nothing is more depressing than working on a sales presentation only to realize that, no matter how great your plan, the corporation isn't interested enough to send people who can take action.

Third, use the language of marketing. You can find excellent university-level "Introduction to Marketing" courses on the Web. You can run through these at your own pace, gleaning what you need to know for your presentation.

The fourth step in preparing for the sale of your partnership idea is to clarify for yourself what you're selling. Have a single sheet of paper—an executive summary—that states concisely what you propose and why. This is as much for your own benefit (once again, keeping you on track) as it is for the folks on the other side of the boardroom table.

The final step in the selling process is to move the potential corporate partner from interest to commitment. This takes time, and rarely happens after one meeting. Because this is a negotiation process, you have to be clear about what is open to compromise and what isn't. Answer their questions as soon and as thoroughly as possible. Continue to press for a decision, but be flexible. The chain of command in the corporate world can be quite bureaucratic. Just don't let the trail get cold.

Once the decision is made, propose a contract and do it fast. Expect that their legal department will need time to look over the terms, and have your attorney plan to do the same. If your board has been kept well informed up to this point, they can take a quick vote to approve the venture, but should not become involved in the actual contract negotiations. That only opens the door for a wavering board member to put a stick in the spokes of an otherwise well-oiled machine. Your new corporate partner will not be impressed if your organization backs away from the relationship at this late stage of the game.

Keep the relationship on track

This task involves several activities. First, get to know your counterparts at your corporate partner to gain a deeper understanding of their objectives. Suggest an informal lunch or a tour of their facilities. Even better, offer a tour of your site and invite them to agency events.

Continually assess the venture by tracking its elements. How much money are you earning? What kind of added exposure are you receiving? Do the results justify the effort? All successful alliances between nonprofits and corporations begin with a short-term relationship that is tested and modified, then the parties involved make longer-term commitments that are reevaluated down the line.

By now it should be obvious: in your relationship with a corporation, there's no moment when you can completely relax. Even if you're successful beyond your expectations, you must always be looking down the road to the next important opportunity with this partner.

Evaluate your results and share the news

Evaluation not only tells you how well your partnership is working; it also helps you develop tools for future corporate partnership pursuits. Identify your mistakes or missteps. Be candid about them and explore how to avoid problems in future marketing co-ventures. Also identify your strengths and consider how to use them better for your next course of action. What have you learned about your partners? What can you expect to encounter among marketing executives you work with in the future?

Evaluation should also be a quantifiable process. Be as detailed as possible about the time your organization has contributed to the marketing partnership, and how that time is valued in terms of dollars. What bottom-line profits were generated for your budget? How are those numbers different from your projections, and why? By reducing certain costs or enhancing certain strategies in the marketing plan, those profits might increase significantly in your next venture.

Several of your constituencies—clients, funders, donors, cooperating nonprofits, and others—deserve regular reporting on the progress of your venture. These people have a history of supporting your organization and they deserve to understand what's going on when you pursue any potentially controversial strategy for earning income. Keep your reports brief, yet respectful. Remember, these folks do not need to know every detail of the partnership. They only need to understand that you are proceeding with integrity and good preparation, while keeping the best interests of the organization at the forefront of your actions.

Like many other nonprofits, Cynthia Madden Leitner and the Museum of Outdoor Arts in Denver have successfully developed corporate partnership ventures. The organization has chosen its partners with integrity. These companies implement admirable business practices congruent with the values of her nonprofit. The museum has realized significant levels of sustainable income and increased awareness of, and support for, its mission.

The biggest challenge, Leitner says, has been to find the right fit: to pursue partnerships with corporations that benefit the organization but do not compromise values and do not contradict the mission in either spirit or practice. "Because we are well informed about our potential partners and the significance of our contributions to the relationship," Leitner adds, "we will continue to be confident. And confidence attracts success."

Off the Streets, Into the Kitchen

FARESTART

SEATTLE, WASHINGTON

WWW.FARESTART.ORG

ANNUAL BUDGET: $1,800,000

EARNED INCOME: 50%

EARNED INCOME STRATEGIES

- EMPLOYMENT TRAINING AND JOB DEVELOPMENT
- SERVICES FOR NONPROFITS AND OTHER INSTITUTIONAL CUSTOMERS
- CONSUMER SERVICES
- PUBLICATIONS
- CONSUMER GOODS: RETAIL
- CONSUMER GOODS: WHOLESALE

The scene: a modest but handsome downtown Seattle restaurant. The tables are covered with white linen, a flower and vase on each one. A row of photos—chefs in uniform, dozens of them, smiling broadly for the camera—encircles the room. One wall is covered with the framed logos of corporate and foundation sponsors, including Starbucks, Boeing, Washington Mutual Savings and Loan, Safeco, Microsoft, plus several local grantmakers. Volunteers in aprons move through the room, fixing the place settings. The restaurant has an air of quiet, competent anticipation.

At 5:30 P.M., the doors open. By 6:00 every table is occupied, the phone is ringing, and the reservation list is full. Like many other downtown bistros, the place is hopping.

Here's the unusual part: in the kitchen, twenty-five homeless and formerly homeless people are preparing an amazing meal while auditioning for some of the city's finest chefs. By the time the evening is over, nearly 200 patrons will have paid just $16.95 for a three-course gourmet meal. Even better, someone in the kitchen will land a new job and with it, a new life.

Welcome to the FareStart Restaurant, where the motto is: Great food, great price, great cause.

FareStart is unique in that it started as a for-profit company. In 1986, David Lee launched a business to provide meals for local antipoverty agencies. He hired homeless people to help with food preparation; over time, the focus of the business shifted to job training. Lee found that, given the limitations of the market, he could not generate enough income to provide the full range of services he wanted to offer his homeless clients. The goal of increasing sales sometimes got in the way of his social mission. So, after much soul-searching—program director Barbara Hill calls it "the moment of truth"—he incorporated as a nonprofit in 1992 to take advantage of potential grants, corporate donations, and individual gifts. Founded as Common Meals, the group changed its name to FareStart in 1998.

Today, the organization provides a wide range of food services, including the following:

- A restaurant, housed near their office and training kitchen, offering a daily lunch buffet and Thursday evening guest-chef dinners

- One off-site restaurant

- 375 evening meals per day to homeless shelters

- 1,000 daily breakfasts, lunches, and snacks for Seattle's day care and Head Start programs

- 150 meals delivered four nights a week to senior citizen centers

- A catering service that generates more than $5,000 per month in revenues

Altogether, FareStart serves more than 300,000 meals each year. Through contracts, customer fees, and product sales, the group earns about 50 percent of its budget. The balance comes from federal grants, corporate gifts, foundation grants, and private donations. Soliciting contributions, Hill says, "keeps us grounded in the community. For that reason, we don't want to become 100 percent self-supporting."

While FareStart is justifiably known for its great meals, food is a means to a more important end: providing work skills and life skills for Seattle's homeless population. "Work skills" means job training for restaurants and commercial kitchens, because that's where the work is. (A recent *Newsweek* story on employment trends was titled, "Learn to Cook.") "Life skills" encompasses everything from how to stay sober—participants must enter the program drug-free and remain that way—to how to rent an apartment.

The strategy works. In a recent year, 150 students graduated from the sixteen-week training; 90 percent found work immediately. After three months, 90 percent of those remained employed, which is extraordinary for any program that combines job training with issues of homelessness and substance abuse.

From trainees to volunteers and staff, FareStart has a profound effect on everyone involved. When asked by the *Seattle Post-Intelligencer* to describe her greatest moment, former executive director Cheryl Sesnon said, "The first time one of our graduates said this program had literally saved his life."[1] Another student told Sesnon, "Before I came to you, the only thing that fit was a pair of handcuffs."

Stories like these make good press. FareStart does an expert job of generating media attention, with coverage in Seattle's daily newspapers, radio, and television stations. A feature in the trade publication *Restaurant Hospitality* told the story of Anthony Garces, who was living under a bridge when he entered the program and now has a job and an apartment. Why a trade magazine? Because Associated Grocers, a major food distributor, donates lots of food to FareStart. Their employees also volunteer on guest chef night. "We studied our options and decided that the partnership was a natural for a food company like AG," former company president Don Benson told *Restaurant Hospitality*. "And our employees have really embraced the concept with their own volunteer efforts."[2]

FareStart promotes the Thursday dinners (and daily buffet lunches) through donated magazine ads, plus e-mail and broadcast fax lists, reaching 30,000 people annually. They collect e-mail addresses and fax numbers through a business card drop, where restaurant patrons can win a drawing for a free meal. They also use table displays with comment cards to capture customer data. Given the daily lunch traffic at two locations, these strategies generate more than 500 customer leads per week. A team of volunteers enters this data into the computer system, which reduces costs.

On a recent evening, it was hard to tell the trainees from the experienced cooks. Chef Walter Pisano of Tulio Ristorante coached students through the menu, which included grilled eggplant stuffed with arugula and goat cheese, roasted chicken breast with shiitake mushrooms, and, for dessert, "drunken fruit with mascarpone zabaglione." Pisano, a calm man who runs a surprisingly calm kitchen, has served as guest chef a half-dozen times and helped several alumni find jobs. "There's a place for everyone," he says, looking around at the students. "This program is tangible—you can see the results."

Restaurant patrons get to share this sense of pride and accomplishment, which helps to build customer loyalty. During an informal graduation ceremony in the dining room, students talk about their time in the program, their plans for the future, and receive a set of professional kitchen knives as a graduation present. The evening ends with a warm round of applause.

When FareStart began as a for-profit business, many employees came from a social service background. Now that the organization is a nonprofit, however, things have flipped completely around: most staff come from the business world, especially the food service industry. This may explain the entrepreneurial air that permeates their headquarters. In addition to selling food, the group has developed a line of products, including restaurant gift certificates ($10 and $20), logo aprons ($15) and caps ($12), wooden spatulas ($3), travel mugs ($10), and holiday cards ($15 for a pack of ten). Their more ambitious projects include a cookbook ($25) and calendar ($14.95) which feature full-color food photos—the kind you see in gourmet magazines—and recipes from participating guest chefs.

FARESTART WORKED WITH ALBERTSONS.COM TO PROMOTE THE COOKBOOK *SAVORING SEATTLE*

The cookbook, *Savoring Seattle,* was self-published in partnership with ACCESS, the Alliance for Committed Civic Engagement and Social Solutions. (ACCESS, a nonprofit, recruits people from the business community to help nonprofits improve their business practices.) To get the books into the stores in time for holiday season, photography, design, and production were completed in a remarkable thirteen weeks. The result: 2,500 sales between Thanksgiving and New Year's Day. Thanks to extensive news coverage, the book has continued to sell, with a new edition of 10,000 copies published the following year.

As part of their agreement with ACCESS, FareStart received 1,500 copies to sell or give away as they pleased. The organization also gets 100 percent of the profits once expenses are covered; hard costs for the most recent printing (design and production) total about $9 per book. After ACCESS takes out an administrative fee to cover their costs, FareStart expects to receive $100,000 from sales of the first two editions of *Savoring Seattle.*

While the money looks good, the publicity may prove even more valuable. According to Tawn Holstra, executive director of ACCESS, "All participants received enormous attention." That includes both nonprofits, the photographer, the designer and especially the chefs, many of whom have their own publicists to help promote the book. In the end, everyone is thrilled and FareStart has cemented relationships with several key partners.

Every FareStart product—from restaurant meals to aprons and cookbooks—links directly to the mission, which emphasizes how cooking skills can be used to build self-reliance and fight poverty. The perfect fit between mission and product is what makes their sales program so successful.

THINGS TO THINK ABOUT

- *Since you're trying to run a business, hire people with relevant business skills and contacts.* FareStart has succeeded, in large part, because their staff members understand restaurant management and promotion, how to work with the food service industry, and so on. Furthermore, many relationships formed in their "business lives" have proven beneficial to the organization in terms of bringing in volunteers, in-kind donations, purchasing discounts, and spreading good will throughout the industry.

- *Reduce your costs with in-kind donations.* To redesign and renovate the restaurant, FareStart solicited $92,000 worth of free goods and services from corporations and small businesses. This is one area where nonprofit enterprises have a distinct advantage, since many of these gifts can be deducted from the donor's taxes.

- *E-mail and broadcast fax lists provide cheap, targeted advertising.* Use door prizes, drawings, and sign-up sheets at events to collect e-mail address and fax numbers—then use them.

- *Corporate partnerships can generate positive news coverage.* Don't forget that prospective business partners want publicity about their good deeds—that's one of the primary reasons they team up with nonprofits. Many have their own in-house publicists or consultants. Use these folks to help get the word out—they will have contacts in media outlets, such as trade publications, that you could never reach on your own. (By the way, mainstream media reporters often read trade magazines for story ideas.)

- *Once you create quality goods or services, client testimonials can give you a competitive edge.* Good stories generate good business. People eat at the FareStart Restaurant because the food is tasty, the price is fair, it's a pleasant venue, it's a good cause, and on graduation night, they get to hear directly from the beneficiaries of the program, which is a moving experience.

- *Many nonprofits assume, in designing a venture, that the good cause will make up for inferior quality and service. It will not.* If the food isn't good, the price isn't fair, or the place is a dump, people will eat elsewhere. Once the restaurateurs provide fair value, however, the fact that it's a good cause and that diners hear from the program beneficiaries defines the unique dining experience at FareStart. That's why they have a waiting list for both customers and volunteer chefs.

Chapter 9

Navigating the tax implications of earned income

Terry Miller

▨   ▨   ▨

Taxes. Everyone hates the subject, but "tax" is how we regulate nonprofits in the United States. When a tax-exempt organization decides to start an income-generating venture, there are possible tax implications. This chapter is a tax planning primer to help you understand the relevant tax law. By giving an overview, the purpose of this chapter is to help nonprofit managers decide whether to seek professional tax counsel from a certified public accountant (CPA) or tax attorney. This chapter is not legal advice, and the author is not a lawyer.

Giving legal advice means applying the law to a set of facts, and every set of facts is different. In this chapter we discuss broad principles, specific applications, and areas of current regulatory enforcement and scrutiny. These include areas of open dispute between the nonprofit sector and the IRS. Especially in such areas, the laws could change very soon; this chapter should be taken as accurate as of 2001. One of the benefits of hiring expert legal counsel is that such experts keep abreast of changes in law and strategy.

Who cares about tax laws affecting nonprofits and commercial activity? In this chapter, the word *nonprofit,* unless otherwise qualified, means a U.S. tax-exempt organization, most likely organized as a nonprofit corporation in one of the fifty states, with officially recognized exemption from federal and state income tax. All tax issues discussed in the chapter affect publicly supported 501(c)(3) organizations. Issues discussed around *public support* relate only to 501(c)(3) organizations that are publicly supported charities. Issues discussed around *unrelated business income* and *commerciality* affect all 501(c) organizations. If your organization is Canadian, skip this chapter and get legal advice from a Canadian lawyer. If your organization is a private foundation, you may wish to read this chapter for insight about your grantees, but private foundation rules are especially tricky and require qualified counsel. If your organization is not incorporated, there may be liability issues to consider before starting a venture; the purpose of being incorporated is to help protect individuals from liability.

Finally, the use of *tax exempt* or *exempt* in this chapter is a reference to corporate income tax, not to exemption from sales, property or other taxes, which rules vary greatly from state to state and city to city.

The commerciality standard and the notion of unrelated business income

Since 1950, there has been a principle in this country that a tax-exempt organization earns its exempt status based on how it is *organized and operated,* not based on what it does with its profits. For example, if you operate a pizza parlor but give all your profits to charity, that does not confer tax exemption on your pizza parlor, no matter how well intentioned the operation. The reason is that it would not be fair to the person down the street who is operating a traditional pizza parlor in an effort to make a buck like any other business. Your nonprofit, enjoying more favorable tax treatment, would be in a position to undercut the competition on price. If your venture idea looks like other businesses in the community, it is important to take a very careful look at the tax issues raised and evaluate information on whether the activity is different from commercial competition.

Let's assume that your nonprofit's proposed pizza parlor distinguishes itself in the following ways: it uses produce grown organically in gardens on formerly vacant lots in the inner city; these gardens expose low-income kids to experiences with gardening and science; the business employs women leaving domestic violence shelters by building job skills. If all these are true, then your venture may be operated sufficiently differently from commercial pizza parlors to merit tax exemption.

Another well-known example of this tension is the relationship of YMCA gyms to for-profit health clubs. In many jurisdictions, private health clubs have challenged the local property tax exemption enjoyed by YMCA gymnasiums, arguing that the Y has become nothing more than a health club competitor and should be taxed accordingly. Inquiry into this issue is also going on in Congress related to exemption from federal income taxes, and most state exemptions follow the federal rules. The YMCAs, of course, counter that fitness is part of public health and improvement of the citizenry, and consistent with their exempt purposes. In response to these pressures, many Ys have added scholarship and outreach programs in an effort to distinguish their fitness operations from competing taxable businesses.

This was not always the law. For the first half of the twentieth century, all receipts were tax free to a charity, whether derived from contributions or from the conduct of business, so long as those funds were used to further the exempt purposes of the charity. This so-called destination test held sway until 1950. By that time, the charitable sector had grown large enough to be perceived as a competitive threat by the business sector.

In response, the business sector mounted a powerful lobbying campaign to limit tax benefits to charities. Also, charitable organizations were pushing the envelope on the destination test. For example, the Mueller Macaroni Company was donated to New York University, which proceeded to operate it quite profitably, setting off substantial protest from commercial entities, which viewed this as unfair competition.

Largely in response to business pressure, Congress enacted the Unrelated Business Income Tax in 1950. The gist of the tax is clear: a charity should pay income tax on income from any commercial business unrelated to its charitable purpose. Unrelated business income (UBI) is income earned from a trade or business that is regularly carried on and is unrelated to the exempt purpose of the nonprofit. The main issues are also apparent: What is a business? When is it related and when unrelated? What are the implications of the concept of "regularly carrying on"? There are, of course, lots of exceptions, exclusions, and other complications.

Finally, if a given commercial venture is very large, compared to the rest of the activity of a nonprofit, it raises a question: Is the overall organization really a tax-exempt nonprofit with some commercial activity, or is it really a for-profit business that does some charitable work? Nonprofits that create larger unrelated ventures often operate those ventures out of taxable subsidiary corporations to avoid this larger commerciality concern.

Scale of the venture

The first thing to think about when assessing the need for professional tax advice is the scale of your planned venture. For example, if the venture might account for $5,000 of a $200,000 budget, these issues are not likely to matter very much one way or the other, and even if mistakes are made in tax reporting, the risk in a tax audit is small. If larger sums of money or a larger percentage of your budget are involved, then you need to be strategic about the tax issues from the beginning.

Use this chapter to get a general idea of the issues involved and then go get started on your idea. If it takes off and grows and actually makes a profit (no small task), then you can hire counsel, do any tax reporting, and reorganize if necessary. The worst case is another tax return to prepare and file and some tax to pay out of the profits on your new venture. There is no legal activity that is forbidden to a nonprofit. Even if you manage to start a business that grows to be huge and successful, your nonprofit can set up a taxable for-profit subsidiary corporation to hold the business and pay taxes on it like any other commercial venture.

However, if, at the start-up stage, you feel certain the commercial activity might end up in a for-profit subsidiary, put it there now. Otherwise, it may be difficult later to transfer the commercial activity from the nonprofit. Second, if your nonprofit needs to broaden its purposes so that the activity is related, this should be done at the outset. These topics are discussed later in this chapter.

Revenue versus support

The first distinction to make is the difference between *revenue* and *support*. Support is money your organization receives as a gift, grant, or contribution to further your purposes. Revenue is money your organization receives because the payer receives something in return. Sometimes a single check can be partly revenue and partly support. For example, if you charge $50 to a dinner and dance and the fair market value of such an event is $20, then the $50 payment is $20 revenue and $30 support. Only the $30 support is deductible to the payer if your organization is a 501(c)(3). This chapter, as well as the rest of this book, is all about generating *revenue*.

For tax purposes, there are three types of revenue: passive investment income, exempt function income, unrelated business income. Unrelated business income is taxable (after deducting related expenses); the other two are not. Following some definition, each of these types of revenue is discussed in more detail.

Passive investment income includes revenue earned as interest and dividends on your bank and investment accounts, gains on sales of investments, royalty income, and rental of real property—land or buildings—that is not debt-financed (mortgaged). Passive investment income is a specific exclusion from the legal definition of unrelated business income, with one exception discussed later concerning payments from subsidiaries.

Exempt function income includes fees derived from activities that are primarily engaged in to further charitable or other tax-exempt purposes and not primarily to earn revenue, as well as certain revenues excluded from the definition of unrelated business income. This type of revenue is often also called *program service revenue*. All groups profiled in this book earn exempt function income.

As we said earlier, most of this chapter is devoted to a discussion of *unrelated business income* and unrelated business income tax (UBIT). Any profits made from an activity that generates unrelated business income are taxable as if the venture were commercial. Your goal in tax planning is to operate and account for any venture in a way to avoid paying UBIT if possible. If the scale of the venture is large in dollars or as a percentage of your budget, professional help will be necessary to determine whether it is possible to avoid UBIT.

Whether earned income is taxable revolves around the commerciality standard, so as a nonprofit manager you can start by asking yourself: "Do we have any business competition for this venture?" If the scale is small, or if you can confidently answer no, you probably don't need counsel.

Passive investment income

The easiest revenue to classify as passive is simple interest and dividends. Royalties and rental income can pose more complicated questions.

ROYALTIES. If your organization allows an unrelated commercial venture to use its goodwill or logo or to publish work that your nonprofit has written, in exchange for a stream of payments, and the nonprofit does nothing to promote the commercial venture, then the revenue is passive royalty income. As of this writing (December 2001), royalties are a big area of dispute between the IRS and nonprofits.

The best-known dispute about royalty income has centered on affinity credit cards. In affinity credit card arrangements, a large nonprofit allows a bank to use its mailing list to market a credit card that carries the logo of the nonprofit and that provides a stream of income to the nonprofit, typically based on a portion of the annual fee plus a very small portion of every transaction charged on the card.

In defining UBI, Section 513 of the Internal Revenue Code specifically exempts income from mailing list rental earned when an exempt organization rents its mailing list to another exempt organization, regardless of how related the mission. In other words, an environmental charity could rent its mailing list, passively, to Mothers Against Drunk Driving, for example, and not have the income counted as taxable. The IRS takes the position that this implies that Congress intended rental of mailing lists to commercial entities to be taxable as unrelated business income. Nonprofits argue that revenue earned by renting a mailing list to any entity is passive royalty income to the renting nonprofit and is therefore excluded from UBI as passive investment income. The IRS counters that services provided by an exempt organization in maintaining the mailing list (keeping the names up-to-date) leads to at least part of the revenue stream being non-passive and therefore taxable as UBI.

In an appropriately passive affinity credit card deal, typically the nonprofit does two things in exchange for the revenue it earns. First, it allows the bank to use its mailing list one or more times. Second, it allows the bank to use its name, logo, and goodwill on the bank's credit cards and promotional literature. (If the nonprofit were to engage in activities promoting the card, the revenue might become UBI because it is not passively generated, but this is not the primary subject of the current tax dispute around affinity cards.) The IRS takes the position that revenue, at least from the rental of the mailing list to the bank, is taxable as UBI. So far, the IRS has lost in court on this issue, but it has not been litigated to the Supreme Court, so nothing is final.

If your organization is considering renting your mailing list and the use of your name and/or logo to a non-exempt organization, and the dollars involved are large, you should seek counsel. There are tactical steps you can take to minimize tax exposure. First, you can structure the deal as two separate deals to minimize the portion of the revenue stream that the IRS would tax if it eventually prevails. Second, you can accurately report the arrangement on annual Forms 990 so as to start the statute of limitations running, and thereby limit how far back the IRS can look to your nonprofit for tax if it prevails in the courts.

RENTAL OF REAL PROPERTY. If your organization owns real property outright and rents it without providing services or renting a bunch of personal property (such as furniture and equipment) in addition to the real property, the revenue is excluded from UBI and therefore not taxable. If the property is debt-financed (mortgaged), then a portion of the income may or may not be taxable UBI, depending on whether the tenant is mission-related to your organization. The idea here is that borrowing money to buy a property and then paying off the mortgage with rental income derived from tenants is a fundamentally commercial activity.

If your organization earns large-scale revenue from renting real property to tenants that are not mission related, then you should seek counsel.

INCLUSION OF PASSIVE INCOME FROM SUBSIDIARIES. There is one key exception concerning the treatment of royalties, rents, and interest paid from a taxable subsidiary to a nonprofit parent. In these cases, if the nonprofit owns more than half of the subsidiary, the income is not exempt from UBI. This keeps the subsidiary from dodging taxable income by booking high expenses paid to the parent.

Exempt function income

There are many ways for a charity to earn revenue from the very activities that promote its exempt purposes. Consider an art museum that is organized for public benefit to promote appreciation of art and is operated to attract as many people to appreciate art as possible. For such a museum, the admission charge would count as an exempt function income (or program service revenue), which in no way would be taxable, even though it is a purely earned income, and the person buying admission is not entitled to any deduction for a charitable contribution.

Passive investment income is fairly easy to define and to spot. Determining whether other types of revenue are exempt function income or unrelated business income can be much more complex. Virtually every type of revenue-generating activity that resembles activities also carried on by businesses has some sort of criteria or rules developed by Congress or the IRS to evaluate whether the activity is UBI.

Unrelated business income

Unrelated business income (UBI) is defined with a three-part definition: income earned from a *trade or business* that is *regularly carried on* and is *unrelated* to the exempt purpose of the nonprofit. Each of the three parts of the definition may provide an opportunity for tax planning. Why is this important? Because net income from UBI (after deducting related expenses) is taxable at the corporate rate, about 35 percent at this writing. Tax planning may allow a venture to be organized and operated in a way that avoids this tax. (Unrelated business income tax is abbreviated as UBIT, and net UBI, which becomes *unrelated business taxable income,* is known as UBTI.)

• *UBI Question 1: Related or unrelated?* The exempt purposes of your nonprofit are shown in the following documents, listed from most important to least important:

- Your articles of incorporation
- Possibly your bylaws
- The original application for recognition of exemption on IRS Form 1023 or 1024
- Any further correspondence with the IRS on this subject
- Your annual Forms 990
- Various internal documents, such as a mission statement or program brochures

Imagine that your organization operates a day care center for children. You decide to sell a fancy—but educational—babysitters' guide for $30 as a fundraising item. If the articles of incorporation and the tax-exemption application say that you are organized to "provide day care to children," then selling the guide is unrelated business activity, and profits (if any) would be taxable. If, however, your articles of incorporation and application say that the organization intends to work in a variety of ways for the welfare of children, including provision of day care, publishing of materials, and educating the public, then selling the guide would generate exempt function income and would not be taxable.

After considering a new venture and your purposes as currently stated, you may decide that it would be best to amend your articles of incorporation to broaden your mission, and to notify the IRS on Form 990 that your activities have changed and explain the new broader charitable mission. If your nonprofit's purposes and activities have changed substantially, you may wish to file a formal request for IRS recognition that the new purposes and activities qualify as exempt.

Special Fragmentation Rule. It is important to keep in mind that when the IRS looks at a complex venture such as a college or museum gift store or bookstore, it will break the venture into small components, or fragments, before applying the UBIT rules. This means it will determine that revenue from the sale of certain individual items is exempt function income or falls otherwise into one or more exemptions from UBI, while revenue from the sale of other individual items is taxable UBI. For example, the museum above that exists to promote appreciation of art might sell a variety of items in its gift store, such as local tourist guidebooks, that are not particularly related to art and art appreciation. The IRS would take the position that revenue from those tourist guides is UBI and net income from those guides is taxable, while it would leave alone the sale of art prints and art books.

• **UBI Question 2: *What is a trade or business?*** This gets to the very heart of the commerciality standard discussed above. Revenue from certain activities has been specifically exempted from the definition of taxable UBI since these activities are by definition not equivalent to commercial ventures:

- Activities substantially conducted by volunteers

- The sale of merchandise, substantially all of which has been donated

- Activity that is carried on by a 501(c)(3) organization primarily for the convenience of members, students, patients, officers, or employees

- The distribution of low-cost items (defined as $7.60 in 2001) as tokens of appreciation for gifts

- Bingo games, defined very specifically

- Certain public entertainment activities, such as festivals or county fairs

- Certain specific types of conventions and tradeshows

Obviously, if your activity might use one of the first three exemptions listed, the question now arises as to the definition of *substantially* or *primarily.* If you're considering a large-scale venture, you should seek counsel.

In addition to the good news about exemptions from UBI based on the definition of *trade or business,* there is bad news. There are certain activities that the IRS considers inherently commercial and unrelated to exempt purposes, including revenue from advertising, revenue from certain sponsorships, and revenue from debt-financed property.

Advertising is a subject on which the IRS has tried to draw a bright line. In nearly all cases, regular advertising revenue (such as in a quarterly newsletter) is reportable as UBI, if gross UBI revenue—before expenses—is more than $1,000. In extremely rare cases, organizations have been able to demonstrate that their advertising itself achieves an exempt purpose. For example, a medical journal might be able to qualify its advertising as exempt from UBI if the advertising is closely related to the journal's articles, is itself truly substantive in content, and educates the reader about new medical and scientific products on the market.

In the case of advertising, the calculation of income and expenses becomes very complicated. First of all, the rules allow for deduction of the proportionate cost of publication and distribution relating to the proportion of the material that is devoted to paid advertising. In other words, advertising space as a percentage of total publication space equals the percentage of production, printing, and distribution cost that may be deducted. However, in some cases the rules require the reporting nonprofit to count as UBI a portion of subscription income (which may be called "membership dues" depending on the facts and circumstances) as well as the advertising income. The bottom line: If your organization has learned how to generate revenue of more than $1,000 from advertising, you need to learn the accounting rules and think through your recordkeeping very carefully. Start with Form 990-T instructions and IRS Publication 598, *Tax on Unrelated Business Income of Exempt Organizations.*

Corporate sponsorships, unless properly structured, run the risk of being treated as advertising. With corporate sponsorships, such as the Mobil Cotton Bowl, businesses agree to provide funds to events such as sports competitions, parades, and public festivals. In exchange for the funds, the sponsor is provided promotional benefits characterized as "acknowledgment," often including the renaming of the event or facility.

In 1993, the IRS made an attempt to tax this revenue as advertising and therefore UBI. It was particularly focused on bowl games. The IRS position is understandable, since most of the businesses paying for sponsorships are counting the payment as a promotional expense rather than as a charitable gift. The sports and festivals lobby, however, was strong enough that it got Congress to pass new Code language (Section 513(i)) and trumped the IRS. The Code now specifically exempts sponsorship payments from treatment as UBI, so long as the "acknowledgment" does not include "advertising [the sponsor's] products or services (including messages containing qualitative or comparative language, price information, or other indications of savings or value, an endorsement, or an inducement to purchase, sell, or use such products or services)." The Code also limits the exemption if the sponsorship payment is contingent on the number of people attending the event or otherwise exposed to the message. There are also limitations on the exemption for publication of sponsorship messages in regularly scheduled and printed material that is not distributed in connection with an event.

Watch out for merchandise for sale. If your organization regularly sells T-shirts, tote bags, baseball caps, and the like emblazoned with its logo, this revenue may be considered UBI by the IRS if it is examined. To be safe from treatment as unrelated business income, merchandise needs to do more than simply promote the organization itself, as far as the IRS is concerned. However, if your name (say, "People to Prevent Toxic Waste"), your logo, or the item itself promotes your mission by carrying a message such as "reduce, reuse, and recycle," then the revenue would be exempt function income. In any case, very few groups report ongoing sales of a few T-shirts as UBI, but on audit the IRS might have a different view, depending on the merchandise, who sells it (volunteers or paid staff), what it says, and how regularly it is sold.

If your new venture is run by volunteers, or involves the sale of donated items, or is truly for the convenience of your members, students, patients, officers, or employees, then you can treat it as exempt function income. If your new venture involves advertising or large-scale corporate sponsorships, you should learn more about the subject before structuring your accounting system or drafting sponsorship agreements.

• *UBI Question 3: What is "regularly carried on"?* Nonprofits and the IRS have argued this issue in many specific cases. In general, an activity done only once a year is not "regular" for this purpose. Some organizations have an annual banquet, member meeting, and program books in which they sell advertising, but they do not sell ads at other times of the year. Such an organization might be able to count the advertising revenue as exempt from UBI. However, the IRS took the position that activities of the National Collegiate Athletic Association (NCAA) in selling advertising in its annual college basketball tournament program book were activities regularly carried on because the program book was so substantial that there was, in fact, a year-round sales effort and advertising staff. The IRS lost to the NCAA in court, but may be waiting for a better set of facts to pursue this issue.

If your venture will be conducted once a year or less, it is likely exempt from UBI and not taxable. If it is large scale and will be conducted more often than once a year, but still only on an occasional basis, get counsel.

If an organization has gross unrelated business income of $1,000 or more, it must file Form 990-T, due annually at the same time as Form 990. Form 990-T starts with the gross unrelated business income and allows deductions for costs associated with the production of that income to determine the net UBTI—unrelated business taxable income. If a nonprofit owes UBIT, it must pay quarterly estimated tax payments. (See also the discussion of cost allocations in the next section.)

Current areas of scrutiny, enforcement, and dispute

As mentioned earlier, a number of areas are currently being debated or carefully enforced by the IRS:

- Corporate sponsorships
- Fitness facilities

- Mailing list rentals
- Affinity credit card arrangements
- Fragmentation
- Travel tours
- Associate member dues
- Cost allocations

We've already discussed corporate sponsorships, fitness facilities, mailing list rentals and affinity credit card arrangements, and the fragmentation rule. Other areas of current attention include travel tours, associate member dues, and cost allocations.

Travel tours being sponsored by colleges, universities, churches, museums, and other nonprofits continue to be challenged by for-profit tour groups, who claim unfair competition. Having a formal educational program—one that is emphasized in the solicitation materials and occupies participants substantially all the time—is the easiest way for nonprofits to avoid UBI.

Associate member dues arise as a UBI issue when a nonprofit organization with specific membership benefits, such as an insurance plan, attracts non-voting members who join solely to access the benefits but are not otherwise part of the program or constituency of the nonprofit.

Regarding *cost allocations,* the IRS believes many organizations are overstating the expenses associated with generating unrelated business income, claiming greater deductions to reduce the amount of tax paid. If your organization reports unrelated business income, you may wish to obtain help with accounting for the costs, particularly so that you take full advantage of allowable deductions.

If your venture is large in scale and involves corporate sponsorships, fitness facilities, mailing list rentals or affinity credit card arrangements, sale of many different items variously related and unrelated to your mission, travel tours, or associate member dues, or you are reporting UBI and filing Form 990-T, then you should keep abreast of rapidly changing laws and enforcement standards.

Public charity status: The public support tests

This is a very complicated subject, not for the faint of heart. If your organization is a 501(c) organization other than a 501(c)(3), you can skip this section.

A 501(c)(3) organization is either a *private foundation* or a *public charity.* Most 501(c)(3) organizations are defined as "not a private foundation" and earn their public charity status because they receive their support from sufficiently diverse sources.

The law restricts and regulates private foundations very carefully, because they are typically charities that have received funding from very few sources and may therefore be tempted to serve the private interests of the key donor or donors. The law assumes a charity is a private foundation unless the organization can prove that it is not.

Exempt function income (or program service revenue) is treated more favorably for the public charity support tests than any other form of earned income. Once again, the scale of the project matters: if your organization has many small contributors and a relatively small-scale earned income venture, it is not likely to create a public support issue.

Creating a taxable subsidiary corporation

When an unrelated business venture takes off and grows, nonprofits sometimes spin off the venture into its own corporation. In most cases, it is proper for the nonprofit to own 100 percent of the stock in such a subsidiary and receive all the after-tax profits. These profits are not treated favorably for the purposes of the public support test, but using a subsidiary can solve other issues:

- Assuming it is a bona fide corporation, the subsidiary corporation may shield the parent organization from liability arising from the venture.

- If unrelated business activities become very large in relation to the amount of charitable activity, having the unrelated business activities in a separate organization prevents a challenge to the parent charity of whether it is really a commercial organization.

- It is easier to account for income and expenses in a separate entity and therefore calculate accurate net income for purposes of calculating taxes.

- Profit-making ventures are sometimes best run by staff who are more interested in making money than in doing good. Organizations may find it easier to spin off a venture so the business can develop its own profit-minded entrepreneurial culture.

If you are feeling overwhelmed by the complexity of the tax rules, remember what we said at the beginning: get started! See if you can make your venture work. If you're concerned about taxes or legal issues, consult an attorney with relevant expertise.

"Our Profit Is Our Vegetables"

THE FOOD BANK OF WESTERN MASSACHUSETTS
HATFIELD, MASSACHUSETTS
WWW.FOODBANKWMA.ORG
ANNUAL BUDGET: $1,700,000
EARNED INCOME: 32%

EARNED INCOME STRATEGIES
• CONSUMER GOODS: RETAIL
• CONSUMER GOODS: WHOLESALE

On a small farm in the New England hills, a local food bank is using an earned income strategy to challenge the way we fight poverty while feeding those in need. Along the way, The Food Bank of Western Massachusetts is also helping to change the face of agriculture by delivering some of the freshest, tastiest, healthiest produce you'll find anywhere.

Founded in 1982, the organization operates in many respects like other food banks: gathering food from local processing plants, distributors, stores, farms, and families and sharing it with soup kitchens, senior citizen programs, halfway houses, rehabilitation programs, and food pantries throughout the region. These 420 partner agencies pay a shared maintenance fee of 14 cents per pound for packaged food, which helps to defray the costs of handling and distribution. This fee—a standard practice among food banks—generates about $250,000 per year in earned income for The Food Bank. During a recent year, food from their programs reached 171,000 people—20 percent of the region's population.

Like their clients, food banks crave fresh fruits and vegetables, which are the most difficult foods to collect, store, and distribute. To address this problem, The Food Bank of Western Massachusetts borrowed an acre of garden space from Hampshire College in the late 1980s to start the Chili Project. Their goal: grow ingredients—onions, peppers, beans, and so on—for vegetarian chili, a nutritious alternative to packaged foods loaded with starch and sugar. Within three years, the garden had expanded to eight acres. In addition to chili ingredients, the land produced fresh vegetables for distribution to the poor. "We discovered," says executive director David Sharken, "that the agencies liked our produce better than our chili."

In 1992, The Food Bank made the leap from gardening to farming, buying 60 acres and an assortment of farm buildings for nearly $1 million. Nearly two-thirds of the cost was covered by a state grant program designed to protect productive farmland from development. Other financing for The Food Bank Farm came from a variety of sources, including individual donors, foundations, corporations, the town conservation commission, and a loan from the Vermont National Bank's social responsibility fund co-signed by a generous donor.

The Food Bank solicited shareholders to underwrite the cost of operating the farm. The process—known as Community Supported Agriculture, or CSA—works like this: in the spring, community members pay a fixed price to buy a share of a season's worth of produce. Once a week, from May through October, shareholders are invited to stop by and select from the 50 varieties of organic vegetables already harvested and cleaned, plus fruits, herbs and flowers. In November and December, participants come by once per month to collect potatoes, squash, and other winter crops from the root cellar. Because the money is paid up front, members share the risk as well as the bounty, though the farm mitigates the risk through crop diversity and extensive irrigation.

Before opening to the public, a dozen families were recruited as a test group for market research. For several months, they picked their own food, cleaned it, ate it, and provided feedback to the farmers. "We learned that for most people, pick your own doesn't work," Sharken says. "Folks are just too busy." So the farm managers budgeted more time and money to gather and clean the produce and raised the price of a share to cover these costs. Once the system was tested and prices established, they began looking for business.

To recruit customers, The Food Bank sent a mailing to all donors, distributed press releases, and placed hundreds of brochures in local churches and community agencies. They set a goal of fifty families; seventy signed up. In the second year, their goal was eighty shareholders; one hundred families joined. With the additional capital provided by the new shareholders, the farmers were able to cultivate more acreage and increase the variety of crops. By the third year, with 220 members signed up, the program was covering its costs from shareholder fees.

Today, 525 shareholders, representing 700 families (some families "share a share"), participate in the program. Sharken believes it to be the biggest CSA in New England and one of the largest in the country. For many participants, abundance is a bigger concern than crop failure. "Your life becomes driven by vegetables," member Carol Pope told the *Boston Globe*. "You get so much, you turn around in your kitchen and you find the vegetables are gaining on you. There's always an eggplant on my tail."[1]

Current rates are $375 for a full share, which feeds a family of three to five people. This works out to ten to twenty pounds of produce for less than $15 per week. A "share-plus" costs $510 and feeds five to seven people. According to an independent study, the same food would cost 60 percent more at the supermarket (non-organic) and more than twice as much at a natural foods store specializing in organic produce.

In a recent year, Food Bank Farm subscribers paid a total of $220,000, which covered the full costs of operations. However, they consumed only half the produce—the rest was given away. Through their share fees, participants paid for 150,000 pounds of vegetables to feed their neighbors in need. As farmer Michael Docter told *Harrowsmith Country Life* magazine, "We're proving that a community-supported farm can be lucrative, except that in our case, we're channeling all our potential profits into food for the needy."[2] Sharken puts it this way: "Our profit is our vegetables."

Carol Rothery, who directs the Northampton Survival Center, has received food from the farm "since the day it opened." During a recent growing season, the Survival Center received an average of 2,500 pounds of produce per month. She and her staff set it out for the 700 families who use the center. The stacks of produce are "a visual delight," she says. "I love it when we open the doors and everyone sees the vegetables—it's just thrilling."

Shareholders choose from a wide array of crops, spanning the alphabet from arugula to zucchini. The Food Bank Farm also purchases eggs, bread, soap, maple syrup, and other items from local farms and businesses, adds a small mark-up, and sells them to shareholders. These incidental sales gross $25,000 (net: $10,000) per year.

Member Keith Davis notes the "astounding difference in taste" between store-bought and farm-harvested vegetables, but he emphasizes that visiting the farm is an integral part of the experience. "It's beautifully landscaped, with flowers everywhere, and there's all these chickens running around, and the kids and their toys, and you get to see your friends…" His voice trails off. "It's not like shopping. It's fun."

The success of The Food Bank Farm comes after several seasons of trial and error. The skills and requirements for running a small business, as opposed to an anti-poverty agency, are dissimilar and sometimes contradictory, which created friction within the organization. "We have two different sets of customers: the shareholders, who are by and large affluent, and the needy," Sharken says. "It took us a while to acknowledge the tensions inherent in serving both." Conflicts arose over internal power and decision-making. As Docter points out, "Farmers need autonomy to make good business decisions and other people on staff don't always have that autonomy." Since farmers work irregular hours—*lots* of hours during the growing season—meetings were difficult to schedule. Office and distribution staff felt disconnected from what was happening out in the fields.

"Once the farm had a life of its own," Sharken says, "we decided to look at all options to address these problems, including a separate organization." Beginning in 1999, farmers Michael Docter and Linda Hildebrand spun off their own company, Cultivating Solutions (csaworks@aol.com) and are doing business as The Food Bank Farm while also consulting with other CSAs. The Food Bank owns the land, the buildings, and half the equipment. The farmers, who rent the land and the buildings, own the balance of the equipment, pay all farm-related expenses, and receive all shareholder fees. By contract, they continue to provide half their produce to The Food Bank, while having the freedom, in Docter's words, "to focus on what we do well. It's been working great." Sharken is also pleased with the arrangement. "From the customer's point of view," he says, "nothing has changed."

With a shareholder renewal rate topping 80 percent—a typical CSA renews 60 to 70 percent of its members from year to year—Sharken isn't concerned about the competition. Without any advertising, The Food Bank has a wait list of families who want to participate next year. However, the organization has been less successful at convincing shareholders to become donors; Sharken estimates that only 5 to 10 percent make an additional gift. "Many assume that their share fee is a contribution," he says. "People forget that only 4 percent of the food we provide to local agencies comes from the farm. It really forces us to focus on public education, teaching people about why hunger exists in the first place."

For Rothery of the Survival Center, the best part of the program is the way it connects the community together in unexpected ways. "People come by to donate used clothing," she says, "and they ask, 'Where did all those vegetables come from?'

"'From The Food Bank Farm.'

"'Oh yeah? I'm a member of The Food Bank Farm.' And they get so excited, because they're part of such a good thing."

THINGS TO THINK ABOUT

As farmer Michael Docter points out, many food banks have failed at CSA farming because of poor planning, inappropriate expectations, inadequate staffing, and impatience. To address these problems, Docter and his colleagues offer the following suggestions, which are relevant for all nonprofit business ventures:

- *Tie all business activities directly to your mission.* "Do what you know," Sharken says.

- *Find the right staff to run the venture.* A social service or community organizing background might not provide the appropriate set of skills.

- *Leave business decisions to people with appropriate training and instincts for the work—especially those who run the business operations day to day.* Give them the autonomy and authority to do their jobs and to fail occasionally. As Sharken points out, you need both "entrepreneurs and maintainers," so make sure your personnel policies are flexible enough to accommodate both.

- *Develop a detailed plan, then give yourself time to learn from experience.* "The learning curve for this work is at least five to ten years," Docter says.

- *Outside subsidies—grants, loans, cash transfers from other organizational bank accounts—can give you a false sense of success.* As Docter puts it, "At some point, you must cut off the subsidy and force yourself to make it work."

Chapter 10

Managing and expanding your venture

❊   ❊   ❊

Most of us chronically underestimate the time it takes to complete anything. This not only applies to simple jobs such as cooking dinner or cleaning the house, but it also holds for larger projects. For example: How long until your new venture begins to break even? (Longer than you realize.) How soon will your board members begin to grumble about "this earned income stuff?" (Sooner than you think.) When will you feel the need to update your résumé and start shopping it around?

Most new businesses take three or more years to turn a profit. In creating a business plan, one of your goals is to determine—given the demand for your product or service, your marketing skills and budget, and your pricing—how much subsidy you'll need. Without a solid plan, you won't be able to raise enough money to run the project until it can pay for itself. If you give up too easily, you might kill a potentially successful business before it's viable. Successful entrepreneurs survive the early years because they have a solid business plan, faith in their abilities, and a willingness to keep working their plan.

Launching a venture requires vision, enthusiasm, and a touch of boldness. Managing and growing it requires a different mix of attributes, including dedication, doggedness, a sense of humor, and a willingness to continually examine, update, and repackage everything you sell. In this chapter, we'll discuss strategies for dealing with success: how to maximize your venture and net more money while being true to your values.

Retaining and retraining staff

While we usually think of "subsidy" in terms of start-up money, more often it means unpaid or underpaid staff time. This is especially true in grassroots groups, where the "privilege" of working for the good of the community is seen as a license to pay less. Sometimes a spouse or partner—whose better-paying job allows another family member to work for low wages—provides the subsidy. Intentional or not, low salaries tend to discriminate against single-income families, especially those with children or other dependents. (How many anti-poverty groups pay near-poverty wages?)

Kay Sohl and her co-workers at Technical Assistance for Community Services provide a useful example. In the early years, they put in long hours at low pay while developing the market for their training and consulting services. They kept the organization afloat with cheap or donated labor. Over the long run, they've learned how competitive salaries and benefits improve morale and reduce turnover, and result in better customer service and greater potential to increase earned income. In other words, happy, well-respected, well-compensated people *net* more money for the organization. TACS now earns up to 75 percent of its annual budget from service and product fees.

For most workers, especially in the nonprofit sector, job satisfaction is even more important than compensation. Unfortunately, it's hard to be satisfied on the job if you don't know what you're doing. Some of your colleagues may have the "sales gene" or relevant experience and can step into the role of entrepreneur. Others will need training. Even seasoned salespeople need a refresher course now and then. Budget time and money for their education. (For a list of training resources, see "Finding and Using Outside Help" in Chapter Three.)

Outsourcing: Expanding your talent pool

In some progressive circles, *outsourcing* is considered a dirty word. In this context, the word refers to firing (or refusing to hire) salaried workers who are entitled to benefits and job protections, and replacing them with independent contractors who are entitled to neither. This analysis is usually applied to large corporations seeking to earn a higher return for stockholders while disregarding the needs of loyal workers. Taken in this way, I agree: outsourcing is irresponsible behavior.

However, I propose a different definition. Rather than replacing your current salaried staff, outsource specific jobs to specialists as needed. Don't have enough work to employ a graphic designer? Contract with a design firm to update your letterhead, brochure, and sales materials. Need marketing or media advice? Work with a consultant. Is the demand for your service growing, but not fast enough to hire another staff person? Find a contractor who's willing and able to help, at least until you can build up the business and hire more staff. In fact, outsourcing can be a good strategy for identifying and auditioning future staff members, even before you have a position to fill.

The Institute for Conservation Leadership (ICL) has nine full-time staff who spend three-quarters of their time delivering services to hundreds of clients. That equation doesn't allow for much individual client contact. To ensure better service, ICL works with independent consultants and trainers. These contractors are hired as needed and increase the range of potential services, since each brings unique expertise (fundraising, board development, volunteer management, and so forth) to the organization. While this arrangement includes substantial costs—as an example, the Institute hosts an annual retreat for participating trainers and consultants—it allows for a lot of flexibility. This strategy also generates new business. Several participating resource people have their own busy practices and refer groups they can't serve to ICL.

Grassroots Leadership, which is led by singer and songwriter Si Kahn, provides an another example. The group contracts with booking agent Josh Dunson of Real People's Music (rpmjosh@aol.com) to negotiate and promote concerts and speaking engagements. The agent receives 20 to 30 percent of the fee—a big slice—but the service, convenience, and professionalism are well worth the expense. If you compare the full cost of completing a task in-house or farming it out to a specialist, you may discover that using a contractor actually nets you more money.

Repackaging your work for new markets and larger sales

When you created your enterprise, you spent a lot of time brainstorming how to turn your assets into saleable services and products. Now that your project is up and running, the brainstorming should continue. (In the truly entrepreneurial workplace, brainstorming never stops.) Once or twice each year, sit down with your colleagues and ask yourselves two questions:

- How can we reformat *what we know* and *what we do* to provide new goods and services to our best customers?

- What about new customers and new markets? How can we reach them? How can we repackage our work to meet their needs?

This is a good opportunity for another round of informal market research. Talk with your customers. What do they like best about your products? Do they have any concerns or complaints? What other goods and services do they need? Then contact prospective customers. Can you identify a fit between their needs and your expertise?

Many of the groups you've been reading about excel at repackaging. Here are some examples:

- The Burns Bog Conservation Society uses its knowledge of bog ecology to produce tours, educational programs, curricula, and books. The content is adapted to meet the specific needs of different audiences, including teachers, students, and nature center visitors—who can be reached in at least three languages.

- Melpomene Institute, which focuses on issues of women's health and physical activity, sells its expertise in several ways: books, videos, brochures, a Web site, a journal, information packets, a resource center, public speaking engagements, workshops, and consultation.

- The Resource Center of the Americas created *Buen Viaje: Mutually Beneficial Tourism* as a school curriculum. The same content was then used to design a half-day seminar for prospective tourists. What's next—a manual for economic development officers? Workshops for travel agents? Curricula translated into other languages? Group tours?

As another repackaging option, try bundling several products or services together for a larger sale. Several organizations—Native Seeds/SEARCH, Women's Bean Project, and the White Earth Land Recovery Project—combine food products into gift baskets. By bundling a textbook, video, and curriculum guide on Chicano history, the SouthWest Organizing Project has created a popular kit for teachers priced at $114.

WHITE EARTH LAND RECOVERY PROJECT'S NATIVE HARVEST REPACKAGES INDIVIDUAL PRODUCTS INTO GIFT BASKETS FOR LARGER SALES

Working with competitors to expand the market

One way to expand your business is to work with your competitors. This may seem counterintuitive—after all, you're competing for the same customers—but if you work together, you can increase the customer base for everyone. Mutual support strategies come in several forms.

Cooperative advertising and promotion

Competitors can band together to purchase ads at a deep discount, reaching more prospects collectively than any business could reach individually. Native Seeds/SEARCH participates in a co-op advertising program sponsored by Fourth Avenue Merchants Association in Tucson. This strategy brings more shoppers to the district, increasing sales for all participants.

The Institute for Conservation Leadership used a related marketing tactic in the Pacific Northwest. Fifteen nonprofit providers, including ICL, worked together on a "Capacity Builders Resource Guide" that was distributed across the region. The brochure profiles each group and their services, some of which overlap. To learn which training and consulting approaches are most effective, these organizations are now testing a common approach for evaluating their work. With more than a thousand environmental groups in the Northwest and perhaps 20,000 in North America, participants are not worried about any of their competitors or collaborators cornering the market.

Referrals

Through their free Helpline service, Technical Assistance for Community Services provides referrals to more than 250 consultants in the Portland, Oregon area. Many later return the favor, referring clients to TACS. Thanks to this symbiotic relationship, Portland has an exceptionally diverse pool of nonprofit helpers. Because of the available talent and programs, local organizations have learned, over time, how to best use training and consulting services—which increases demand for these services. By helping each other, would-be competitors are building up business for the entire "consulting sector."

A COOPERATIVE BROCHURE PROFILES FIFTEEN PACIFIC NORTHWEST NONPROFIT RESOURCE PROVIDERS AND THEIR SERVICES

Niche marketing

Our Community Bikes, which sells inexpensive bicycles built from cast-offs and spare parts, has turned potential competitors—other bike shops—into suppliers. The commercial shops donate unused bicycle components to OCB. While all these businesses sell bicycles, they're targeting different niches: cheap used bikes as opposed to expensive new ones. Indeed, the commercial stores view OCB as a potential customer-generator, since some folks who start with inexpensive bicycles choose to trade up later.

Managing supply and demand

When launching a new venture, it's hard to locate the balance between supply and demand. Without a sales history, you must rely on sales projections. Without a marketing history, you don't know which methods work best for reaching your target audience.

If you over-promote and demand exceeds supply, customers will request products or services that have already sold out. When turned away, most will never contact you again. On the other hand, if you under-promote and supply exceeds demand, you're stuck with a lot of inventory, idle staff, and a cash-flow problem.

Consider Native Harvest, a project of the White Earth Land Recovery Project. Native Harvest sells food and craft items gathered, grown, and made by indigenous producers. In the case of their homemade products, such as wild rice and maple syrup, the nonprofit faces several bottlenecks between the harvest and the consumer: outdated, finicky processing equipment; a seasonal workforce; insufficient staff for packaging and shipping orders; and not enough work space to prepare and store the foods. These barriers are interrelated; they could hire more staff but don't have the physical space for them to do their jobs.

This is a recipe for a marketing headache. "If we're out there marketing," says Donna Cahill of Native Harvest, "we have to be able to produce." For example, she would like to service more wholesalers, but she's wary about meeting wholesale demand—one year, the organization ran out of wild rice.

To address the supply and demand question, you have several options:

• *Do thorough market research.* Find out everything you can about similar enterprises—even if they're located in other communities. How many customers do they have? Do they service wholesale accounts? Which months are the busiest? If they sell products, how much inventory do they keep in stock? Which marketing strategies work best? If customers order out-of-stock items, how does the business resolve that problem? Talk with your peers and learn from their successes and mistakes.

- *Test-market your products first.* Before you invest a lot of time and money to roll out a new venture, try your goods or services with a small target audience. What do they think of the product? How much they would spend to purchase it? Test-marketing will allow you to predict demand with a bit more confidence.

- *Find ways to augment the supply of popular goods and services.* Locate a back-up supply in case you run out. As discussed above, you may need to outsource some of the work to contractors you know and trust.

- *Time your marketing efforts.* Don't promote your products until you're sure you can meet the demand yourself or you've found a back-up source.

- *Don't spend money until you have to.* Try not to invest in inventory until you can measure the demand. Don't assume that bulk purchasing will save you money—if you end up with a bunch of unsold goods, you'll lose money. Test-market first.

- *Raise funds to expand your capacity.* If your demand chronically exceeds your supply, from a business perspective, that's a great problem. With proven demand, you're in a good position to raise money to enlarge your operations.

Second-stage financing

Looking back at Native Harvest, each of their barriers to expansion can be traced, in some measure, to lack of capital. They don't have enough money to buy new equipment, hire more permanent staff, or add more space. Without "second-stage financing"—in other words, funding to make a successful venture even more successful—many small businesses and nonprofit ventures cease to grow.

If you can demonstrate that demand exceeds supply—if more people want what you're offering than you can service—you can go out and raise more money. Furthermore, you'll be negotiating from a position of strength. Since you now have an established track record, lenders or investors can make decisions based on real results and not just speculation.

Arm yourself with a strong case: sales records and projections, testimonials, and a plan for increasing and managing your supply to meet the increased demand. Then prepare your financials. In dealing with any lender or investor, your financial statements are always the most important documents. There are many reasons to keep good books, and this is one of them: to expand your business, you will need to show your accounts to potential funders.

For ideas on where to find capital, see Chapter Six.

The value of modest expectations

To build your enterprise for the long haul while protecting your sanity, begin with a realistic outlook. "Understand one thing," writes Jed Emerson in *New Social Entrepreneurs*. "You are not going to end poverty in America, you are not going to create a cash cow, and you are probably not going to be able to create a utopian work environment."[1]

On the other hand, nonprofit ventures can help you move your mission, increase your independence, and engage your constituents. By selling your expertise, you'll create new opportunities to educate and activate your community. Your colleagues will appreciate the added income, too. Dreams can come true as long as you keep your expectations modest and you're willing to put in the work.

In the preceding pages, we've introduced strategies to help you elevate a successful venture to the next level of success. In Chapter Eleven, we'll look at failure: four examples of ventures that didn't work out, and what you can learn from them.

Radical Self-Defense

THE CENTER FOR ANTI-VIOLENCE EDUCATION

BROOKLYN, NEW YORK

WWW.CAE-BKLYN.ORG

ANNUAL BUDGET: $516,000

EARNED INCOME: 20%

EARNED INCOME STRATEGIES

• CONSUMER SERVICES

• TRAINING AND CONSULTING FOR NONPROFITS AND OTHER INSTITUTIONAL CUSTOMERS

In a Brooklyn dojo, where women, teenage girls, and children learn martial arts, a red line is painted on the floor. On one side, the city: raucous, competitive, and often dangerous. On the other side, the dojo: calm, cooperative, and safe. When students cross that line and enter the workout room, they are encouraged to relax and reflect, to draw strength from their inner selves and from each other. "This haven feeling," says former associate director Lucy Grugett, "is hard to find in New York."

If the dojo sounds like some sort of silent meditation zone, think again. According to Grugett, the best part of the work is "We get to yell." "Learning how to yell was an amazing experience," student Cathy Marshall told the *New York Blade News*. "They talk about taking up space with your voice. I was like, 'What?' I feel like I really found my voice."[1]

Annie Ellman and Nadia Telsey created Brooklyn Women's Martial Arts in 1974 to teach women karate for self-defense. Martial arts classes were, and remain, a means to a greater goal: teaching skills to prevent violence, providing a supportive environment for survivors of violence, and examining the social and political factors that encourage violence. In the words of Ellman, who continues to serve as executive director, "Martial arts training is an effective tool for helping women prevent, counter, and heal from the traumas of violence."

The first classes were held in day care centers, living rooms, and church basements. From the beginning, the organization charged fees to generate income. "Fee for service is central to what we do," says Grugett.

In the early 1990s, the group became The Center for Anti-Violence Education to reflect the mission better and reach a broader audience, including boys and the gay-lesbian-bisexual-transgender community. "The old name sounded too narrow," says Grugett, who worked with the organization for fifteen years. Because of their long history and name recognition, classes are still marketed under the banner of Brooklyn Women's Martial Arts.

The Center runs a number of programs:

1. *On-site classes.* These include self-defense, karate, and tai chi chuan for women; self-defense and karate for teenage girls; and the children's empowerment project for boys and girls ages six to fourteen, featuring goju karate and self-defense. Programs for teenage girls and survivors of violence are free. The women's karate class costs $35 to $85 per month. The children's program is charged on a sliding scale. "We've never turned anyone away for lack of money," Grugett says. "On the other hand, we've never had a concern about charging people who have more money." More than 100 women take the basic self-defense course each year; 150 participate in the karate and tai chi programs.

The Center operates with a strong feminist philosophy. "We're the radicals," says administrative director Brenda Jones proudly. Lesbians founded the organization, and many students, staff, and board members are lesbians, though women of any sexual orientation are welcome and many straight women participate. While the Center defined its constituency for political reasons, as opposed to marketing reasons, it has turned out to be a wise marketing decision.

Because of the quality of the classes and the safe haven aspect of the dojo, a number of students have attended for three years or more. First and second-generation customers—mothers and daughters—are beginning to take classes together. The dojo also serves as a networking hub for the lesbian community, where students share referrals on everything from gynecologists to carpenters. Some women have found life partners there. Over time, the Center for Anti-Violence Education has become an important institution for New York's substantial lesbian population. As Christine Quinn of the New York City Gay and Lesbian Anti-Violence project told the *Blade News,* "They're a tremendous resource for the community."[2]

2. *Off-site classes.* Center instructors lead self-defense and violence-prevention workshops for a variety of nonprofits, especially hospitals and colleges. During an average month, they conduct four or five courses for clients such as the Park Slope Safe Homes Project, New York Asian Women's Center, Brooklyn College, Project Reach Youth, Natural Resources Defense Council, Safe Horizon, Barnard College, and Sista to Sista. Clients pay up to $500 for a two-hour seminar, though workshops are often provided for free to small community groups such as churches and tenant organizations.

The best-paying clients are colleges, hospitals, and victim services agencies.

According to Grugett, the Center has also marketed to home health care agencies—whose mostly female staff work in the homes of strangers—and corporate offices, but without much luck. In the case of one large corporation, she says, they discovered they were inadvertently "stepping on the toes of their in-house security department," and the contract didn't pan out.

A number of other at-risk populations, including the physically and mentally disabled, could benefit from anti-violence training. The Center is considering expanding services to these groups, while also weighing issues of cost, staffing, and other resources.

3. *Youth programs.* The Center has developed a number of programs specifically for youth, including Teen Women's Initiative and the Children's Empowerment Project. Most workshops take place at the dojo, while others are offered in the community. These programs are subsidized through grants—"Youth funding is easier to raise," Grugett says—and are offered for free or on a sliding scale.

Grugett sees youth as a big arena for the organization's growth. "We've always had a commitment to kids," she says, pointing out that they offered free child care from the beginning, "but now, even more." Grugett and her colleagues are now struggling to measure their effectiveness in this area. "How do we quantify success?" she asks. "Are kids getting in fewer fights? Are they better able to reach out for support when they need it? We don't know yet."

4. *Curriculum development and train-the-trainer programs.* A few years ago, the Center created a violence-education curriculum for the national nonprofit Girls, Inc. to use in their chapters across the country. For an additional fee, the Center then trained Girls, Inc. staff to implement the curriculum.

After more than two decades of work on violence prevention, The Center for Anti-Violence Education has developed substantial knowledge and useful strategies. (In legal terms, these are known as intellectual property.) The next challenge, says Grugett, "is to replicate ourselves. These kind of [curriculum development and train-the-trainer] programs are our biggest hope for future growth."

5. *Government contracts.* The Center for Anti-Violence Education received a two-year, $130,000 contract from the New York State Department of Health under the category "Innovative Strategies to Address Violence Against Women." (As Annie Ellman wrote in the Center's newsletter, *Update,* "Amazing—a government category that recognizes us!"[3]) The state funding was used to provide free self-defense, karate, and tai chi classes to survivors of sexual assault, domestic violence, or childhood abuse and to sponsor an ongoing support group. With underwriting from foundations and the New York City government, the organization continues working with rape crisis centers and domestic violence programs throughout the city.

The Center also raises money through more traditional means, including mailings to parents of kids in the children's program. One successful approach is a "thirteenth month" fee requested from students who sign up for a year-long course. Overall, about 25 percent of their students are also donors, which is an excellent conversion rate. In 2000, the Center raised more than $100,000 from twenty-fifth anniversary events and appeals—their best year ever.

Ultimately, everyone associated with the organization would love to put an end to violence and put themselves out of business. As one supporter wrote, "The Center for Anti-Violence Education...effectively envisions and engenders a world that simply does not include violence against women and children as a given." This passionate statement is elevated by the word *effectively*—their programs work.

What's the best way to advertise? Be good at what you do.

THINGS TO THINK ABOUT

• *What types of customers do you want? Be specific.* Marketing professionals call this "niche marketing" or "segmenting your market." Because of the group's politics and interests, The Center for Anti-Violence Education has chosen to serve a multiracial community of women, especially lesbians, and children. This distinguishes their product from the many commercial dojos in the city. As Lucy Grugett points out, "Our students can't get *this* elsewhere."

As your business grows, you may have the opportunity to expand your market to reach new types of customers. You must ask yourselves the question, "Who do we want to serve?" at every stage of growth. The children's programs, for example, are designed to reach a broad cross-section of kids, so admission is balanced by age, gender, and income.

• *Word of mouth is the best source of new business.* To promote their classes, The Center for Anti-Violence Education distributes lots of flyers and sets up tables at Brooklyn street fairs. "If we haven't been doing outreach," Grugett says, "it has an effect." However, they've found that current and former students, who know and value the classes, are responsible for most new customers.

While the Center doesn't provide incentives to promote word of mouth, some businesses give "finder's fees" or discounts. Others offer free gifts or services. (Convince a friend to sign up for Working Assets phone service and you'll receive a discount on your next phone bill or a coupon for free Ben & Jerry's ice cream.) How can you use *your* relationships with customers to create new business?

Chapter 11

When bad ventures happen to good groups

■   ■   ▩

No book about commerce would be complete without a discussion of business ventures that went wrong. The vast majority of small businesses fail, and nonprofits are not immune from the usual problems: poor market research, products and services no one really wants, insufficient capital, inadequate customer service, limited funds for marketing and promotion, inflexibility, no contingency plan. Indeed, because of their orientation as non-businesses (and in some cases, anti-businesses), nonprofits are particularly prone to these troubles, plus a few others: underpricing and ambivalence.

What follows is a brief look at several organizations, including two discussed earlier in this book, whose enterprises didn't work out as planned. By most measures, these groups are extremely successful. Indeed, their ability to overcome poor business decisions or bad luck is a testament to their resiliency and the value of their programs. Even though these ventures didn't meet expectations, the following case studies can be read as success stories.

"Don't let individual setbacks inhibit your ability to take on risk," says Richard Oulahan of Esperanza Unida. "Don't look at them as failures, but as part of an important sequence of learning events."[1] Rick Ufford-Chase of BorderLinks concurs: "We've learned everything the long way by doing it wrong," he says. "We've succeeded in spite of ourselves." Given the inevitable mistakes and missteps on the road to profitability, how will you apply what you've learned? These organizations adapted and survived.

Institute for Local Self-Reliance

WASHINGTON, D.C., AND MINNEAPOLIS, MINNESOTA • WWW.ILSR.ORG

The Institute for Local Self-Reliance (ILSR), founded in 1974, has a long and distinguished history researching and promoting sustainable communities, including work on energy, food systems, and solid waste. Senator Paul Wellstone called ILSR "One of this country's leading practical thinkers in the area of sustainable economic development."

The group began in a Washington, D.C., townhouse, where they experimented with solar collectors and hydroponic gardens. For a while they financed their work by growing sprouts—alfalfa, lentil, and mung bean sprouts—in the basement and selling them to food cooperatives and grocery stores. At their peak, says co-founder and vice president David Morris, they were selling 400 pounds per week. After writing a how-to manual, they spun off the sprout business to other organizations.

Then came Kohoutek. The Kohoutek Comet, seen en route to our solar system in the mid-1970s, was all over the news. "They kept saying, 'It's going to be brighter than the moon,'" Morris remembers. "Brighter than the moon! That got our attention." Being an enterprising group, ILSR commissioned graphic artist Laura Seldman to create three T-shirt designs with the motto, "Kohoutek Cometh." They presented their designs to the Hayden Planetarium in New York; the gift shop manager took one look and ordered 500 shirts. "We flipped out," says Morris. "We thought, 'This is too easy.'"

Dazzled by the prospect of big sales, ILSR purchased 10,000 blank shirts from a wholesaler and transformed their three-story townhouse—the former sprout nursery—into an assembly plant for screening and drying T-shirts. Their design was featured in the *Washington Post*. John Belushi wore one on *Saturday Night Live*. The shirts sold out as fast as they were made. "People were lining up outside our door to buy," Morris says. Eventually, 5,000 were sold at $6 to $7 each.

"The only problem," he says, "was the damn comet."

The Kohoutek craze began in the fall, but with every passing month the comet was downgraded. By the time it actually arrived four months later, it was almost invisible to the naked eye. The astronomers had made a terrible call, the public lost interest in something they couldn't even see, and ILSR was stuck with 5,000 blank T-shirts and a bunch of silk screen equipment.

Despite the astronomical misinformation, this story has a happy ending. The leftovers were sold, at a deep discount, to a cooperative of women artists that prospered in the neighborhood for another twenty years. The shirts were put to good use and ILSR made its investment back. Having survived its adventures in commerce, the organization has grown to include two offices, eighteen staff, and an annual budget of $1.3 million.

THINGS TO THINK ABOUT

- Nature is unpredictable—just ask anyone who's had to cancel an outdoor fundraising event due to bad weather. (That's why they sell rainy day insurance.) The moon will rise on schedule, but clouds might obscure it. If your earned income strategy depends on the cooperation of the natural world, watch out. "Our enormously profitable idea," says Morris, "was based on an untrue assumption: the comet would be brighter than the moon."

- It's cheaper to buy in bulk—until you get stuck with the unsold goods. Before you buy a lot of *anything* for resale, test-market your products first.

- Think net, not gross—then factor in your time. The Institute for Local Self-Reliance grossed $25,000 to $30,000 on "Kohoutek Cometh" T-shirts. Once the cost of goods, promotion, and miscellaneous expenses were subtracted, they netted about $3 per shirt. "On a per hour basis," says Morris, "we could have made more money washing cars."

CASE EXAMPLE

Oregon Fair Share

PORTLAND, OREGON • WWW.OREGONACTION.ORG

I began my fundraising career in 1980 as a door-to-door canvasser with Oregon Fair Share in Portland. Fair Share was a statewide citizen action group working on a variety of economic and social justice issues, including utility rate reform, community reinvestment, and reducing toxic waste.

Not long after I was hired, the group opened a thrift store to diversify income. I remember lively debates about what to name the new business. The staff favored political names, such as "Lefty's Leftovers" or "What's Left?" that reflected the mission of the organization. Not wanting to scare off apolitical (or even right-wing) customers, the board choose the more neutral "Organized Thrift." The storefront served a working-class neighborhood with lots of foot traffic and a substantial Fair Share membership. A staff member managed the shop with help from a team of volunteers.

From the beginning, the project was saddled with inappropriate expectations. "When Fair Share opened its thrift store," writes Charles Cagnon, "its members believed that the business was going to cure all the organization's financial problems. Staff had to stress to the membership that this was not going to be the case."[2] In fact, the business plan projected net income of $1,000 per month, which would have provided only 5 percent of the organization's annual budget.

The business never reached that level of profitability and was closed within a year. Besides overly optimistic sales projections, the project faced a number of other obstacles. Gathering goods to sell was a never-ending job; staff and volunteers were forever calling members for hand-me-downs and sorting through cast-offs from other stores. (The manager was not above climbing into trash bins in search of saleable merchandise.) Preparing the merchandise was equally time-consuming. As Cagnon writes, "Staff members who are accustomed to being organizers find it boring to perform such tasks as ironing shirts for sale."[3] More subtly, the enterprise had no promotional plan and did little to distinguish itself from other thrift shops. Local members supported the store, but Fair Share needed to reach beyond the membership for support and never found an effective way to do so.

Despite the failure of the thrift shop, Oregon Fair Share continued its community organizing into the 1990s, when it shut down. Subsequently, a new organization—Oregon Action—was founded to build on Fair Share's history and values, and is now organizing public interest campaigns focusing on corporate responsibility.

THINGS TO THINK ABOUT

- If your enterprise is unrelated to your mission—in other words, if the sole purpose of the project is to make money—it's much harder to maintain enthusiasm over the long haul. Stick to earned income strategies that reflect your mission, programs, and values.

- Develop a promotional plan and budget money to implement it. Without regular promotion, your business will falter.

- Untrained volunteer labor can only take you so far. In the case of a retail shop with fixed hours, reliable, trained staff—either salaried or volunteer—are essential.

- Temper your big ideas with reasonable expectations, then prepare your financial projections accordingly. You may discover that your ideas create lots of work, but only a modest financial return.

Our Community Bikes

VANCOUVER, BRITISH COLUMBIA • WWW.PEDALPOWER.ORG

Our Community Bikes was founded in 1993 to promote "pedal power" for cleaner air, reduced reliance on gasoline and other fossil fuels, and a sustainable, locally based economy. As staff member Richard Andrews hastens to add, riding a bike is also a lot more fun than sitting in traffic chewing on your fingernails.

Much of their work takes place in a neighborhood storefront. Staff and volunteers assemble cycles from donated parts, fix bikes, help customers who want to do their own in-shop repairs, and lead classes on bicycle repair and commuter safety. Using spare parts and lots of ingenuity, they also create pedal-powered machines that are used overseas for a variety of tasks, such as grinding corn and coffee. A self-described "temple of the pedal," Our Community Bikes earns 100 percent of its budget from sales of goods and services.

In 1995, Better Environmentally Sound Transportation (BEST), the original sponsor organization of Our Community Bikes, opened the Main Station Bikes boutique at a regional transportation center near downtown Vancouver. Their goal was to serve bicycle commuters with emergency repairs and a range of accessories: clothing, helmets, rain gear, racks and baskets, travel bags, lights, maps, water bottles, and so forth. This second location never drew enough business to cover the costs and, after lots of tinkering, was shut down two years later.

In retrospect, says Andrews, the problems are easy to identify. First, the business plan overlooked many expenses, so the budget didn't reflect the real costs of doing business. Second, they promised the funders that the new shop would be profitable after the first year. That was unrealistic. Third, they were undercapitalized and didn't have enough money to fully stock the store and promote their goods and services. Fourth, the location didn't work for retail sales. Fifth, they were paying too much rent. Sixth, their management style was too informal. Finally, he says, they never found the right mix of products to bring in the customers they needed. "We offered lots of accessories," he says, "but no bikes."

After Main Station Bikes shut down, the former manager opened a successful commercial shop in the same district. Why did he succeed where Main Station Bikes had failed? He found a smaller, cheaper space. He affiliated with another thriving cycling business and was able to tap into an established customer base. He offered a different combination of goods and services that provided bigger profit margins. The new line included higher-priced accessories (Andrews calls this stuff "bike geek candy") and full service repairs. In the end, he reached a market that Main Station Bikes had missed.

THINGS TO THINK ABOUT

- Nonprofits often sell goods and services that nobody wants to buy. In other words, their products are chasing the market, instead of the other way around. Main Station Bikes would have benefited from better market research. One possible strategy: surveying bicycle commuters passing through the transportation center and asking what they needed.

- In any business plan (or strategic plan or grant proposal—any document that tries to predict the future), the most important piece is the budget. If the numbers don't reflect reality—in other words, if you haven't done your budgeting homework—your business is likely to fail.

- Another common problem in nonprofit ventures is undercapitalization: not having sufficient funds on hand to build the business. Remember, it takes three to five years for most small businesses to show a profit. How much money will you need to make it to profitability, and where will you find the money?

CASE EXAMPLE

The Food Bank of Western Massachusetts

HATFIELD, MASSACHUSETTS • WWW.FOODBANKWMA.ORG

The Food Bank of Western Massachusetts does what all other food banks do: collect and distribute foods and other necessities to those in need. By establishing The Food Bank Farm to grow fresh produce and underwriting that farm by selling subscriptions to local families (known as "community-supported agriculture"), they have perfected a unique strategy to provide fresh vegetables to their 420 partner agencies and the people they serve. As executive director David Sharken likes to point out, "our profit is our vegetables."

In 1991, The Food Bank began a two-year process to create and market a line of commercial foods to generate income for their programs. As the *Daily Hampshire Gazette* wrote, "First came the food bank. Then the food bank farm. Now comes the food bank product line."[4] The planning process included market research, selecting the products, identifying and contracting with suppliers, getting approval from the U.S. Food and Drug Administration, designing and manufacturing the packaging, and working with regional distributors and retailers to put the products in grocery stores. Start-up costs totaling $20,000 came from the organization's cash reserves.

The Food Bank chose to enter the consumer foods business, in part, because of long-standing relationships with distributors and grocers. These relationships paid off quickly. Several stores agreed to waive the slotting fees they typically charge to place products on their shelves.

In 1993, The Food Bank launched its first item—microwave popcorn—under the brand name Food Bank Foods. As former executive director Catherine D'Amato told *The Berkshire Eagle,* popcorn was chosen because of its popularity, long shelf life, and relatively high profit margin: $4 to $5 per case of 12 boxes.[5] As part of the initial promotion, the organization mailed free samples to all the newsrooms in the region. Not surprisingly, they got a lot of media coverage, including photos of the package. *The NonProfit Times,* a national publication, featured the project as a model nonprofit enterprise.[6]

Sales were strong at the beginning but quickly tapered off. With no advertising budget and no designated staff person—"We needed a popcorn czar," says Sharken—consumers forgot about the product. "We never answered the question, 'What do you do after the initial media hit?' You need someone to keep massaging the promotion."

Another issue was quality control. "It tasted bad," Sharken says. "It wasn't good popcorn." The scale of the venture also created problems. Given their budget and staffing limitations, The Food Bank focused on stores in western Massachusetts. Unfortunately, this regional approach didn't provide many economies of scale. With each package netting about 40 cents, the group had to sell lots and lots of popcorn to make a significant profit.

Given all these obstacles, the product never found many regular customers. After a year of poor sales, Food Bank Foods Microwave Popcorn was pulled from the stores.

Despite the problems, Sharken remains convinced that the concept has merit, especially if it could be duplicated on a larger scale. "Maybe," he muses, "through our national network, America's Second Harvest." Based on his experience with both the farm and popcorn sales, he offers smart advice for would-be entrepreneurs: whatever you sell, make sure it relates to your mission.

THINGS TO THINK ABOUT

- The goodwill you gain from your social mission will only carry you so far. Customers may give you a chance because they agree with your politics or programs, but if your product doesn't meet their needs or the quality is poor, they won't come back.

- If you're serious about earning significant income, somebody has to take responsibility for managing and promoting the business. Popcorn won't sell itself; *nothing* sells itself. Without an "enterprise advocate," your business will languish.

- Marketing never ends. Even successful brands need to keep their products in front of the public. Marketing experts suggest that you dedicate a percentage of your gross sales income—typically 7 to 12 percent—on marketing. The more you sell, the more you should spend to keep your customers coming back.

Food and Power

GEORGIA CITIZENS COALITION ON HUNGER
ATLANTA, GEORGIA
WWW.GAHUNGERCOALITION.ORG
ANNUAL BUDGET: $450,000
EARNED INCOME: 12%

EARNED INCOME STRATEGIES
- CONSUMER GOODS: RETAIL
- EMPLOYMENT TRAINING AND JOB DEVELOPMENT

"There is power in controlling your source of food," says Sandra Robertson, looking out the window of her community center in Atlanta's south end. On a formerly weedy patch of ground, the rich, reddish-brown soil has been plowed and fertilized with compost. Organic vegetables grow in neat rows: cucumbers, green beans, tomatoes, cabbage, squash, melons. Volunteers wearing big hats tend to the crops, weeding and watering and chasing away the bugs.

The Georgia Citizens Coalition on Hunger (also known as the Hunger Coalition), founded in 1974, works to end hunger, poverty, and homelessness throughout the state. The coalition includes more than 50 organizations and 750 individuals. As Robertson, the executive director, told Sara Bullard, a writer for the Ford Foundation, "We try to protect the basic rights of all citizens to adequate food, shelter, access to transportation, and child care."[1] Through advocacy, training, and community organizing, the Hunger Coalition works to ensure that low-income people have the resources, skills, and political and economic clout to achieve self-sufficiency.

In 1994, after years of advocating with government agencies to do a better job of meeting the needs of the poor, the Hunger Coalition began a visioning process with welfare recipients. Robertson remembers, "We asked ourselves, 'What would the perfect world look like?'" The answer included fresh vegetables and good clothing at affordable prices. From this seed of an idea, they launched the Umoja Thrift Store and Indoor Farmer's Market. *Umoja*, in Swahili, means "unity."

Their building, adjacent to a high school, covers 15,000 square feet, roomier than many grocery stores. The property includes five acres of usable land. Thanks to the generosity of the owner, the Community Foundation of Greater Atlanta, they have "an indefinite lease at $1 per year," says Robertson. Renovations cost $250,000; 60 percent was covered by the foundation, other contributors, and donations of labor and materials. Interestingly, the facilitator who led the visioning process located the building. "We just started talking about it," Robertson says, "and it happened."

Of course, life is never that simple. Once the site was secured, the Hunger Coalition launched an ambitious plan to create new jobs for low-income neighbors, provide food and clothing for the community, and eventually earn enough income to cover their costs. A market study commissioned by the coalition identified only forty-four businesses within a two-mile radius. Only half sold any sort of food, and most of these were convenience stores and gas stations. Given the limited competition, the market appeared wide open.

Oxfam America, an international hunger relief organization, provided an initial grant of $60,000 to cover planning and start-up costs. Umoja opened in 1996 with a big celebration. Then things went downhill fast. Thanks to over-optimistic sales projections and undercapitalization—not enough start-up money—the Hunger Coalition was forced to lay off employees within six months. Faced with the crisis, staff and board pulled together, raised more money, refined the business plan, delayed some projects, and worked harder at promotion. Several staff members filed for unemployment insurance, looked for other jobs, and managed the store in their spare time. All but one stayed on to volunteer until the cash flow improved.

When asked about the secret to their survival, Sandra Robertson laughs. "We prayed a lot," she says, citing daily prayer sessions led by the volunteers. "We came through stronger and more determined. All businesses have to endure times like that." Hubert Sapp, a former program officer at Oxfam, concurs. "They've learned lesson after lesson. It's been an ongoing laboratory."

The thrift store carries a typical collection of second-hand clothing and household goods, plus hair care products and an assortment of African crafts. Snack foods—pizza, popcorn, and candy—are also available. During a recent visit, the farmer's market, which occupies a portion of the same big hall, offered a wide range of produce, including potatoes, green beans, corn, cabbage, chilies, eggplant, kiwis, cantaloupes, onions, tomatoes, collard greens, grapes, pineapples, lemons, nectarines, plums, and strawberries. Some crops are raised in the garden, others are purchased from local farmers, and the remainder are bought from a wholesaler.

Buying and selling vegetables, says Robertson, is not for the faint of heart. "The first year, we didn't have a clue" about quantities and pricing. "Snap beans went from $10 a bushel to $30 in a week. You learn about the peaks and valleys."

One reason for planting a market garden, she says, was to even out the costs and pass those savings on to the customers.

On most items, the Umoja Indoor Farmer's Market can underprice Atlanta grocery stores by 10 to 50 percent. Every Saturday, prices are reduced even further to move these perishable foods. When asked about undercutting other stores, she says, "Look at our volume. We're not a threat to anyone's business." Indeed, other retailers occasionally use Umoja as a supplier by buying at the Farmer's Market, marking up the price, and reselling the produce. Sales for thrift store and grocery items total $100 to $150 per day—well below daily expenses of $300—so the Hunger Coalition still has a way to go before this project breaks even.

The Umoja Thrift Store and Farmer's Market is set back from the street, down a long driveway behind the high school. The casual shopper will not find it easily, which presents a marketing challenge. "A lot of people don't know we're here," Robertson says. Given her limited budget, promotional options have included flyers, news articles, word of mouth, and a small sign on the street. New marketing strategies include newspaper ads, radio, and possibly television. "We're building these costs into the budget," she says, "because we have to do it. Without advertising, we can't grow." Staff is also working with the immediate neighbors—the school—to sell fruit and snacks to the students.

Working with several public agencies, the Hunger Coalition also organizes a series of outdoor farmer's markets in Atlanta's public housing communities. These outdoor markets address two problems simultaneously through what Sapp,

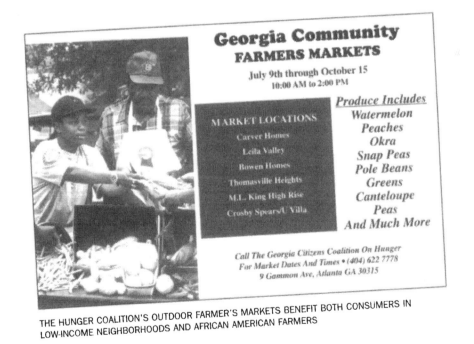

THE HUNGER COALITION'S OUTDOOR FARMER'S MARKETS BENEFIT BOTH CONSUMERS IN LOW-INCOME NEIGHBORHOODS AND AFRICAN AMERICAN FARMERS

formerly of Oxfam, calls "a two-way win that helps both sides of the equation." First, consumers in low-income neighborhoods often pay higher prices for poor quality food. By purchasing directly from the growers, residents get fresh produce at a much lower cost. Second, African American farmers "have always had a difficult time economically," says Jerry Pennick of the Federation of Southern Cooperatives. As he told the *Atlanta Journal/Atlanta Constitution*, "They have not had equal access to credit or markets. For the farmers, [this program] provides a reliable market."[2] By selling directly to consumers, growers get a better price for their vegetables, which helps them pay their bills, hang on to their land, and keep farming.

For the Hunger Coalition, these earned income strategies are simply a means to an end: community empowerment and self-sufficiency. "We as black farmers have to take a hold of what's important to us," Jerry Fields told the *Journal/Constitution*. "And that's our people."[3] Sandra Robertson puts it this way: "We're creating community pride," she says, "and you can't measure that in dollars and cents."

THINGS TO THINK ABOUT

• *If you can't handle the risk, don't go into business.* Despite their best efforts, the Georgia Citizens Coalition on Hunger almost shut down the Umoja Thrift Store and Indoor Farmer's Market due to slow sales. Like many novices, their staff overestimated income and underestimated costs. (At least three out of four small businesses fail—now you know one of the main reasons this happens.) Through diligence and persistence, and an ongoing subsidy provided by grants and donations, they were able to keep the doors open and develop the business. With increased advertising, they expect to break even by the end of 2002. However, the lesson is clear: don't risk a major earned income project if you can't afford to lose money.

• *Before you launch, make sure you have enough funding to tide you over until you're profitable.* Nearly all nonprofit ventures are undercapitalized, and many promising projects are abandoned for lack of operating money.

• *If you don't promote your goods or services, no one will buy them.* When calculating the costs of launching and running your venture, include realistic line items for advertising and other promotional strategies.

• *Location, location, location.* Because of its off-the-street location, the Hunger Coalition has a hard time drawing customers to the thrift store and farmer's market. One solution: bring the food to the customers. Since their mission is to empower low-income Atlanta residents, they've established seasonal farmer's markets in several public housing communities across the city. These popular events benefit both the farmers, who get a fair price for their crops, and consumers, who can buy food at a substantial discount. Price plus convenience equals sales.

• *Time-sensitive merchandise must be priced to sell.* Nobody wants rotten vegetables, so once a week, the Umoja Indoor Farmer's Market reduces prices by 50 percent. Because they sell produce below cost on "discount day," they lose money on some items, but at least they're generating income instead of compost. If you offer time-sensitive goods or services, the longer you wait, the less they're worth. You can't sell moldy fruit, a sweater is less valuable in the summer than in the winter, and a ticket to last night's concert is worth absolutely nothing today. Adjust your prices accordingly.

Chapter 12

Lessons learned along the way

If you've made it this far, you've already learned how to brainstorm, select, plan, finance, launch, market, and manage your new venture. It's a lot to learn! In case you're feeling overwhelmed (or if you're just flipping through the book, looking for the good parts), here's a summary of the common wisdom. These "top tips" are drawn from the experience of the nonprofit entrepreneurs profiled in this book.

Top tips for earned income

Mission first

Lead with your mission... Nonprofit managers and activists often worry that their social goals will be corrupted through the practice of commerce. They fear that the "money tail" will start wagging the "mission dog," and are afraid to risk the quality of their work or their reputations in pursuit of cash.

This legitimate concern is easily addressed by putting your mission first. If a prospective venture doesn't fit your values, don't do it. Furthermore, if no one is passionate about the project—passionate means really, really enthusiastic—don't do it. Without energy and commitment, even the most lucrative ideas will fail. Successful ventures are all about love, not money.

...But don't forget your customers. Many nonprofits assume that the value of their cause—the rightness of their mission—will somehow compensate for mediocre quality or service. The goodwill created by your work might bring people through your door the first time, but if your service stinks, your products are of poor quality, or your customers' needs are not met, they won't be back. Honor your mission by taking care of your customers.

Mobilize the right team

Recruit board members who understand enterprise. A resistant or uneducated board can sink your earned income project. Look for people with relevant business experience who also love your mission. While corporate contacts may prove helpful, don't forget self-employed businesspeople, including artists and other cultural workers.

Put the right people in charge, then give them the time, space, and money to do their jobs. For starters, you'll need an "enterprise advocate" with primary responsibility for managing the venture. Hire someone with relevant business skills, or provide training for the passionate but inexperienced. Don't meddle—leave business decisions to the folks who operate the business. Give them the freedom to experiment and occasionally fail.

To paraphrase David Sharken of The Food Bank of Western Massachusetts, some of us are good at creating new projects, while others excel at maintaining long-time initiatives. To create an entrepreneurial organization, your personnel policies must be flexible enough to honor and accommodate both the entrepreneurs and the maintainers.

Managing a business could interfere with your salary scale, since people with business expertise tend to receive better compensation than community organizers or social service providers. To solve this problem, get creative. Perhaps you can put your venture manager on contract for the first year, or pay her through a salary-plus-bonus arrangement. If the venture succeeds, you might generate enough revenue to raise *everyone's* pay.

The value of planning

Write a plan, then use it. I'm not convinced that every nonprofit venture requires an official, by-the-numbers business plan. It's a matter of scale—the larger the venture, the more detailed the plan. At the very least, however, you'll need an informal planning document that describes the purpose of the business, a profile of your customers, how you plan to reach and service them, how you'll manage the project, and how the finances will play out. This plan becomes your guide for raising money, managing the enterprise, serving your customers, and evaluating your success.

Take control of your finances. In any planning document, especially a business plan, the most important component is the budget. If the numbers don't reflect reality, your venture is likely to fail.

- Do your projections. A detailed cash flow analysis can help you figure out when to spend money, when to save it, and when you'll need an outside subsidy, such as a grant or a loan. At Native Seeds/SEARCH, holiday shoppers provide half the annual sales income in the final quarter of the year. As a result, the group has learned to build up the bank balance in the winter and reduce expenses during the summer.

- Determine how much start-up money you will you need. Where will it come from? Once again, caution is advised. Nearly all nonprofit ventures are undercapitalized, and many promising ideas fail for lack of ready cash. If you can't find a way to adequately finance the venture, don't do it.

- Keep track of the numbers, month by month. If you don't know how much money you're earning and spending—the difference is your profit or loss— you can't evaluate and adjust your pricing, marketing strategy, staffing, and so forth. Review the numbers monthly.

Know your strengths, know your market

Define your niche. What makes your work unique? What can you do that no one else can do? Do you have special access to a specific market? What qualities set your organization apart, and how will those qualities be reflected in your goods and services?

You cannot do everything for everyone. The more you specialize—focus on one or two things, and do them exceptionally well—the better your odds for success. Just be sure that the marketplace wants (even better, demands) your specialized products.

Do your market research. In the world of social change enterprise, perhaps the most common problems arise from "products chasing the market" instead of the other way around. Before launching a venture, do your homework.

Don't underprice your work. Nonprofit organizations have a bad habit of undervaluing their work by either giving it away or assuming that everyone else is as broke as their staff members. These are two fatal mistakes. "When clients don't blink," says Dianne Russell of the Institute for Conservation Leadership, "I wonder, are we charging enough?" The answer: probably not.

Any successful earned income program must begin with the assumption that customers will pay a high enough price to cover your costs and generate a profit. Use market research to determine "what the market will bear." If that price won't net enough money to make it worth the trouble—*think net income, not gross income,* and factor in your time—pick another venture. As an alternative, look for third party payers (foundations, corporations, or donors) who can subsidize the difference.

To develop new products and reach new customers, repackage your expertise. Repackaging can take several forms. One option is to cluster current services or products and sell them as a set. For example, individual nonprofit management workshops can be combined into a workshop series. Another option is to take the content from one format (a workshop), re-create it in a different format (book, video, "toolkit"), and offer it to the same customers. A third option is to repackage the same content in a different format to reach new customers (workshop in a second language, workshop geared to a specific profession or population).

The trick is to look at what you know and what you do, determine all the audiences that could benefit from your expertise, conduct market research, and package your knowledge to best meet their needs.

Sell to businesses, nonprofits, the government—think retail last. The majority of commerce is conducted among businesses and institutions—*not* by selling to individual consumers. Your best audience may be other nonprofits, businesses, or government agencies. As customers, they're more reliable and predictable. They budget purchases in advance and tend to buy in larger quantities.

Think creatively about how you can serve institutional customers. The Resource Center of the Americas provides Spanish lessons and cultural awareness programs to judges and the metropolitan newspaper, while Our Community Bikes offers on-site bicycle commuter classes for local corporations and government agencies.

Promotional savvy

Create a unified look to help "brand" your organization and your venture. Your "look" is a big part of your identity, so plan to invest some time and money. At least one group profiled here devotes a quarter-time staff position to graphic design. As a result, their promotional materials are clear, consistent, and attractive. As an alternative, hire a professional designer whom you admire and trust. Once you've found design elements that work, stick with them.

Use multiple strategies to market your goods and services. Novice entrepreneurs rarely budget enough time, money, or attention to marketing. Successful promotion is based on *variety* and *repetition*: employing several approaches simultaneously, and using them over and over. Marketing never ends.

The most effective marketing strategy is a happy customer. When it comes to sales promotion, nothing beats word of mouth: a referral from a satisfied client. The first and most important step in any marketing program is customer satisfaction. To boost word of mouth, consider incentives for people who tell their friends: for example, a gift or a "finder's discount." Ask your best customers for testimonials, then use them in your marketing materials.

Good media mean good marketing. The organizations featured in this book all manage successful earned income programs and—not coincidentally—they also get great news coverage. The commercial media influence many more prospects than grassroots groups can ever reach with their modest promotional budgets. Furthermore, a good news story (even a bad news story) confers an air of legitimacy.

The lesson: look for the news handles in your work. Cultivate local reporters and editors. Make the news.

To build your business, build business relationships

Work with your competitors to expand the market. If the idea of competition makes you uncomfortable, here's an antidote: turn your competitors into your allies. Work with them on joint marketing programs that build awareness of your good and services.

Choose business partners who share your values. Apply this litmus test to both the businesses you patronize and any potential corporate marketing agreements. When you buy goods and services, for instance, use union vendors whenever possible. If you're considering cause-related marketing, examine your prospective partner's policies on health and safety, workplace organizing, environmental impact, and so on.

Consider the partnership between Grassroots Leadership and Rounder Records; they jointly produced three music and storytelling CDs. The record label was created to celebrate traditional folk music from around the world. "We've always had a sense of mission," says co-founder Bill Nowlin of Rounder, and that mission dovetails nicely with the work of the nonprofit. Of course, it helps that Si Kahn, executive director of Grassroots Leadership, and former board member John McCutcheon are both musicians who have long-standing business relationships with Rounder. They built those relationships, in large part, because the company mirrored their personal and professional values.

The same can be said of booking agent Josh Dunson of Real People's Music, who has represented Kahn since 1981. "I come from a community organizing background," he says. "My family was active in the labor movement, so I feel a real kinship with Si." These relationships endure because the people involved share deeply held personal beliefs, and because everyone does their work with competence and respect.

The cash register is the voting booth

While earned income strategies are loaded with risk—the potential for dissension, financial losses, erosion of your social mission—they also offer great rewards. With diligence and imagination, you can develop new ways to involve your members, promote your issues, educate the public about your work—and increase your budget. There are endless opportunities to combine sales with activism.

"The cash register," Paul Hawken has written, "is the daily voting booth in democratic capitalism."[1] When we enter the marketplace as nonprofits—our missions and passions and anger and hope held before us like shields—we acknowledge this reality, like it or not. Rather than being defensive, we can take our cue from Hawken: "Business offers us rich and important ways to improve the world. Every transaction in the scheme of things is small, incremental, seemingly inconsequential, but each moment has the potential to create real change."[2]

Notes

Chapter One

1. War Resisters League, www.warresisters.org, July 2, 2001.

2. United for a Fair Economy, www.ufenet.org, Dec. 31, 2000.

3. G. Aeschliman, "Saving the Earth, Saving Our Souls," *Enough!* (Center for a New American Dream), Winter 2000–2001, p. 11.

4. P. Hawken, *The Ecology of Commerce* (New York: HarperCollins, 1993), p. 76.

5. R. Steckel, *Filthy Rich: How to Turn Your Nonprofit Fantasies into Cold, Hard Cash* (Berkeley: Ten Speed Press, 2000), p. 14.

6. J. Emerson and F. Twersky (eds.), *New Social Entrepreneurs: The Success, Challenge, and Lessons of Non-Profit Enterprise Creation* (San Francisco: Roberts Foundation, 1996), p. 417.

7. Steckel, *Filthy Rich*, p. 15.

8. Hawken, *Ecology of Commerce*, p. 1.

9. Esperanza Unida, *Replication Manual* (Milwaukee: Esperanza Unida, 1999), p. 9.

Bad Jokes, Great Service: Our Community Bikes

1. A. Sullivan, "Recycled Cycles Spin Big Profits," *Vancouver Courier,* Oct. 26, 1997, p. 15.

2. Sullivan, "Recycled Cycles," p. 15.

3. R. Andrews, "Laughing Children and Fat Chickens: Our Community Bikes in Guatemala!" *Spoke 'n' Word* (Better Environmentally Sound Transportation), Spring–Summer 1998, p. 21.

4. The M. K. Gandhi Institute for Nonviolence, www.gandhiinstitute.org, Jan. 21, 2002.

Chapter Two

1. C. Cagnon, *Business Ventures of Citizen Groups* (Helena, Mont.: Northern Rockies Action Group, 1982), p. 2.

2. J. Flanagan, *Successful Fundraising* (Chicago: Contemporary Books, 2000), p. 54.

3. Flanagan, *Successful Fundraising,* p. 55.

4. J. Flanagan, "Generating Income from Customers and Clients," *Grantsmanship Center Magazine,* Summer 1999, p. 25.

5. Theatre Communications Group, www.tcg.org, July 2, 2001.

6. E. Skloot, "The Growth of and Rationale for Nonprofit Enterprise," in E. Skloot (ed.), *The Nonprofit Entrepreneur: Creating Ventures to Earn Income* (New York: Foundation Center, 1988), p. 3.

7. Flanagan, *Successful Fundraising,* p. 49.

8. L. Davis and N. Etchart (eds.), *The NGO Venture Forum: Profits for Nonprofits* (Santiago, Chile: NESsT, 1999), p. 32.

9. Quoted in B. Shore, *Revolution of the Heart: A New Strategy for Creating Wealth and Meaningful Change* (New York: Riverhead Books, 1995), p. 93.

10. National Center for Social Entrepreneurs, www.socialentrepreneurs.org, July 13, 2000.

11. Cagnon, *Business Ventures,* p. 23.

12. J. L. Fix and N. Lewis, "Growth in Giving Cools Down," *Chronicle of Philanthropy,* May 31, 2001, p. 29.

13. H. Sternberg, "Internet Resources for Grants and Foundations," *C&RL NewsNet* (American Library Association), May 1997.

14. J. Emerson and F. Twersky (eds.), *New Social Entrepreneurs: The Success, Challenge, and Lessons of Non-Profit Enterprise Creation* (San Francisco: Roberts Foundation, 1996), p. 14.

15. Flanagan, *Successful Fundraising,* p. 47.

16. For a different angle on nonprofits, earned income, and continuums— their version is called the "social enterprise spectrum"—see J.G. Dees, J. Emerson, and P. Economy (eds.), *Enterprising Nonprofits: A Toolkit for Social Entrepreneurs* (New York: Wiley, 2001), p. 15.

17. "No Good Deed Goes Unpunished," *Board Member* (National Center for Nonprofit Boards), June 1998, p. 6.

Flavors of the Desert: Native Seeds/SEARCH

1. A. E. Nevala, "In the Southwest, a New Plant Reserve Protects the Mother of All Chilis," *National Wildlife,* Feb.–Mar. 2000, p. 14.

Chapter Three

1. B. Shore, *Revolution of the Heart: A New Strategy for Creating Wealth and Meaningful Change* (New York: Riverhead Books, 1995), p. 67.

2. W. A. Duncan, *Looking at Income-Generating Businesses for Small Nonprofit Organizations* (Washington, D.C.: Center for Community Change, 1982), p. 8.

3. R. Steckel, *Filthy Rich: How to Turn Your Nonprofit Fantasies into Cold, Hard Cash* (Berkeley, Calif.: Ten Speed Press, 2000), p. 209.

4. Esperanza Unida, *Replication Manual* (Milwaukee: Esperanza Unida, 1999), p. 63.

5. L. Rocawich, "The Progressive Interview: Si Kahn," *The Progressive,* Apr. 1994, p. 29.

6. N. Haycock, "Stepping Out in the Marketplace: The Pitfalls of Earned Income for the Small Nonprofit," in E. Skloot (ed.), *The Nonprofit Entrepreneur: Creating Ventures to Earn Income* (New York: Foundation Center, 1988), p. 148.

Capitalism with a Conscience: Global Exchange

1. M. L. LaGanga, "Traveling with a Moral Compass," *Los Angeles Times,* June 23, 1997, p. 21.

2. B. Strubbe, "Reality Trek," *Orange Coast,* Sept. 1997, p. 62.

3. Strubbe, "Reality Trek," p. 63.

4. Global Exchange, www. globalexchange.org, Sept. 29, 1999.

5. LaGanga, "Traveling with a Moral Compass," p. 21.

6. LaGanga, "Traveling with a Moral Compass," p. 21.

Chapter Four

1. The brainstorming and evaluation process presented here has been freely adapted, with permission, from R. Steckel, *Filthy Rich: How to Turn Your Nonprofit Fantasies into Cold, Hard Cash* (Berkeley: Ten Speed Press, 2000).

2. J. Emerson and F. Twersky (eds.), *New Social Entrepreneurs: The Success, Challenge, and Lessons of Non-Profit Enterprise Creation* (San Francisco: Roberts Foundation, 1996), p. 398.

3. J. Kitzi, "Recognizing and Assessing New Opportunities," in J. G. Dees, J. Emerson, and P. Economy (eds.), *Enterprising Nonprofits: A Toolkit for Social Entrepreneurs* (New York: Wiley, 2001), p. 51.

4. W. A. Duncan, *Looking at Income-Generating Businesses for Small Nonprofit Organizations* (Washington, D.C.: Center for Community Change, 1982), p. 5.

5. E. Skloot, "The Venture Planning Process," in E. Skloot (ed.), *The Nonprofit Entrepreneur: Creating Ventures to Earn Income* (New York: Foundation Center, 1988), p. 39.

6. J. C. Levinson, *Guerrilla Marketing: Secrets for Making Big Profits from Your Small Business,* 3rd ed. (Boston: Houghton Mifflin, 1998), p. 31.

7. E. Arrick and M. Virtue/African American and Latino Art Museum Working Group, *The Earned Revenue Handbook: A Guide for Museums with Culturally Defined Collections* (West Chester, Pa.: Cornerstone Consultants, 1997), pp. 13–14.

8. C. Cagnon, *Business Ventures of Citizen Groups* (Helena, Mont.: Northern Rockies Action Group, 1982), p. 27.

9. L. Pinson and J. Jinnett, *Anatomy of a Business Plan* (Chicago: Dearborn, 1999), pp. 49–50.

10. M. Virtue and J. Delgado/African American and Latino Art Museum Working Group, *The Museum Shop Workbook* (West Chester, Pa.: Cornerstone Consultants, 1996), p. 11.

11. Speech to the Georgia Center for Nonprofits, Atlanta, Ga., June 18, 1998.

Chapter Five

1. C. Massarsky, "Business Planning for the Nonprofit Enterprise" in E. Skloot (ed.), *The Nonprofit Entrepreneur: Creating Ventures to Earn Income* (New York: Foundation Center, 1988), p. 73.

2. Massarsky, "Business Planning," p. 74.

3. W. A. Duncan, *Looking at Income-Generating Businesses for Small Nonprofit Organizations* (Washington, D.C.: Center for Community Change, 1982), p. 13.

4. L. Pinson and J. Jinnett, *Anatomy of a Business Plan* (Chicago: Dearborn, 1999), pp. 15–16.

5. Pinson and Jinnett, *Anatomy of a Business Plan,* p. 8.

6. W. LaDuke, "The Wild Rice Moon," *Whole Earth,* Winter 1999, pp. 78–79.

How to Build a Working Neighborhood: Esperanza Unida

1. J. Dresang, "Esperanza Unida Gives Former Welfare Mom a Lift," *Milwaukee Journal Sentinel,* Sept. 25, 1997.

2. Esperanza Unida, *Replication Manual* (Milwaukee: Esperanza Unida, 1999), pp. 31–32.

3. P. Nero, "Getting It Together," *Milwaukee Journal,* Oct. 16, 1994.

4. Quoted in Esperanza Unida, *Community and Funders Report* (Milwaukee: Esperanza Unida, 1998), p. 2.

5. Esperanza Unida, *Replication Manual,* p. 9.

6. Esperanza Unida, *Replication Manual,* p. 28.

7. J. V. Cano, "Agency's Training Programs Have Helped Community," *Milwaukee Sentinel.*

8. www.grass-roots.org, July 12, 2000.

9. K. M. Knapcik, "Class Imparts Confidence in Job Seekers," *Milwaukee Journal Sentinel.*

10. C. Newman, "Book Learning," *Business Journal,* Apr. 2, 1999, p. 11.

11. Esperanza Unida, *Replication Manual,* p. 25.

12. Esperanza Unida, *Replication Manual,* p. 36.

Chapter Six

1. W. A. Duncan, *Looking at Income-Generating Businesses for Small Nonprofit Organizations* (Washington, D.C.: Center for Community Change, 1982), pp. 6–7.

2. E. Skloot, "How to Think About Enterprise," in E. Skloot (ed.), *The Nonprofit Entrepreneur: Creating Ventures to Earn Income* (New York: Foundation Center, 1988), p. 35.

3. E. Arrick, "Financing the Enterprise," in Skloot (ed.), *Nonprofit Entrepreneur,* p. 107.

4. Duncan, *Looking at Income-Generating Businesses,* p. 14.

5. Esperanza Unida, *Replication Manual* (Milwaukee: Esperanza Unida, 1999), p. 60.

6. R. Steckel, *Filthy Rich: How to Turn Your Nonprofit Fantasies into Cold, Hard Cash* (Berkeley: Ten Speed Press, 2000), p. 145.

7. *Philanthropy News Digest* (Foundation Center), Apr. 17, 2001.

8. E. Arrick, "Financing the Enterprise," p. 97.

Reclaiming History/Reclame La Historia: SouthWest Organizing Project

1. E. Arrick and M. Virtue/African American and Latino Art Museum Working Group, *The Earned Revenue Handbook: A Guide for Museums with Culturally Defined Collections* (West Chester, Pa.: Cornerstone Consultants, 1997), p. 13.

2. P. Gonzales and R. Rodriguez, "Chicano History Book Banned in Vaughn," *Voces Unidas* (Southwest Organizing Project), Apr. 1997, p. 19.

Chapter Seven

1. "Six Interruptions Every Hour," *Fast Company,* Mar. 2000, p. 218.

2. J. C. Levinson, *Guerrilla Marketing Attack: Strategies, Tactics, and Weapons for Winning Big Profits for Your Small Business* (Boston: Houghton Mifflin, 1989), pp. 17–18.

3. G. J. Stern, *Marketing Workbook for Nonprofit Organizations,* 2nd ed. (St. Paul, Minn.: Amherst H. Wilder Foundation, 2001), p. 7.

Crossing Borders: Borderlinks

1. R. Ufford-Chase, "Glimpsing the Future: Why Christians Must Resist the Global Economy," *The Other Side,* Jan.–Feb. 1997, pp. 13–14.

2. Ufford-Chase, "Glimpsing the Future," p. 14.

3. R. D. Kaplan, "Travels into America's Future: Mexico and the Southwest." *Atlantic Monthly,* July 1998, p. 52.

4. BorderLinks, www.borderlinks.org, July 15, 2000.

5. Y. Chlala, "Bienvenidos a La Frontera: Building Bridges at the U.S.–Mexico Border," brochure, Amnesty International USA.

Off the Streets, Into the Kitchen: FareStart

1. S. Phinney, "Food Talk: Cheryl Sesnon, FareStart Director," *Seattle Post-Intelligencer,* Nov. 4, 1998, p. C1.

2. G. L. Oberst, "From Homelessness to Hope," *Restaurant Hospitality,* Apr. 1998, p. 31.

"Our Profit Is Our Vegetables": The Food Bank of Western Massachusetts

1. B. J. Roche, "Feeding New Englanders, and the Needy Too," *Boston Globe,* Aug. 20, 1995, p. 47.

2. P. Dunphy, "Food for All," *Harrowsmith Country Life,* June 1994, p. 38.

Chapter Ten

1. J. Emerson and F. Twersky (eds.), *New Social Entrepreneurs: The Success, Challenge, and Lessons of Non-Profit Enterprise Creation* (San Francisco: Roberts Foundation, 1996), p. 416.

Radical Self-Defense: The Center for Anti-Violence Education

1. A. Askowitz, "The Good Fight," *New York Blade News,* Apr. 24, 1998, p. 1.

2. Askowitz, "Good Fight," p. 8.

3. A. Ellman, "From Executive Director Annie Ellman," *Update* (Center for Anti-Violence Education), Spring 1998, p. 1.

Chapter Eleven

1. Esperanza Unida, *Replication Manual* (Milwaukee: Esperanza Unida, 1999), p. 17.

2. C. Cagnon, *Business Ventures of Citizen Groups* (Helena, Mont.: Northern Rockies Action Group, 1982), p. 46.

3. Cagnon, *Business Ventures,* p. 46.

4. S. Pfarrer, "Popcorn with a Purpose," *Daily Hampshire Gazette,* July 2, 1993, p. 1.

5. M. J. Tichenor, "Food Bank Popcorn to Boost Program for the Needy," *Berkshire Eagle,* July 2, 1993.

6. C. Massarsky, "Food for Thought—and Profit," *NonProfit Times,* Mar. 1994.

Food and Power: Georgia Citizens Coalition on Hunger

1. S. Bullard, "United States: A Coalition Is Helping Americans Understand Human Rights and Deepen Their Commitment to the Struggle," *Ford Foundation Report,* Fall 1998, p. 26.

2. M. R. Williams, "From Rural Fields to Urban Tables," *Atlanta Journal/Atlanta Constitution,* July 31, 1997, p. 3.

3. J. Blake, "Farmers' Market in Housing Projects Makes Connection That Feeds Body, Soul," *Atlanta Journal/Atlanta Constitution,* Sept. 14, 1996.

Chapter Twelve

1. P. Hawken, *The Ecology of Commerce* (New York: HarperCollins, 1993), p. 213.

2. Hawken, *Ecology of Commerce,* p. 136.

Resources

⬛ ⬛ ⬛ ⬛ ⬛ ⬛ ⬛ ⬛ ⬛ ⬛ ⬛ ⬛ ⬛ ⬛ ⬛ ⬛

Business planning

Anatomy of a Business Plan, 4th ed., Linda Pinson and Jerry Jinnett, 1999. 274 pages. $21.95. Dearborn, 155 North Wacker Drive, Chicago, IL 60606–1719. 312/836–4400, www.dearborn.com.

> *Written in simple, straightforward language, this book features a thorough section on preparing financials. Includes two complete business plans.*

Business Plan Pro 2002, $99.95. PaloAlto.com, 144 East Fourteenth Street, Eugene, OR 97401. 888/PLANPRO, www.paloalto.com.

> *The best-selling software for creating business plans. Includes financial planning templates and 200 sample plans. An affiliated Web site, with lots of business planning information, is www.bplans.com.*

The Business Road Map to Success, www.sba.gov/starting/indexbusplans.html.

> *This self-paced outline and tutorial from the Small Business Administration will help you create a business plan.*

Business Planning (for nonprofits or for-profits), www.mapnp.org/library/plan_dec/bus_plan/bus_plan.htm.

> *This Web site, assembled by consultant Carter McNamara, includes dozens of links to business planning information.*

Business and marketing plans, www.morebusiness.com/templates_worksheets/bplans/

> *Links to even more sample plans.*

How to Write a Business Plan, 5th ed., Mike McKeever, 1999. 256 pages. $29.95. Nolo Press, 950 Parker Street, Berkeley, CA 94710. 800/992–6656, www.nolo.com.

> *An easy-to-follow, step-by-step guide to business planning, with forms and samples.*

Kauffman Center for Entrepreneurial Leadership, Ewing Marion Kauffman Foundation, www.entreworld.com.

This Web site is a good resource for developing and managing a business.

The Museum Shop Workbook, Mary Virtue and Jane Delgado/The African American and Latino Art Museum Working Group, 1995. 28 pages. $15. Cornerstone Consultants, 1236 Waterford Road, West Chester, PA 19380. 610/696-8149, www.cornerstoneconsultantspa.com

A simple, clear, concise guide to creating and managing a store. Includes a great summary of how to create financial projections, with easy-to-use worksheets.

Preparing a Business Plan, www.ctcnet.org/ch9.htm.

The Community Technology Center Network, which hosts this Web site, is a consortium of 500 independent technology centers where people get free or low-cost computer access. The chapter posted on this Web page is excerpted from their start-up manual for new centers.

Commerce, capitalism, and business ethics

Business Ethics, P.O. Box 8439, Minneapolis, MN 55408. 612/879–0695, www.business-ethics.com.

This magazine promotes and explores ethical business practices as they relate to environmental protection, worker rights, corporate responsibility, "wealth discrimination, the unearned privileges of the financial elite," and other issues. Free e-mail newsletter.

Business for Social Responsibility, 609 Mission Street, 2nd Floor, San Francisco, CA 94105. 415/537–0888, www.bsr.org.

BSR is a membership organization for businesses seeking to demonstrate respect for ethical values, people, communities, and the environment. Their sister organization, Canadian Business for Social Responsibility, can be reached at 620-220 Cambie Street #121, Vancouver BC V6B 2M9. 604/323–2714, www.cbsr.bc.ca.

Growing a Business, Paul Hawken, 1987. 251 pages. $12. Simon & Schuster, 1230 Avenue of the Americas, New York, NY 10020. www.simonsays.com.

The Ecology of Commerce: A Declaration of Sustainability, Paul Hawken, 1993. 272 pages. $13. HarperCollins, 10 East Fifty-Third Street, New York, NY 10022. 212/207-7000, www.harpercollins.com.

If you're concerned about how commerce might corrupt your organization or skew its mission, these books by Paul Hawken provide a useful perspective on the relationship between business and social change.

Funding, loans

Environmental Support Center, 1500 Massachusetts Avenue, N.W., Suite 25, Washington, DC 20005. 202/331–9700, www.envsc.org.

> *The mission of the Environmental Loan Fund, managed by ESC, is to stabilize, increase, and diversify the long-term funding base of environmental organizations by providing working capital for fundraising and earned income projects.*

Independent Press Association, 2729 Mission Street, Suite 201, San Francisco, CA 94110. 877/INDYMAG, www.indypress.org.

> *IPA, which calls itself "the antidote to monopoly media," manages a revolving loan fund. The fund provides up to $30,000 to member publications only (nonprofit and for-profit) to expand marketing efforts. Small grants are also available for business planning.*

National Community Capital Association, 620 Chestnut Street, Suite 572, Philadelphia PA 19106. 215/923–4754, www.communitycapital.org.

> *NCCA, whose motto is "capital for economic, social, and political justice," is the national umbrella organization for community development loan funds and other social lenders. They can put you in touch with lenders in your region.*

The PRI Directory: Charitable Loans and Other Program Related Investments by Foundations, 2001. 155 pages. $75. New York: The Foundation Center. 800/424–9836, www.fdncenter.org.

> *This directory lists nearly 200 foundations that provide loans, sometimes known as program-related investments. In a recent year, half of their loan funds went to capital projects: building construction, renovation, land purchase, and equipment.*

International organizations

Ashoka: Innovators for the Public, 1700 North Moore Street, Suite 2000, Arlington, VA 22209. 703/527–8300, www.ashoka.org.

> *For more than 20 years, Ashoka has promoted social entrepreneurship as a strategy for tackling social, economic, and environmental problems around the world, especially in developing countries.*

Nonprofit Enterprise and Self-sustainability Team (NESsT), Jose Arrieta 89, Providencia, Santiago, Chile. +562/222–5190, www.nesst.org.

> *NESsT works in Latin America and Central Europe to promote what it calls "self-financing" of nonprofits through earned income. The group sells reports and case studies (in English) and sponsors an international conference.*

Marketing

Donordigital.com, 182 Second Street, 4th Floor, San Francisco, CA 94105. 415/278–9444, www.donordigital.com.

> *This consulting firm specializes in online fundraising, advocacy, and marketing for progressive nonprofits and businesses. Free e-mail newsletter available.*

Guerrilla Marketing: Secrets for Making Big Profits from Your Small Business, 3rd ed., Jay Conrad Levinson, 1998. 388 pages. $13. Houghton Mifflin, 222 Berkeley Street, Boston, MA 02116. 800/225-3362, www.houghtonmifflin.com.

> *This book is both a marketing manifesto and a how-to guide. Levinson is one of the masters of modern marketing and the "Guerrilla" books (15 titles and counting) are his franchise.*

Marketing Workbook for Nonprofit Organizations, 2nd ed., Gary J. Stern, 2001. 193 pages. $30. Amherst H. Wilder Foundation, 919 Lafond Avenue, St. Paul, MN 55104. 800/274–6024, www.wilder.org.

> *Like all the other Wilder Foundation books, this one is clear, informative, and easy-to-use, with lots of useful worksheets. Even if you're not selling goods or services, this book will help you clarify your goals, identify your audiences, and meet your mission more effectively.*

1001 Ways to Market Your Books, 5th ed., John Kremer, 1998. 704 pages. $27.95. Open Horizons Publishing, P.O. Box 205, Fairfield, IA 52556. 800/796-6130, www.bookmarket.com.

> *Practical, hands-on, and incredibly thorough. If you're selling or planning to sell publications, buy this book.*

Media relations

How to Tell and Sell Your Story: A Guide to Media for Community Groups and Other Nonprofits, 1997. 64 pages. $7. Center for Community Change, 1000 Wisconsin Avenue, N.W., Washington, D.C. 20007. 202/342–0567, www.communitychange.org.

How to Tell and Sell Your Story—Part 2: A Guide to Developing Effective Messages and Good Stories About Your Work, 1998. 48 pages. $7. Center for Community Change, 1000 Wisconsin Avenue NW, Washington, DC 20007. 202/342–0567, www.communitychange.org.

Making the News: A Guide for Nonprofits and Activists, Jason Salzman, 1998. 320 pages. $19.95. Westview Press/Perseus Books, 5500 Central Avenue, Boulder, CO 80301. 800/386–5656, www.westviewpress.com.

SPIN Works! A Media Guide Book for the Rest of Us, Robert Bray, 2000. 115 pages. $18.95. SPIN Project, 77 Federal Street, 2nd Floor, San Francisco CA 94107. 415/284-1420, www.spinproject.org.

> *These four books are all written by and for grassroots activists and contain practical, hands-on strategies for working with the news media.*

Media training

Safe Energy Communication Council, 1717 Massachusetts Avenue NW, Suite 106, Washington, DC 20036. 202/483–8491, www.safeenergy.org.

SPIN Project, 77 Federal Street, 2nd Floor, San Francisco, CA 94107. 415/284–1420, www.spinproject.org.

We Interrupt This Message, 160 Fourteenth Street, San Francisco, CA 94103. 415/621-3302 and 226 West 135th Street, 4th Floor, New York, NY 10030. 212/694–1144, www.interrupt.org.

> *These three organizations provide high-quality media training for activists.*

Nonprofit enterprise

Business Ventures of Citizen Groups, Charles Cagnon, 1982. 51 pages. Northern Rockies Action Group, Helena, MT. (This report is out of print, and NRAG no longer exists.)

> *An early study of earned income strategies used by progressive advocacy organizations.*

The Cathedral Within: Transforming Your Life by Giving Something Back, Bill Shore, 1999. 292 pages. $21.95. Random House, 1540 Broadway, New York, NY 10036. 212/782-9000, www.randomhouse.com.

> *Strategies to end hunger and poverty and improve the lives of children through social enterprise.*

Community Wealth Ventures, 733 Fifteenth Street, N.W., Suite 600, Washington DC 20005. 202/478–6570, www.communitywealth.com.

> *This consulting firm is a for-profit subsidiary of Share our Strength, a nonprofit that works to end hunger through corporate partnerships and other entrepreneurial approaches.*

Denali Initiative, 1815 Metropolitan Street, Pittsburgh, PA 15233. 412/322-1773, www.denaliinitiative.org.

> *Based at the Manchester Craftsmen's Guild, which is often cited as a model nonprofit enterprise, the Denali Initiative is a fellowship and training program for nonprofit leaders interested in social enterprise.*

Earned Revenue Handbook: A Guide for Museums with Culturally Defined Collections, Mary Virtue and Ellen Arrick/The African American and Latino Art Museum Working Group, 1995. 34 pages. $15. Cornerstone Consultants, 1236 Waterford Road, West Chester, PA 19380. 610/696–8149, www.cornerstoneconsultantspa.com

> *While this workbook focuses on museum retailing, it contains useful information for any kind of nonprofit retail venture, with an excellent chapter on selling to the education market.*

Enterprising Nonprofits: A Toolkit for Social Entrepreneurs, J. Gregory Dees, Jed Emerson, and Peter Economy, 2001. 330 pages. $34.95. John Wiley & Sons, 605 Third Avenue, New York, NY 10158. 212/850-6000, www.wiley.com/nonprofit.

> *A thorough discussion of nonprofit ventures focusing on issues of organizational readiness. A second volume—they had so much to say, it wouldn't fit in one book— is due in 2002.*

Filthy Rich: How to Turn Your Nonprofit Fantasies into Cold, Hard Cash, Richard Steckel, 2000. 240 pages. $16.95. Ten Speed Press, P.O. Box 7123, Berkeley, CA 94707. 800/841-BOOK, www.tenspeed.com.

> *Fine chapters on brainstorming and evaluating venture ideas and a compelling case for using corporate money for nonprofit ventures.*

Institute for Social Entrepreneurs, 9560 Dogwood Circle, Eden Prairie, MN, 55347. 952/942-7715, www.socialent.org.

> *Jerr Boschee, a leader in the field of nonprofit enterprise, manages this consulting and training organization.*

Looking at Income-Generating Businesses for Small Nonprofit Organizations, William A. Duncan, 1982. 25 pages. Center for Community Change, 1000 Wisconsin Avenue, N.W., Washington, DC 20007. 202/342–0567, www.communitychange.org. (Out of print.)

> *One of the few publications on this topic geared to the needs and limitations of grassroots groups.*

National Center for Social Entrepreneurs, 5801 Duluth Street, Minneapolis, MN 55422. 800/696–4066, www.socialentrepreneurs.org.

> *NCSE provide training and publications for nonprofits interested in exploring and building their entrepreneurial capacity.*

National Gathering for Social Entrepreneurs, 320 West 13th Street, New York, NY 10014, 212/645-8111, www.natlgathering.org.

> *Through periodic conferences, a Web site, and other strategies, the National Gathering provides a forum for social entrepreneurs to share ideas.*

New Social Entrepreneurs: The Success, Challenge, and Lessons of Nonprofit Enterprise Creation, Jed Emerson and Fay Twersky, eds., 1996. 417 pages. Free. Roberts Enterprise Development Foundation, P.O. Box 29266, San Francisco CA 94129. 415/561–6677, www.redf.org.

> *This report details the early experience of the Roberts Enterprise Development Foundation, a key participant in the social venture philanthropy movement. The foundation helps nonprofits in the San Francisco Bay Area to start and run mission-related businesses.*

The Nonprofit Entrepreneur: Creating Ventures to Earn Income, Edward Skloot, ed., 1988. 170 pages. $19.95. The Foundation Center, 79 Fifth Avenue, New York, NY 10013. 800/424–9836, www.fdncenter.org.

> *An early, important book on this topic. Includes a chapter on "the pitfalls of earned income for small nonprofits."*

Revolution of the Heart: A New Strategy for Creating Wealth and Meaningful Change, Bill Shore, 1995. 167 pages. $19. Putnam, 375 Hudson Street, New York, NY 10014. 800/788-6262, www.penguinputnam.com.

> *Bill Shore is the founder of Share Our Strength and a leader in the field of cause-related marketing. This book recounts his personal history while presenting a rationale for nonprofit enterprise.*

Roberts Enterprise Development Fund, P.O. Box 29266, San Francisco CA 94129. 415/561–6677, www.redf.org.

> *REDF promotes social entrepreneurship nationally and internationally, and funds a select group of enterprising nonprofits in the San Francisco region.*

Social Entrepreneurs Alliance for Change (SEA Change), 215 Leidesdorff Alley, 4th Floor, San Francisco, CA 94111. 415/291–9900, www.sea-change.org.

> *SEA Change promotes alliances among entrepreneurial nonprofits, funders, and the business community.*

Quick index
Earned income strategies for nonprofits

■　■　■　■　■　■　■　■　■　■　■　■　■　■　■　■

Are you interested in selling to a specific market or learning more about a particular earned income strategy? Use this quick index to identify the relevant organizations profiled in this book.

Consumer goods: retail

Consumer goods: wholesale

Consumer services

Employment training and job development

Performance and public speaking

Publications (p. 57)

Services for nonprofits and other institutional customers

Training and consulting for nonprofits and other institutional customers

Travel and tourism

Index

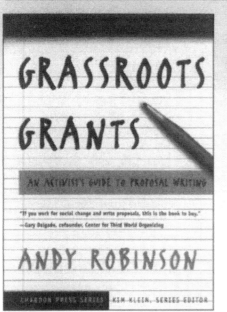

RESOURCES FOR SOCIAL CHANGE

AVAILABLE FROM JOSSEY-BASS AND CHARDON PRESS

Raise More Money

The Best of the Grassroots Fundraising Journal

Kim Klein and Stephanie Roth, Editors
Paper 214 pages
ISBN 0-7879-6175-2 $28.00

This collection offers a wealth of tips and strategies, as well as guidance on how small nonprofits can raise money from their communities, reduce their dependence on foundations or corporations, and develop long-term financial stability.

Fundraising for the Long Haul

FOURTH EDITION

Kim Klein
Paper 176 pages
ISBN 0-7879-6173-6 $20.00

In this companion to her classic *Fundraising for Social Change,* Kim Klein distills her 25 years of experience and wisdom to provide practical guidance for sustaining a long-term commitment to social change for organizations that are understaffed and underresourced.

Fundraising for Social Change

FOURTH EDITION

Kim Klein
Paper 416 pages
ISBN 0-7879-6174-4 $35.00

This classic how-to fundraising text teaches you what you need to know to raise money from individuals. Learn how to set fundraising goals based on realistic budgets; write successful direct mail appeals; produce special events; raise money from major gifts, planned giving, capital campaigns, and more.

Ask and You Shall Receive

A Fundraising Training Program for Religious Organizations and Projects

Kim Klein
Paper
ISBN 0-7879-5563-9 $23.00

A self-study course in the basics of grassroots fundraising written specifically for groups raising funds for religious organizations and projects. (Includes a Leader Manual and a Participant Manual.)

Inspired Philanthropy

Tracy Gary
Paper 122 pages
ISBN 0-7879-6176-0 $20.00

Learn how to match your giving with your values. No matter how much or little you have to give, you'll learn how to create a giving plan that will make your charitable giving catalytic.

TO ORDER, CALL (800) 956-7739 OR VISIT US AT
www.josseybass.com/go/chardonpress